Andreas Mattig

Industrial Dynamics and the Evolution of Markets in the Mutual Fund Industry

GABLER RESEARCH

Andreas Mattig

Industrial Dynamics and the Evolution of Markets in the Mutual Fund Industry

GABLER

RESEARCH

Bibliographic information published by the Deutsche Nationalbibliothek
The Deutsche Nationalbibliothek lists this publication in the Deutsche Nationalbibliografie; detailed bibliographic data are available in the Internet at http://dnb.d-nb.de.

Doctoral thesis, St. Gallen University 2009

1st Edition 2009

Editorial Office: Claudia Jeske | Sabine Schöller

Gabler is part of the specialist publishing group Springer Science+Business Media.
www.gabler.de

Cover design: KünkelLopka Medienentwicklung, Heidelberg
Printed on acid-free paper
Printed in Germany

ISBN 978-3-8349-1938-0

Table of Contents

Zusammenfassung

Die vorliegende Dissertation beschäftigt sich mit der Industriedynamik und der Evolution von Märkten in der Anlagefondsindustrie. Das Ziel besteht darin, diese dynamischen Effekte zu verstehen, zu erklären und aus den Erkenntnissen Handlungsfelder abzuleiten. Als Ausgangspunkt dient ein Model, in welchem etablierte Unternehmen auf Innovationen reagieren. Diese Innovationen eröffnen neuen Wettbewerbern einen Marktzugang, womit bestehende Industriestrukturen verändert werden. Der zentrale Aspekt liegt auf einer Mehr-Ebenen Betrachtung. Diese beleuchtet die Empfindlichkeit der Reaktion auf die Innovation nicht nur auf die Industriestruktur-Ebene, sondern auch auf die Ebene der vielfältigen (Kooperations- und Wettbewerbs-)Beziehungen innerhalb und zwischen den bereits im Markt etablierten Unternehmen. Auf der Basis dieses Modells werden in einem weiteren Schritt zwei Aspekte der Industriedynamik gemessen und erklärt:

Der erste Aspekt konzentriert sich auf das Problemfeld des schrittweisen Eindringens neuer Produkte und neuer Prozesse. Dieses Problemfeld wird auf der Basis eines evolutions-ökonomischen Modelles bearbeitet und illustriert, wie die Marktbeherrschenden Firmen gewisse Innovationen (vor allem im Produktbereich) kopieren und dadurch neuen Wettbewerbern den Marktzugang verwehren. Daneben zeigt sich jedoch auch, dass sich über die Zeit eigentliche „Baublöcke" oder „Module" der Industriearchitektur herausbilden. Diese Module bestehen aus Abhängigkeiten zwischen spezifischen Fähigkeiten der Unternehmen und deren verfügbarer (Verarbeitungs-)Kapazität. Veränderungen der Marktarchitektur tendieren dazu, solchen Modulen zu folgen. Der zweite Aspekt der Industriedynamik beschäftigt sich mit abrupten Veränderungen der Marktsituation, wie sie durch regulatorische Veränderung oder durch die Etablierung neuer Technologien möglich erden. Die Arbeit fokussiert dabei auf den Vertriebskanal von Anlagefondsfirmen und fragt, weshalb die Einführung von elektronischen Märkten nicht zu der erwarteten Verschiebung im dominanten Verkaufskanal geführt hat. Dabei tritt die Bedeutung der Fähigkeiten zur Abschöpfung des durch eine neue Technologie generierten Zusatznutzens und zur Koordination und Kontrolle von unternehmensübergreifenden Netzwerken hervor. Der letzte Teil dieser Dissertation widmet sich konsequenterweise der Möglichkeiten dieser Koordination und Kontrolle am Beispiel von (Outsourcing-)Netzwerken. Die Arbeit bedient sich dazu einer Referenz aus dem Retail-Banking.

Die gewonnenen Erkenntnisse der verschiedenen Untersuchungen fliessen in eine abschliessende Gesamtbetrachtung ein und dienen als Grundlage für einen anwendungsorientierten Diskussionsrahmen. Dieser Diskussionsrahmen soll es ermöglichen, das dritte Ziel der Disseration zu erreichen, d. h. mögliche Handlungsfelder für Anlagefondsfirmen zu definieren.

Abstract

This thesis attempts to understand, explain and influence market evolution and industry dynamic processes in the mutual fund market. The joint model that guides the discussion is based on the dynamics of entry and allows shifts in the industry architecture to be tracked as the existing structures are hit by different triggers of change. Triggers of change are modeled by two generic types of exogenous innovation, which are labeled gradual and disruptive. We argue that market leaders are forced to reorganize themselves as a reaction to disruptive innovation, and that they are likely to adjust their product portfolio and pricing policy in the case of gradual innovation in order to deter new entrants.

Based on this argument, we contribute by building a formal model to discuss innovation-triggered shifts in the mutual fund industry architecture, and by developing a corresponding measurement approach. This approach tracks product expansion along evolutionary pathways, or disruptive readjustments along jumps in implicit bid-ask spreads. When discussing newly evolving market structures, the competitive environment and entry dynamics are at the heart of the analysis and discussion. The more complex a market structure is and the more segmented decisions are taken from an organizational stance, the more the decision space and dynamics of entry become opaque.

We argue that the perception of innovation and the resulting entry deterrence strategies are key drivers behind structural industry formation, and we propose a model of an incumbent's response to innovation-driven entry. Subsequently, we measure the expected impacts of the model by looking at gradual and disruptive innovation events in the industry. Gradual innovation is addressed in Chapter 6, by the application of evolution metrics, which allows us to partition the effects of gradual change along basic building blocks of closely interdependent process-capability nodes. The impact of disruptive innovation can be analyzed well, when discussing the reasons for stickiness in the key bottleneck of the fund industry, which is its distribution function (Chapter 7). In both cases, the transition is analyzed along the shifting performance and cost structures per trade. The results allow insights into the microstructures and the dynamics of the industry and emphasize the role of network control for value appropriation. This notion of network control is the focus of Chapter 8. Referring to developments in retail banking operations, we look at the challenge of bridging the widening gaps in operational risk as disintermediation moves forward, and we evaluate different modes of governance to do so. The thesis concludes with a summary and an integrative framework that allows to discuss the managerial options arising from industrial dynamics.

1 Introduction

This thesis deals with industrial dynamics and market evolution in the mutual fund industry. Both these concepts are rooted in the notion of industry architecture. Industry architecture can be loosly described as the combination of industry structure (both in terms of fragmentation, as well as in terms of the boundaries of the firms in the market), channels of interaction or relation (across the bounded firm segments and between firms) and the nature of these interactions. Structures and relations are not stable concepts. So change in regulation, in demand, in technology or in riskiness may easily affect previously existing configurations. These adjustments are referred to when using the term "industrial dynamics". Industrial dynamics analyzes the forces and directions of changes in industry architecture and may lead to the evolution of (new intermediary) markets wherever boundaries of firms change or new gaps open. The theory and methodology to cope with such tasks is very broad in scope and ranges from concepts that are rooted in classical micro economics to research strands that draw from sociology and the management literature. Industry dynamics and market evolution are thus key concepts that can be used to discuss and assess the implications of competitive pressure in a holistic way, and serve as a strong tool to point towards emerging strategic options.

When talking about competitive pressure and change in the industry – Why should one look at the mutual fund industry context? Especially as industry practioniers (e.g. KPMG) keep referring to this industry as one of high overall growth and prosperous outlooks in its annual investment surveys (KPMG, 2007a, 2007b).

Despite a long history of growth and strong evidence that this growth in net new money will continue (DEUTSCHE BANK, 2006; ICI, 2008), the dominant players within the industry now find themselves faced with changing competitive conditions. Evidence for such a change in competitive positions is found in steadily decreasing profit margins, as reported by the large established players over the last couple of years (DEUTSCHE BANK, 2006). These decreasing margins have so far resulted in additional M&A activity to bolster economies of scale, but clear reasons for the ongoing trend have so far hardly been discussed systematically at a firm level, and even less so at the industry level (BATIZ-LAZO, 2007; DEUTSCHE BANK, 2006). Despite this outlook, mutual funds are continuing to gain importance when measured by banks increasing their staff and marketing commitments (ICI, 2008). Since 1998 the market for mutual fund solutions has doubled in size from 9.6 trillion USD to 18 trillion USD – solely for the U.S.. Internationally the growth has been even more spectacular, especially in some emerging countries (WALTER AND

Sisli, 2007). This strong market growth is in line with the eagerness of many investors to capitalize on the benefits of mutualized investment schemes, but contrasts sharply with the shrinking margins observed at the firm level. Apparently, de novo entry into this industry occurs without a clear concept with respect to value propositions and is merely overshadowed by the top-line growth of the market (Ramos, 2007). Furthermore, the industry is changing considerably: regulatory environments are beeing newly defined, especially in Europe, and customers' increasing sophistication affecting the established product offering. Changing rules and demand structures are just two of the factors that are expected to alter the industry structure over the coming years (Oxera, 2006). Thereby, changes in the industry structure are not only relevant for the involved firms, but they also have an impact on securities prices to some extent, as costs to analyze, trade and allocate them depend very much on the organization structure through which they are handled. This is a classical field of the micro market structure debate (O'Hara, 2007).

So far, the focus of mutual fund research has been driven by data availability and as a result almost remained restricted to the U.S., where discussion has centered on the analysis of investment strategies, valuation issues and micro market effects of large trading orders by funds. The issue of industry structure and the redesigning of firm boundaries for mutual funds has been conceded almost entirely to the domain of practical oriented reports (KPMG, 2007a), leading to a lack of theoretical and empirical discussions and an over-emphasis of "best practice" cases. This leaves room for an academic contribution in this field, especially since the existing management literature has already raised important issues that might broaden the financial perspective of the industry, but that so far has been restricted to a separated environment in terms of audience. Siggelkow (2002), for instance, introduced the idea that it is mainly the interplay of different value drivers and path dependency that determine the logic of competition in (mutual fund) markets, and authors such as Dosi or Tirole (1988) laid the grounds for this kind of discussion at the very onset of the industrial organization discussions. However, an integrated perspective that introduces these management traditions into the large finance-based mutual fund literature remains to be found.

From a practical perspective, observed problems like the pressure on margins and the complexity of a wide set of evolutionary drivers that emerge from the management discussion, press for a more comprehensive view as well, albeit here the emphasis lies more on corporate strategy formation issues than on a comprehensive theory set.

This thesis attempts to track the strategic environment changes relevant for corporate strategy and mutual fund competition issues by first highlighting the industry logic, and second, by observing dynamic shifts in the market structure and the triggered reactions of the dominant market players. The input of the approach is seen by the introduction of "innovation types" as an impetus for dynamic changes. Variance of the innovative effect allows the discussion to be linked to the two dominant theory fields: the dynamic role of capabilities from a network and evolutionary economics point of view and the more static discussion framework proposed by new institutional theory. The aim is to address the market by building on a comprehensive concept of industry dynamics and market evolution in the mutual fund context. Thereby, the principle of "comprehensiveness" is met by developing a research design that shares:

(i) one joint theoretical model to understand the market dynamics from a decision perspective (incorporating capability and resource investment decisions),

(ii) one joint measurement framework for empirical work to track the dynamics and

(iii) one joint application framework for strategic discussions that emerge from the results.

The guiding central argument is that the underlying dynamics in the mutual fund industry are dominated by the entry and exit of new competitors, launch and stop of product issuance and overall growing supply (of net new money inflows into the industry). These shifts are influenced by changes in technology, regulation and financial intermediation demands, as well as by the (tactical) response of incumbents to the corresponding entry-threats. Response structures thereby reflect existing channels of interaction or transaction-process stickiness and allow us to observe inter-and intra-firm relations and industry structure change across a multi-faceted industry.

The topic fits well into the current debate on organizational structures and micro-foundations. In this context, the effects of innovation on vertically integrated industry systems (Wolter and Veloso, 2008) and the interaction of transaction economics and capability discussions (Jacobides, 2008) are an actively discussed topic. The applied research process that leads towards this goal starts with an outline of the industry, describes then the industry's processes and economic logics and leads to a general model of reaction to change. Change is thereby seen as an anticipated threat of innovation that a new entrant introduces into the system. Along the two basic lines of reaction (gradual and disruptive change), we then empirically track evidence for partitioning in the process-capability nexus of product development and in distribution channel choice. After we have indicated potential new intermediary markets that may emerge, we discuss the governance and risk aspects before linking newly evolved markets to the overall industrial system.

With this approach, the thesis seeks to contribute to a formalized framework for identifying, the building blocks of industrial dynamics. Such building blocks are not only sensitive to change but also prone to strategic (re-)positioning at the firm level. In more detail and in the context of the general framework of "responsiveness" to innovation, we provide evidence for product and technological change and discuss the implications of such changes from an operational risk perspective. Illustration 1 depicts the structure of the thesis.

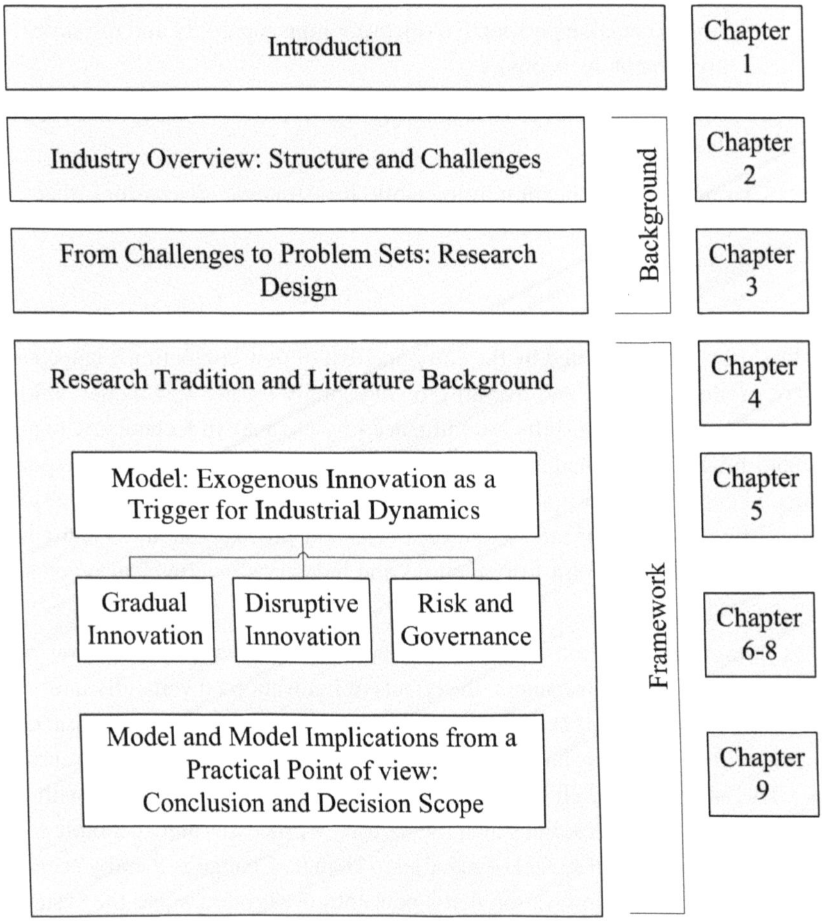

Illustration 1: Structure of the Thesis

Preliminary Comments

Several of the chapters in this thesis have already been published or presented at conferences: An early version of chapter 5 was presented at the 25th DRUID celebration conference in Copenhagen in 2008. Chapter 6 originated from a working paper by MATTIG AND WUEST, 2008. A subsequent version of this was presented at the DRUID Winter Conference 2008 in Aalborg. Chapter 6 is now an extended version of this early draft, which benefited from good feedback. Both DRUID papers can be retrieved in their original form from the organization's databank (www.druid.dk).

Chapter 8 is an extended version of the paper "Modes of Governance in Business Process Outsourcing: Executive versus market's perspective" published in 2008 by the IEEE as one proceeding from the 41st HICCS conference in Hawaii.

I would especially like to acknowledge the contribution of Dr. Simone Westerfeld, who was a co-author for the working paper "Why do electronic markets not (yet) prevail?". Chapter 7 largely follows the concept of this working paper.

2 The Mutual Fund Industry

Over the last few decades, many asset management firms have experienced levels of decreasing or low profitability. Strategic decisions in asset management firms are thus being increasingly confronted with the need to anticipate changes in the industry structure and the dynamics of these changes to (re)position itself along the four core criteria of success in that very industry. These four key factors can be illustrated by providing access to hard-to-get securities at a product level, in offering superior diversification potential and sufficient liquidity to customers when looking at portfolios, and fourth, in differentiating oneself at a firm level by means of lower transaction costs. One concept that allows these demands to be met by the general asset management industry is collective investment schemes, such as mutual funds.

Access to hard-to-get securities can be obtained as collective investment units can take advantage of opportunities that may otherwise be too expensive or require too much time and research effort to learn about. The main factor that attracts investors to rely on collective asset management schemes, however, is not only the smooth way to handle specific assets, but much more the cost efficient path towards an increased scope for diversification. Diversification is a basic investment principle. By investing for instance in mutual funds with different investment strategies, customers invest in a broad basket of stocks, bonds and cash whose investment returns often move independently or with significant correlation to each other. Besides the characteristics that are directly related to product or portfolio aspects, an investor seeks to invest in agents and markets where he can control the risk to some extent, and where the costs stay competitive, i.e. where it is worth entrusting money to an external agent instead of doing research and trading on a stand-alone basis. Here, liquidity and transaction cost are the focal features. Liquidity provides the necessary means to sell your shares quickly and at a fair price. For most mutual funds, the fund company itself is always ready to buy back your shares. As a side effect (and/or cause) of being "liquid", mutual funds trade many more shares than the average investor does. Therefore, brokers are often willing to accept lower transaction fees as a necessary cost of doing business with mutual funds.

Individual investors can (to some extent) profit from these conditions by pooling their market power in collective investment units. The fund industry that has emerged around these investor-friendly features is based on tried and tested principles – investor protection, simplicity, functionality, transparency and trust. These principles (along with a sufficient marketing effort by fund promoters and banks) has become extremely popular and allowed mutual funds to establish themselves. As the industry has grown more popular and competition levels increased along, asset managers have been forced to seek new ways to improve their profitability. This is clearly one main factor why the mutual fund industry has been a pioneer in industrializing, globalizing and risk focusing asset management. "It seems inevitable that this process will continue with the industry's growing maturity and that mergers will increase. Whether eventually just a small number of fund management companies and institutional asset managers will survive and dominate the global fund business remains to be seen. As new brands, business models, products, services and performance promises arise; the fund industry will continue to be confronted with a demanding and dynamic environment" (HÄMMERLI , 2003, p. 37).

Mutual Fund Definition, Size and Scope

In the simple terms of the U.S. Securities and Exchange Commission's (SEC) investor communication, "A mutual fund is a company that pools money from many investors and invests the money in stocks, bonds, short-term money-market instruments, other securities or assets, or some combination of these investments" (SEC, 2008). Collective investment companies such as mutual funds are highly regulated. The entities are established as "open-end-companies" and represent one way to manage money through a pooled investment vehicle. The funds are thereby managed by focusing on costs (with passive investment strategies) or by focusing on distinct capabilities, e.g. in research, trading execution or in brokerage services for distinct securities in the case of actively managed entities.

Comparision of Expense Ratios between
Actively and Passively Managed Mutual Funds

Fund Category	Actively Managed	Passively Managed
U.S. Equity		
Large Growth	1.49%	0.14%
Large Value	1.40%	0.21%
Small Growth	1.71%	0.23%
Small Value	1.54%	0.23%
Int. Equity		
MSCI World	1.73%	0.31%
Emerging Market	2.09%	0.48%
Europe	1.78%	0.27%
Pacific Region	1.95%	0.34%
Bonds		
High Yield	1.25%	0.15%
Intermediate Term	1.07%	0.18%
Short Term	1.01%	0.18%
REITs	1.62%	0.21%

1) Data "Active": Morningstar and Lipper, Inc.
2) Data "Passive": Vanguard
3) Ratios are Averages of the respective Class and do not include trading cost and bid-ask spreads

Table 1: Comparison of Expense Ratios between Actively and Passively Managed Mutual Funds; Data (Mesa Management, 2008)

The history of such pooled investment vehicles dates back to Europe in the late 1700s. According to K. Geert Rouwenhorst in The Origins of Mutual Funds, "Dutch merchant[s] and broker […] invited subscriptions from investors to form a trust […] to provide an opportunity to diversify for small investors with limited means" (Rouwenhorst, 2004, p. 7). The emergence of such pooling initiatives spread to England in the 1800s, when legislative change in the form of the Joint-Stock Companies Acts of 1862 and 1867 permitted investors to share in the profits of an investment enterprise and limited investor liability to the amount of investment capital devoted to the enterprise. In response to this regulatory change, the Foreign and Colonial Government Trust formed in London in 1868 (Riley,1990).

This trust resembled the mutual fund model in its basic structure, providing "the investor of moderate means the same advantages as the large capitalists [...] by spreading the investment over a number of different stocks." (Rouwenhorst, 2004).

When looking for the very start of the mutual fund industry, the literature generally disputes whether to refer to the Swiss Société Civile Genève d' Emploi de Fonds, which was established in 1849, to the Foreign and Colonial Government Trust formed 1864 in London that coined the term of an "investment" fund, or to the Massachusetts Investors Trust that was formed in Boston in March 1924 as the first "real" mutual fund (Rouwenhorst, 2004; Russel, 2007). All these early collective investment vehicles certainly introduced important innovations to the investment company concept by establishing a simplified capital structure, a continuous offering of shares, the ability to redeem shares rather than hold them until dissolution of the fund, and a set of clear investment restrictions and policies.

Since these early times the concept has gained increased attention, led to accelerated growth rates over time as even more of these collective schemes were allowed in additional countries. And later, financial market liberalization led to a higher demand for securities investments. Until today, the market has evolved from an innovative niche into a liquid multi-dollar business. As of yearend 2007, more than 26 trillion USD were invested in mutual fund schemes worldwide (Table 2). Thereby, the U.S. and Europe continued to claim leading shares of the market, although Asia's share saw rapid growth as well. As in many other financial service industries, the literature largely agrees (Ramos, 2009; Walter, 1999b; Walter and Sisli, 2007) that this development, initiated by a product innovation was fuel ed and shaped by market openings and (re-)regulation efforts across time and countries. Thereby, not only the opening and liberalization of national markets played a role, but also the change in local regulation. This can be observed in many cases, e.g. for the U.S., where the rise of Individual Retirement Accounts (IRAs) and Thrift Plans (TSPs – personal retirement saving plans) in 1982 bolstered the use of mutual funds in multiple ways (Duca, 2001). In these national cases, tax law changes are often seen as the single most important driver for change. The (institutional) asset management industry is often referred to as one of the largest and most dynamic parts of the global financial services sector today and in the years ahead (Walter, 1999a).

Table 2: Worldwide Total Net Assets of Mutual Funds, Data ICI (see p. 12–15)

When looking at this market growth over time and comparing effects across regions, growth drivers and factors influencing market and underlying industry structure are more difficult to track. This has led to the interest in the industry structure and their underlying drivers. From a descriptive point of view, there are three important features to be mentioned. First, new sales versus the performance of existing investments, second, regional divergence in growth rates and third, regional patterns in the mutual fund industry structure. When looking at the new fund share – performance ratio on a worldwide base - one could think of two basic motivations for growing assets under management: first, an overall growth of the market, driven by performance and new inflows and second, a relative growth in? market share. Assuming that people worldwide have a similar attitude towards risk aversion, the average investment strategy preference should be equal. Hence, based on capital market theorems, the performance of all the funds in any region should not be different from others in terms of stock market development. (Due

to the equal risk characteristics of the population, it can be assumed that each market offers funds that invest across different international stock and bond strategies). Additionally, the base of assets under management can grow by an increasing net new money inflow as it is attracted by the issuance of appealing new products. From such a product innovation or customer demand perspective, new money inflow differs widely as taxation, transaction costs and investment opportunities vary. This affects the relative incentive for investors to buy mutual fund products. Table 3 displays market growth and net new inflows (labeled sales in the terminology of the ICI) across countries. Based on this data, we provide an initial top-level analysis on the heterogeneity of the industry with respect to drivers of asset growth, growth disparities among countries and prima facie differences in firm characteristics across various geographical markets.

Table 3: Worldwide Growth of Mutual Funds (Performance and Net new Inflows/Sales), calculations based on ICI Data (see p. 16–19)

When analyzing the market growth (dynamics) of the mutual fund industry, the general notion of average global equality in risk aversion seems to hold. The total growth across the different regions co-moves closely, indicating no distortions complete different risk and market performances. At the same time, growth potential (i.e. net sales driven market growth) is developing at a higher pace in emerging countries, and – maybe surprisingly – also in the U.S., which is already the single largest mutual fund market. The growth rates are plotted in Table 4.

Worldwide Total Net Assets of Mutual Funds[1]
(millions of U.S. dollars, end of year)

		2000	2001	2002
World		**11,871,028.00**	**11,654,868.00**	**11,324,128.00**
Americas		**7,424,112.00**	**7,433,106.00**	**6,776,289.00**
	Argentina	7,425.00	3,751.00	1,021.00
	Brazil	148,538.00	148,189.00	96,729.00
	Canada	279,511.00	267,863.00	248,979.00
	Chile	4,597.00	5,090.00	6,705.00
	Costa Rica	919.00	1,577.00	1,738.00
	Mexico	18,488.00	31,723.00	30,759.00
	United States	6,964,634.00	6,974,913.00	6,390,358.00
Europe		**3,296,016.00**	**3,167,965.00**	**3,462,999.00**
	Austria	56,549.00	55,211.00	66,877.00
	Belgium	70,313.00	68,661.00	74,983.00
	Czech Republic	1,990.00	1,778.00	3,297.00
	Denmark[2]	32,485.00	33,831.00	40,153.00
	Finland	12,698.00	12,933.00	16,516.00
	France	721,973.00	713,378.00	845,147.00
	Germany	238,029.00	213,662.00	209,168.00
	Greece	29,154.00	23,888.00	26,621.00
	Hungary	1,953.00	2,260.00	3,992.00
	Ireland	137,024.00	191,840.00	250,116.00
	Italy	424,014.00	359,879.00	378,259.00
	Liechtenstein	N/A	N/A	3,847.00
	Luxembourg	747,117.00	758,720.00	803,869.00
	Netherlands	93,580.00	79,165.00	84,211.00
	Norway	16,228.00	14,752.00	15,471.00
	Poland	1,546.00	2,970.00	5,468.00
	Portugal	16,588.00	16,618.00	19,969.00
	Romania	8.00	10.00	27.00
	Russia	177.00	297.00	372.00
	Slovakia	N/A	N/A	N/A
	Slovenia	N/A	N/A	N/A
	Spain	172,438.00	159,899.00	179,133.00
	Sweden	78,085.00	65,538.00	57,992.00
	Switzerland	83,059.00	75,973.00	82,622.00
	Turkey	N/A	N/A	6,002.00
	United Kingdom	361,008.00	316,702.00	288,887.00

2003	2004	2005	2006	2007
14,048,311.00	**16,164,795.00**	**17,771,027.00**	**21,823,455.00**	**26,199,448.00**
7,969,541.00	**8,792,450.00**	**9,763,921.00**	**11,485,012.00**	**13,442,653.00**
1,916.00	2,355.00	3,626.00	6,153.00	6,789.00
171,596.00	220,586.00	302,927.00	418,771.00	615,365.00
338,369.00	413,772.00	490,518.00	566,298.00	698,397.00
8,552.00	12,588.00	13,969.00	17,700.00	24,444.00
2,754.00	1,053.00	804.00	1,018.00	1,203.00
31,953.00	35,157.00	47,253.00	62,614.00	75,428.00
7,414,401.00	8,106,939.00	8,904,824.00	10,412,458.00	12,021,027.00
4,682,836.00	**5,640,452.00**	**6,002,261.00**	**7,803,906.00**	**8,983,244.00**
87,982.00	103,709.00	109,002.00	128,236.00	138,709.00
98,724.00	118,373.00	115,314.00	137,291.00	149,842.00
4,083.00	4,860.00	5,331.00	6,490.00	7,595.00
49,533.00	64,799.00	75,199.00	95,620.00	105,225.00
25,601.00	37,658.00	45,415.00	67,804.00	81,136.00
1,148,446.00	1,370,954.00	1,362,671.00	1,769,258.00	1,989,690.00
276,319.00	295,997.00	296,787.00	340,325.00	372,072.00
38,394.00	43,106.00	32,011.00	27,604.00	29,807.00
3,936.00	4,966.00	6,068.00	8,523.00	12,577.00
360,425.00	467,620.00	546,242.00	855,011.00	951,371.00
478,734.00	511,733.00	450,514.00	452,798.00	419,687.00
8,936.00	12,543.00	13,970.00	17,315.00	25,103.00
1,104,112.00	1,396,131.00	1,635,785.00	2,188,278.00	2,685,065.00
93,573.00	102,134.00	94,357.00	108,560.00	113,921.00
21,994.00	29,907.00	40,122.00	54,065.00	74,709.00
8,576.00	12,014.00	17,652.00	28,957.00	45,542.00
26,985.00	30,514.00	28,801.00	31,214.00	29,732.00
29.00	72.00	109.00	247.00	390.00
851.00	1,347.00	2,417.00	5,659.00	7,175.00
1,061.00	2,168.00	3,035.00	3,171.00	4,762.00
N/A	N/A	N/A	2,484.00	4,219.00
255,344.00	317,538.00	316,864.00	367,918.00	396,534.00
87,746.00	107,064.00	119,059.00	176,943.00	194,955.00
90,772.00	94,407.00	116,669.00	159,515.00	176,282.00
14,157.00	18,112.00	21,761.00	15,463.00	22,609.00
396,523.00	492,726.00	547,103.00	755,156.00	944,536.00

Worldwide Total Net Assets of Mutual Funds[1]
(millions of U.S. dollars, end of year)

Asia and Pacific		**1,133,979.00**	**1,039,236.00**	**1,063,857.00**
	Australia	341,955.00	334,016.00	356,304.00
	China	N/A	N/A	N/A
	Hong Kong	195,924.00	170,073.00	164,322.00
	India	13,507.00	15,284.00	20,364.00
	Japan	431,996.00	343,907.00	303,191.00
	Korea, Rep. of	110,613.00	119,439.00	149,544.00
	New Zealand	7,802.00	6,564.00	7,505.00
	Pakistan	N/A	N/A	N/A
	Philippines	108.00	211.00	474.00
	Taiwan	32,074.00	49,742.00	62,153.00
Africa		**16,921.00**	**14,561.00**	**20,983.00**
	South Africa	16,921.00	14,561.00	20,983.00

[1] *Fund of Funds are not included except for France, Italy, and Luxembourg after 2003. Data include home-domiliced funds, escept for Hong Kong, Korea, and New Zealand, which include home markets only*

[2] *Before 2003, data include special funds reserved for institutional investors.*

N/A = not available

Note: Components may not add to total because of rounding. For more mutual funds and statistics, visit ICI's website at www.ici.org/stats/mf/arcglo/index.html.

Sources: Investment Company Institute, European Fund and Asset Management Association, and other national mutual fund associations

Table 2: Worldwide Total Net Assets of Mutual Funds, Data ICI

1,361,473.00	**1,677,887.00**	**1,939,251.00**	**2,456,511.00**	**3,678,330.00**
518,411.00	635,073.00	700,068.00	864,254.00	1,192,992.00
N/A	N/A	N/A	N/A	434,063.00
255,811.00	343,638.00	460,517.00	631,055.00	818,421.00
29,800.00	32,846.00	40,546.00	58,219.00	108,582.00
349,148.00	399,462.00	470,044.00	578,883.00	713,998.00
121,663.00	177,417.00	198,994.00	251,930.00	329,979.00
9,641.00	11,171.00	10,332.00	12,892.00	14,924.00
N/A	N/A	N/A	2,164.00	4,956.00
792.00	952.00	1,449.00	1,544.00	2,090.00
76,205.00	77,328.00	57,301.00	55,571.00	58,323.00
34,460.00	**54,006.00**	**65,594.00**	**78,026.00**	**95,221.00**
34,460.00	54,006.00	65,594.00	78,026.00	95,221.00

Worldwide Growth of Mutual Funds: Performance and Sales
(millions of U.S. dollars, end of year)

	2001		2002		2003	
	Growth	**Sales**	**Growth**	**Sales**	**Growth**	**Sale**
World	**-2%**	**8%**	**-3%**	**2%**	**24%**	**3%**
Americas	**0%**	**9%**	**-9%**	**2%**	**18%**	**1%**
Argentina	-49%	N/A	-73%	N/A	88%	N/A
Brazil	0%	N/A	-35%	-16%	77%	20%
Canada	-4%	8%	-7%	2%	36%	2%
Chile	11%	N/A	32%	N/A	28%	20%
Costa Rica	72%	N/A	10%	N/A	58%	N/A
Mexico	72%	N/A	-3%	2%	4%	17%
United States	0%	9%	-8%	2%	16%	1%
Europe	**-4%**	**7%**	**9%**	**5%**	**35%**	**7%**
Austria	-2%	12%	21%	8%	32%	6%
Belgium	-2%	N/A	9%	N/A	32%	N/A
Czech Republic	-11%	-16%	85%	33%	24%	2%
Denmark[2]	4%	23%	19%	17%	23%	19%
Finland	2%	17%	28%	24%	55%	31%
France	-1%	13%	18%	12%	36%	9%
Germany	-10%	8%	-2%	4%	32%	3%
Greece	-18%	5%	11%	0%	44%	15%
Hungary	16%	N/A	77%	N/A	-1%	N/A
Ireland	40%	N/A	30%	N/A	44%	N/A
Italy	-15%	-4%	5%	-3%	27%	2%
Liechtenstein	N/A	N/A	N/A	N/A	132%	100%
Luxembourg	2%	15%	6%	7%	37%	12%
Netherlands	-15%	N/A	6%	N/A	11%	N/A
Norway	-9%	4%	5%	1%	42%	16%
Poland	92%	N/A	84%	N/A	57%	N/A
Portugal	0%	4%	20%	4%	35%	10%
Romania	25%	63%	170%	160%	7%	-37%
Russia	68%	N/A	25%	N/A	129%	N/A
Slovakia	N/A	N/A	N/A	N/A	N/A	N/A
Slovenia	N/A	N/A	N/A	N/A	N/A	N/A
Spain	-7%	0%	12%	1%	43%	16%
Sweden	-16%	5%	-12%	7%	51%	10%
Switzerland	-9%	6%	9%	-1%	10%	-2%
Turkey	N/A	N/A	N/A	N/A	136%	N/A
United Kingdom	-12%	5%	-9%	3%	37%	6%

2004		2005		2006		2007	
Growth	Sales	Growth	Sales	Growth	Sales	Growth	Sales
15%	**3%**	**10%**	**6%**	**23%**	**7%**	**20%**	**7%**
10%	**2%**	**11%**	**5%**	**18%**	**7%**	**17%**	**11%**
23%	N/A	54%	N/A	70%	N/A	63%	N/A
29%	1%	37%	2%	38%	7%	42%	4%
22%	5%	19%	8%	15%	7%	22%	11%
47%	38%	11%	N/A	27%	22%	34%	19%
62%	N/A	-24%	N/A	27%	N/A	-14%	N/A
10%	2%	34%	19%	33%	24%	32%	16%
9%	2%	10%	5%	17%	7%	15%	11%
20%	**5%**	**6%**	**8%**	**30%**	**7%**	**25%**	**1%**
18%	8%	5%	16%	18%	3%	17%	-4%
20%	N/A	-3%	N/A	19%	N/A	16%	N/A
19%	-2%	10%	13%	22%	1%	21%	3%
31%	19%	16%	20%	27%	8%	30%	3%
47%	25%	21%	17%	49%	29%	49%	5%
19%	6%	-1%	6%	30%	10%	22%	-3%
7%	-3%	0%	4%	15%	-4%	10%	-5%
12%	0%	-26%	-18%	-14%	-30%	-12%	-10%
26%	N/A	22%	35%	40%	-1%	38%	29%
30%	N/A	17%	N/A	57%	N/A	46%	N/A
7%	-8%	-12%	-4%	1%	-13%	-1%	-18%
40%	27%	11%	11%	24%	6%	30%	21%
26%	13%	17%	21%	34%	18%	33%	12%
9%	1%	-8%	-9%	15%	0%	9%	-5%
36%	13%	34%	28%	35%	12%	42%	13%
40%	N/A	47%	N/A	64%	N/A	63%	N/A
13%	2%	-6%	5%	8%	-6%	7%	-18%
48%	97%	51%	36%	127%	89%	134%	38%
58%	N/A	79%	N/A	134%	N/A	117%	N/A
04%	56%	40%	51%	4%	-17%	50%	22%
N/A	N/A	N/A	N/A	N/A	N/A	N/A	26%
24%	12%	0%	8%	16%	-1%	17%	-6%
22%	6%	11%	7%	49%	6%	37%	1%
4%	-2%	24%	10%	37%	10%	29%	9%
28%	N/A	20%	N/A	-29%	N/A	1%	N/A
24%	2%	11%	4%	38%	6%	32%	0%

Worldwide Growth of Mutual Funds: Performance and Sales
(millions of U.S. dollars, end of year)

	2001		2002		2003	
	Growth	**Sales**	**Growth**	**Sales**	**Growth**	**Sale**
World	**-2%**	**8%**	**-3%**	**2%**	**24%**	**3%**
Asia and Pacific	**-8%**	**1%**	**2%**	**-3%**	**28%**	**-1%**
Australia	-2%	N/A	7%	N/A	45%	N/A
China	N/A	N/A	N/A	N/A	N/A	N/A
Hong Kong	-13%	2%	-3%	3%	56%	2%
India	13%	23%	33%	28%	46%	39%
Japan	-20%	-2%	-12%	-15%	15%	-2%
Korea, Rep. of	8%	11%	25%	12%	-19%	-16%
New Zealand	-16%	N/A	14%	-4%	28%	0%
Pakistan	N/A	N/A	N/A	N/A	N/A	N/A
Philippines	95%	116%	125%	124%	67%	49%
Taiwan	55%	N/A	25%	-2%	23%	13%
Africa	**-14%**	**11%**	**44%**	**12%**	**64%**	**25%**
South Africa	-14%	11%	44%	12%	64%	25%

Table 3: Worldwide Growth of Mutual Funds (Performance and Net new Inflows/Sales), calculations based on ICI Data

2004		2005		2006		2007	
rowth	**Sales**	**Growth**	**Sales**	**Growth**	**Sales**	**Growth**	**Sales**
15%	**3%**	**10%**	**6%**	**23%**	**7%**	**20%**	**7%**
23%	**4%**	**16%**	**5%**	**27%**	**7%**	**27%**	**9%**
23%	N/A	10%	N/A	23%	N/A	23%	N/A
N/A	N/A	N/A	N/A	N/A	N/A	N/A	N/A
34%	1%	34%	0%	37%	1%	43%	1%
10%	1%	23%	15%	44%	29%	34%	47%
14%	6%	18%	19%	23%	21%	23%	21%
46%	26%	12%	8%	27%	13%	34%	24%
16%	-1%	-8%	-5%	25%	-2%	16%	2%
N/A	N/A	N/A	N/A	N/A	N/A	N/A	135%
20%	15%	52%	32%	7%	-17%	28%	-1%
1%	-12%	-26%	-28%	-3%	-8%	-10%	-2%
57%	**19%**	**21%**	**17%**	**19%**	**14%**	**36%**	**12%**
57%	19%	21%	17%	19%	14%	36%	12%

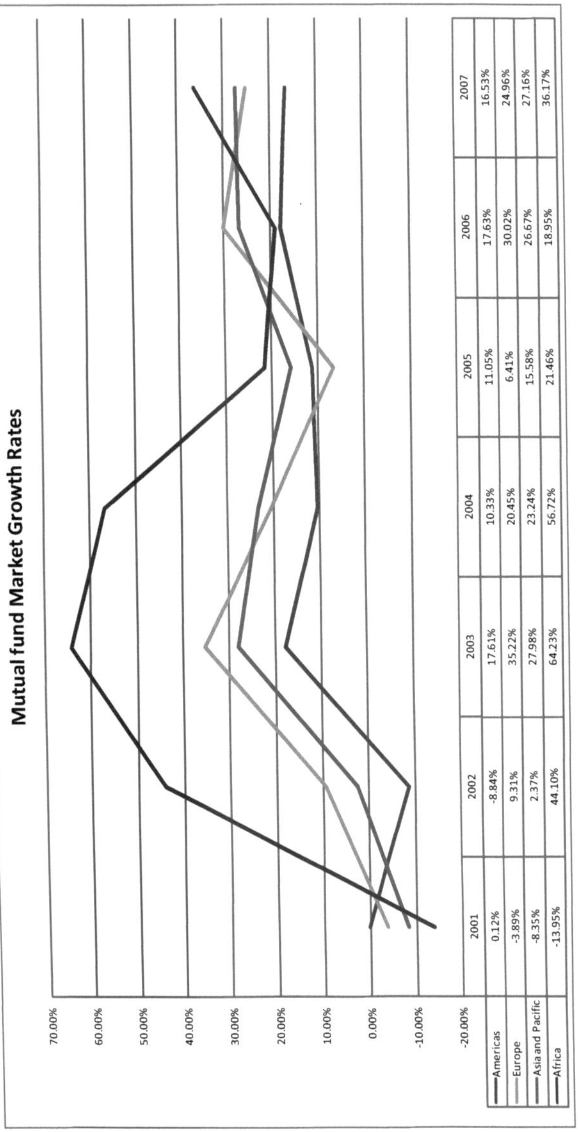

	2001	2002	2003	2004	2005	2006	2007
Americas	0.12%	-8.84%	17.61%	10.33%	11.05%	17.63%	16.53%
Europe	-3.89%	9.31%	35.22%	20.45%	6.41%	30.02%	24.96%
Asia and Pacific	-8.35%	2.37%	27.98%	23.24%	15.58%	26.67%	27.16%
Africa	-13.95%	44.10%	64.23%	56.72%	21.46%	18.95%	36.17%

Table 4: Mutual fund Market Growth Rates, calculations based on ICI Data

When looking at the reasons behind these regional and worldwide growth rates, we cannot only distinguish between performance driven market growth and net new sales or money inflows, but also between the reasons that may lay behind net inflows in general. One often quoted explanation of net new inflows is the increase in demand both from emerging countries and/or developed market regulatory change as discussed earlier, but also from demographic effects. With respect to demographic factors, two factors can increase the use of mutual funds. Firstly, the aging baby boom generation raises the share of the population preparing for retirement and thereby increases demand for saving and investment products. Second, a generally longer life expectancy might increase an individual's willingness to engage in institutional saving designs as a means to prepare for his retirement. Besides regulatory ease and demographic factors that cater to the "base line" of mutual fund industry growth, one might also argue for a more momentum driven event. The observed positive returns could trigger the inflow of net new money into the sector as more people become aware of opportunities. We find in this respect some correlation for such a relationship at the country level, if we simply look at year-to-year correlations between performance and inflows. Furthermore, this correlation seems to (even?) decrease over time. This observation stresses the continuous challenge of substitution that threatens market participants in asset management. Over the last couple of years, structured products have been the realization of such a threat. New money inflows have been increasingly guided towards this substitutional market segment and consequently, structured products gained a bigger share of the market? despite the steady and positive performance of the established mutual funds. The corresponding results are displayed in Table 5.

	2001	**2002**	**2003**	**2004**	**2005**	**2006**	**2007**	**Over Time**
Year-to-Year	0.94	0.93	0.83	0.95	0.79	0.89	0.63	
Level of Significance	*0.00*	*0.00*	*0.00*	*0.00*	*0.00*	*0.00*	*0.00*	*0.01*
Year-to-t-1		0.53	(0.04)	0.02	0.61	0.48	0.55	
Level of Significance		*0.0245*	*0.42*	*0.124*	*0.245*	*0.245*	*0.345*	*0.23*
Year-to-t-2			0.33	0.69	(0.01)	0.56	0.57	
Level of Significance			*0.314*	*0.245*	*0.424*	*0.245*	*0.244*	*0.29*

Table 5: Auto Correlations between Performance and New Inflows, calculations based on ICI Data

The Mutual Fund Complex and its Roles

The mutual fund industry is, as indicated in this general overview, a highly regulated sector. At the firm level, hence, relatively stable and fixed complexes and accompanying roles are fund characteristic. To summarize, the industry stretches along the functions of (legal) fund origination, fund management, fund administration, custodian services for the invested portfolio, and fund distribution. Illustration 2 depicts a typical mutual fund complex, including its principal service providers. The basic mechanism of the complex is stable across different fund markets, and accordingly, the products issued are largely homogenous in structure (GLAUS, 1997).

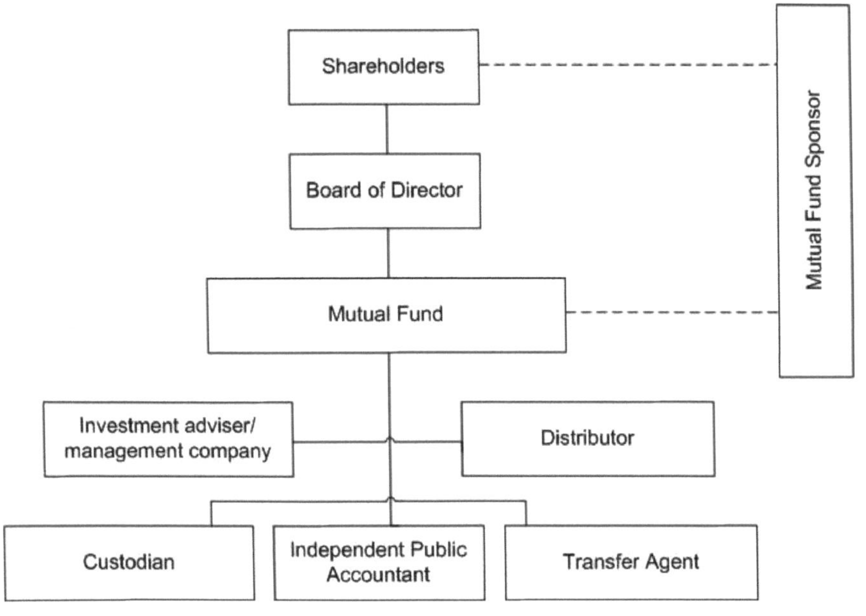

Illustration 2: The Mutual Fund Complex (KPMG, 2007a)

As depicted in Illustration 2, the main roles in the mutual fund complex are governing parties represented by shareholders, by fund sponsors, by the board of directors, the collective investment vehicle itself, and the operating entities. The operating entities consist of a management company, which does research and develops a strategy and allocates the funds' portfolio, a distributor who markets and sells (new) shares, transfer agents, and custodians and accountants who execute and track the fund flows.

Thereby, the board of directors is elected by the fund's shareholders to govern the fund, and its role is primarily one of oversight. The board of directors is not usually involved in the day-to-day management of the fund company. Portfolio management is taken care of by investment advisors who are independent of the board. They are constrained by a fund's investment objectives and policies as stated in the registration statement, which it files with its regulators and the prospectus that is written based on these filings for the investors. A fund's administrator is often an affiliate of the fund, typically the investment advisor, but could also be an unaffiliated third party. The services it provides to the fund have a type of supervisory function with respect to other servicers that cater to the fund's needs, as well as ensuring that the fund's operations comply with applicable regulatory requirements.

Mutual fund firms are very often subsidiaries of banks, but they do not hold a banking license themselves. Therefore, they are required by law to protect their portfolio securities by placing them with a custodian. Mutual funds and their shareholders also rely on the services of transfer agents to perform the various corporate actions required throughout the year. These include maintaining records of shareholder accounts, calculating and distributing dividends, and preparing and mailing shareholder account statements and tax information. Some transfer agents also prepare and mail statements confirming shareholder transactions and account balances, and maintain customer service departments, including call centers to respond to shareholder inquiries. These services are often performed by outside servicers or by large banks.

When describing the organization of the mutual fund industry processes, it becomes clear that they are very much centered on product complexity and segmented strictly along the logic of the ultimate "fund sponsors" (Glaus, 1997). Fund sponsors are the categories of investors that provide the necessary funding for the set-up of each investment product. Thereby, the segmentation is to some extent system-inherent as most financial regulators. Often the fund sponsor is equal to the fund firm, which starts to invest some of its own money into a new unit to ensure that interests of shareholders are aligned, to show commitment and

Average Fund Size (AuM/Fund)
(end of year)

		2000	2001	2002
World		**229.74**	**218.37**	**209.72**
Americas		**585.68**	**552.69**	**488.06**
	Argentina	32.85	17.13	4.84
	Brazil	70.83	60.44	35.11
	Canada	171.80	146.29	127.29
	Chile	31.92	28.76	29.67
	Costa Rica	7.53	13.71	13.58
	Mexico	60.62	90.64	84.50
	United States	854.03	839.85	775.15
Europe		**129.24**	**115.86**	**120.00**
	Austria	74.41	71.80	82.77
	Belgium	76.59	65.96	65.72
	Czech Republic	28.43	27.35	43.38
	Denmark[2]	82.45	75.01	82.79
	Finland	52.69	47.03	52.94
	France	101.06	93.83	108.73
	Germany	241.16	198.39	191.55
	Greece	110.02	88.80	102.39
	Hungary	22.71	25.39	44.36
	Ireland	101.95	116.98	131.29
	Italy	438.48	339.83	352.52
	Liechtenstein	N/A	N/A	34.66
	Luxembourg	122.80	114.63	116.94
	Netherlands	197 84	151 66	148 78

2003	2004	2005	2006	2007
257.44	**291.13**	**312.50**	**352.82**	**394.87**
572.48	**625.17**	**709.38**	**793.44**	**869.40**
10.30	12.66	18.13	27.59	28.17
61.18	77.15	112.82	144.06	182.01
179.32	216.07	289.39	321.03	342.69
20.66	23.44	20.45	19.11	19.40
21.35	9.16	7.31	10.18	12.94
85.44	85.54	113.59	143.28	179.59
912.43	1,008.20	1,116.59	1,282.64	1,497.20
164.07	**192.47**	**199.68**	**235.40**	**255.13**
105.62	123.46	123.73	135.27	129.63
80.66	92.41	82.90	88.63	90.54
70.40	91.70	104.53	124.81	115.08
123.83	153.19	159.66	193.56	210.45
102.82	134.49	136.38	180.33	214.08
145.34	173.36	175.65	218.64	241.38
263.16	284.34	275.82	283.84	254.50
144.88	164.53	129.60	111.76	129.60
41.00	51.20	66.68	52.94	59.33
182.22	223.96	256.81	337.82	328.29
473.06	448.10	435.28	457.83	454.21
65.23	73.35	69.85	74.31	64.20
167.85	203.67	226.50	276.33	305.75
157.80	188.44	183.22	229.51	253.16

Average Fund Size (AuM/Fund)
(end of year)

		2000	2001	2002
World		**229.74**	**218.37**	**209.72**
	Norway	42.71	36.88	36.92
	Poland	20.08	31.60	51.10
	Portugal	85.07	82.27	117.46
	Romania	0.50	0.42	1.35
	Russia	4.78	5.82	6.53
	Slovakia	N/A	N/A	N/A
	Slovenia	N/A	N/A	N/A
	Spain	71.20	63.35	72.64
	Sweden	153.41	129.27	113.27
	Switzerland	225.70	242.73	161.37
	Turkey	N/A	N/A	24.80
	United Kingdom	204.42	181.08	161.66
Asia and Pacific		**86.18**	**85.51**	**98.56**
	Australia	N/A	N/A	
	China	N/A	N/A	
	Hong Kong	200.74	178.65	174.44
	India	57.72	51.46	65.27
	Japan	154.67	119.95	111.55
	Korea, Rep. of	13.42	16.78	25.46
	New Zealand	12.85	11.16	13.01
	Pakistan	N/A	N/A	N/A
	Philippines	6.00	10.55	22.57
	Taiwan	111.37	159.43	177.07
Africa		**50.66**	**34.18**	**45.62**
	South Africa	50.66	34.18	45.62

Table 6: Average Fund Size and Scale Potential

2003	2004	2005	2006	2007
257.44	**291.13**	**312.50**	**352.82**	**394.87**
58.65	73.66	95.76	103.18	146.20
76.57	92.42	117.68	184.44	242.24
168.66	187.20	170.42	178.37	165.18
1.45	3.79	4.74	7.72	9.51
6.45	6.41	9.40	15.81	13.46
28.68	54.20	70.58	73.74	88.19
N/A	N/A	N/A	25.88	39.80
103.34	124.09	118.59	113.73	134.88
180.92	232.24	256.59	373.30	408.71
205.83	245.21	228.76	261.93	310.90
58.74	75.47	79.13	54.83	76.90
234.35	288.14	325.66	396.82	459.18
116.95	**144.43**	**156.05**	**182.25**	**247.75**
N/A	N/A		N/A	N/A
N/A	N/A		N/A	1,272.91
265.64	339.23	456.41	574.21	704.32
85.14	83.37	91.11	124.40	195.64
133.42	156.53	178.05	210.27	238.24
18.09	26.74	27.34	31.37	38.33
17.12	20.20	18.35	21.03	23.96
N/A	N/A	N/A	69.81	77.44
37.71	39.67	45.28	40.63	52.25
190.04	173.77	124.84	124.32	127.90
73.95	**100.57**	**106.31**	**104.03**	**114.59**
73.95	100.57	106.31	104.03	114.59

guarantee an initial funding to start business. The target group to which funds can be marketed, once they are sponsored and running, is defined by regulators and regulatory guidelines, (e.g. by the KAG in Switzerland). Therefore, the potential investors in question are restricted by the scope of the asset management strategy. The two basic investor categories are retail investors and private clients, and/or institutional investors (WALTER, 1999b).

The investors channel the required funding from foundations, endowments and other reserves either into direct investments or into different categories of collective investment schemes. The most important by size are pension plans and mutual funds. However, pension plans – once established – again represent institutional investors, which may engage as (indirect) sponsors of mutual funds. As different investors may favor different treatment in terms of customized tax and fee structures, most funds offer access to specific investment strategies through multiple types of asset claims, i.e. share classes. The business logic of mutual funds lies in attracting sufficient volume from sponsors and investors in order to leverage on economies of scale. Limits to these economics of scales are given by the distribution capacity (i.e. the regulatory boundary to market a product) and the transaction and management capacity (i.e. the research and trading base upon which a fund firm can leverage). Besides mere size, capability may be the second important lever, allowing knowledge spillovers from research and product development to be used to increase a firm's scope. Internationally, the U.S. seems to be the most dominant market, not only in market size, but also in the average volume managed by each fund. It is very likely that these two factors are most probably closely correlated. Table 6 depicts a cross-country comparison of average fund volume managed by funds and allows a basic glimpse of the competitive structure that rests beneath the various regulatory schemes.

Table 6: Average Fund Size and Scale Potential (see previous p. 24–27)

The Mutual Fund Value Chain and Functionality

In the case of the mutual fund industry, or more general financial services, (temporary) stability in the industry architecture is constrained by different functions that need to be provided during every "production", i.e. financial intermediation process. There exist a number of slightly differing classifications (BERNET, 2003) for this intermediation or production process. We refer here to a concept of four functions as outlined by FREIXAS AND ROCHET (1997) as these authors have already applied the intermediation concept to the specific case of mutual funds directly under this classification: payment services)

(ii) Transforming assets

(iii) Managing risks

(iv) Processing information and monitoring borrowers

Not all of these functionalities need to be performed autonomously to "produce" financial services – but all the functionalities have to be present in a closed intermediation system. In the case of asset management functionality, mutual fund firms are generally viewed as potential vehicles to "produce" liquidity, asset transformation, risk management and fund processing; these products can be substituted by various other types of vehicles (e.g. classical investment companies). Thus, the industry architecture in mutual fund markets is simply a sub-architecture of the dominating money management functionality. Accordingly, the structure and performance of the money management industry has to be discussed "by the nature of the conduits through which the financial assets of the ultimate savers flow [...] and through the liabilities of the ultimate users of finance" (WALTER AND SISLI, 2006, p. 6). Under the more general perspective of asset management, mutual funds are thus always threatened by the functional substitution of other more efficient or more specialized instruments that support broadly similar functions, independent of what vehicle or financial instrument is favored to provide the intermediation services. In this sense, the mutual fund industry does not exist as an industry of its own. More specifically, it is a sub-industry of the much broader asset management industry. Within this market, mutual funds eventually evolved by efficiently bridging gaps in the intermediation processes. This bridging is characterized by solutions for specific groups of retail customers who could not otherwise achieve the same quality of service (risk-return-performance) as institutional managers.

The asset management industry is analyzed predominantly along product types (performance and brand arguments) and cost issues. This is also true for the sub-type of mutual fund competition. Consequently, from a strategic management point of view, discussions focus on the width and depth of vertical and horizontal boundaries of the firms. In this environment, mutual funds compete with alternative intermediation solutions, as well as with other mutual funds that are offered both under a joint "parental" organization and by third parties (banks). The critical resources are the customer deposits. They are the very onset of every theoretical argument to characterize competitive environments for a mutual fund industry (Boot and Schmeits, 2005).

When pursuing deposits, the competitive landscape seems to be very unleveled. There are clear differences between countries in terms of how mutual funds (and other investment vehicles) are distributed and in how their origination process is organized. These differences are closely interlinked with the local comparative industry growth and its historical (legal) structures (Walter, 1999a). For instance, European fund distribution is strongly dominated by bank-branch diffusion (e.g. Germany 80%; France 70% or Spain 61%), where independent advisors or electronic market places and exchanges have gained higher importance in the UK (50%) or the U.S. (45%) based on industry statistics (Fischer and DenOtter, 2007; ICI, 2008). Not before European legislation will have pressed for decreasing barriers to trade in financial products and a more stringent control of vertical competition, did new firms enter the markets and – most interestingly – many of them focused on direct fund distribution. Examples are "Direkt Anlage" in Germany or "Virgin Direct" in the UK when only looking at intra-country distribution, or "Fidelity Investments" and "Fleming Flagship" in the case of cross-border

distribution. Another trend that has emerged is the scarcity of certain clustered capabilities or the prevalence of an existing transaction capacity that provokes an increased separation of fund administration, fund management and fund origination (white-labeling).

Processes and role involvement along the value chain

The process view of mutual fund firms can be depicted relatively straightforwardly. Every investment vehicle has to be produced and distributed. In between, the vehicles – or more precisely the assets invested by the vehicles - are to be managed by an integrated bank or by a network of cooperating specialists. The complete process can be illustrated along an idealized industry value chain. Thereby, we follow the notion that the value of any end product or service is built up in stages. Along these stages of production, labor can be divided within and across companies. By analyzing the value chain, an organization can gain a better understanding of the key capabilities involved in creating the products or services it is involved with (Jacobides, 2008a). For this reason, the value chain can be regarded as a complete transformation model overlaid by the necessary support functions.

Illustration 3: The Mutual Fund Industry Production Chain; Data DenOtter (2007)/Interviews *(see page 32)*

Our depiction of the mutual fund value chain is based on our industry observation. We attributed an average range for value appropriation along the value chain. It should be noted that value creation and value appropriation are not aligned. Whilst product innovation may create substantial value, it can only appropriate limited value. The picture is quite the opposite for distribution. Distributors only generate limited additional value, but they control the bottleneck (of the industry as it is today. This allows them to extract a proportion of value that is relatively high, compared to the work that has to be invested (once a sales network is established).

Thus, value appropriation does not necessarily have to follow the value creation by the industry. For instance, value might be generated in the design and development of distinct products, but is only captured when these products are distributed to the final customer. Consequently, there is a strong incentive for a production unit to be linked closely with the distributory function, in order to recoup the cost of the underlying activity. This is easily illustrated as distribution is the task across the entire value chain that commands the largest share of the created value, while production and new product issuance in contrast can appropriate a relatively small portion of the overall fees. The special position of the distributors can be seen in their intra-firm bargaining power, as they control the critical interface to the clients. Finally, fund management is the other strong player in the value chain. It controls the dominant share of generated value by an accrued volume in trading and portfolio management. Another aspect is the timing of claims the different functions can lay on the generated value. Production functions usually get their claimants at product issuance, whereas management and distribution functions share the annual fee income, which is generally calculated on the net asset value (NAV) of the products.

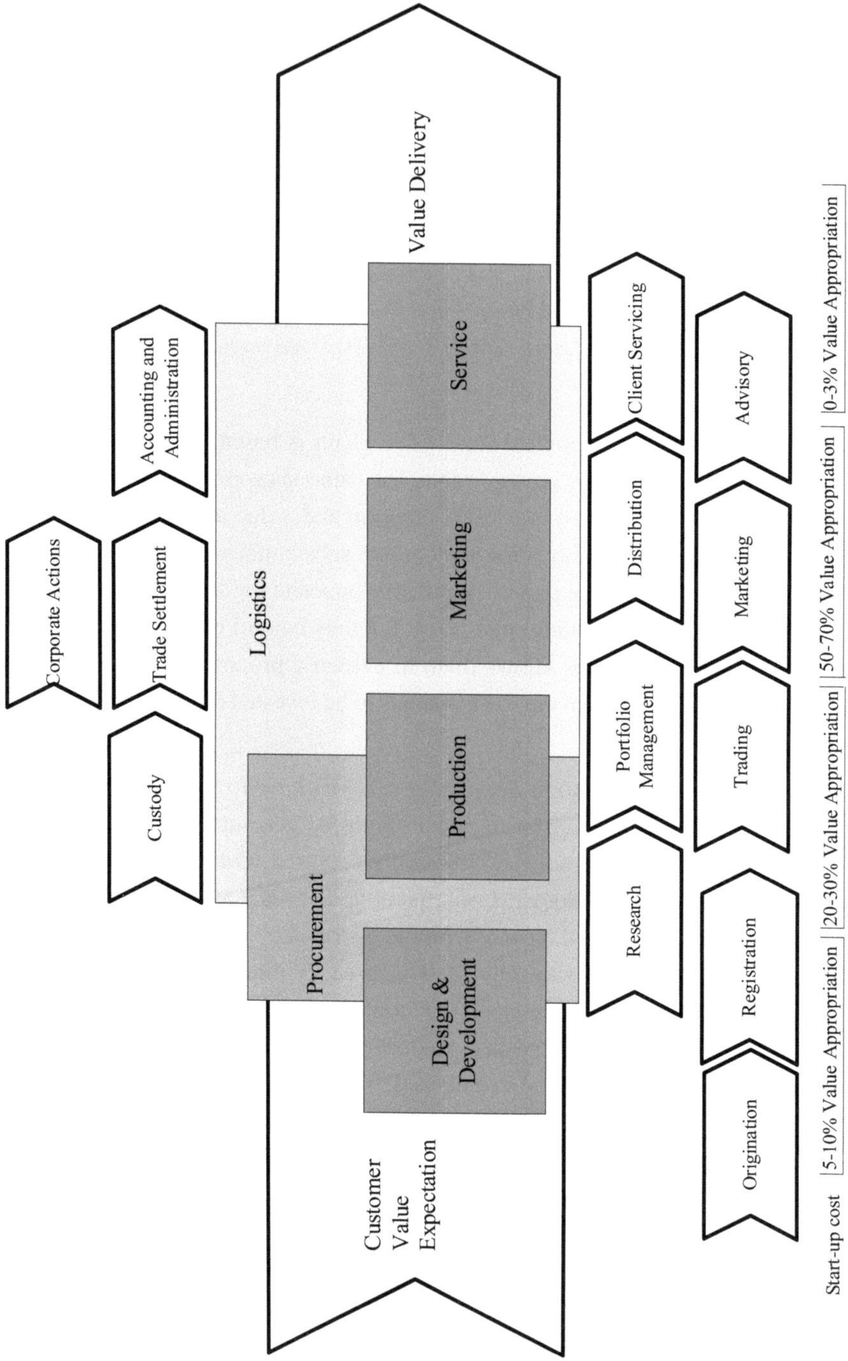

Illustration 3: The Mutual Fund Industry Production Chain; Data DenOtter (2007)/Interviews

Current Trends: Challenges for Efficiency

When looking at current worldwide industry structure, mutual fund complex and value chain, increasing efficiency and new regulatory schemes emerge as the most apparent fields of change. For this reason, the current bottle neck in value appropriation, the distribution function, may be a good starting point. Currently, distribution channels can range from in-house platform of banks, OTC trading between different intermediaries, up to mutual fund shares that are effectively traded at exchanges (Deutsche Bank, 2007). These modes of exchange also define the interaction between product types that are dependent on the degree of product standardization. That linkage can be illustrated by standardized product types with low risk features that are traded over mutual fund exchanges ("supermarkets") such as (exchange trade funds) ETFs (Fischer and DenOtter, 2007) and hedge fund shares that have to be acquired on a per-case basis after undergoing a complete due diligence process and agreement to lock-up periods for trading in the vehicles. Whilst both of these product types do not normally qualify as "mutual funds", they may serve as strong illustrations of the two extremes in type of capability enhanced versus transaction efficient products and their accompanied trading mechanism.

When asking industry practitioners about current trends and challenges, they refer to three major factors: First, the demand push "towards simple and transparent products at lower cost", the regulatory challenge of opening European markets and increased supervision and compliance cost, and third, basically as a consequence of demand and regulatory pressure, a call for more efficiency. Thereby, efficiency goes in hand with specialization and collaboration across the value chain. Most of the challenges have to be met by increasing (operational) efficiency – and hence by rethinking current positioning along the traditional integrated value chain. Potential changes in this value chain of mutual funds can thereby at first glimpse be identified at the level of altered overall industry structure (e.g. a more oligopolistic or more competitive setting) that could be triggered by regulatory adjustments mainly and altered organization that corresponds more smoothly to market demands and executes demand more swiftly and more efficiently.

These non-regulatory factors call for capability development in product innovation and risk management just as much as for lowering transaction cost and improving overall efficiency. Especially where transaction efficiency drives product characteristics, standardization and volume (i.e. potential market size) become central features of analysis. Here, there are a number of ongoing trends to be witnessed, mainly driven by the European market integration: The main levers for increased efficiency can here be seen in the initiatives to standardize notification procedures and sales prospectuses, or in the more convenient market access for third-country mutual funds, the so called fund passports.

Besides the general initiatives of European Union directives, there are two more actions that are often discussed as a potential means to increase competition and industry efficiency across markets. Both are, however, for the time being, to some extent restricted by regulators. Fund mergers and asset pooling by mutual fund firms are two elements that might impact the landscape where they are admitted. Whilst the first might lead to increased scales directly, pooling of assets might allow new options in financial disintermediation in the asset management industry as a whole. With respect to mergers, there is obviously a considerable savings potential to be tapped, which cannot be replaced by outsourcing arrangements as possible today. As for the second, asset pooling would represent an even more desirable tool for reducing operational costs and rationalizing small subscale products more swiftly and across single fund firms. Particularly entity pooling in the shape of "Master Feeder"-structures appears to be a highly practical way to obtain better market access within closely knit regulatory rooms, such as Europe, at lower costs. Both options, just as well as facilitated and improved market access through standardized prospects and procedures might enhance competition to the ultimate benefit of investors. However, for now they do not yet form significant building blocks for industrial architecture (re-)design.

Industry Architecture and Building Blocks for change

General theories for discussing industry structures and competition rest upon two dominant paradigms. The Structure-Performance-Conduct (SPC) assumption and the Efficient Hypothesis Construct (EHC). The former describes competitive outcomes (i.e. heterogeneity in positioning and performance of the firms) as the consequence of the dominant industry structure (e.g. an oligopolistic setting). The analysis under the SPC is a form of static observation of industry outcomes, as it focuses on the equilibrium state of an industry and compares this state with attributes of firms that happen to be in the market at such moments. The approach is thus mainly suitable to compare different equilibrium outcomes along different time periods or across different countries. The second attempt proposes a correlation between an emerging structure and the ex-ante observed firm heterogeneity (e.g. with distinct respect to firm efficiency). Therefore the efficiency hypothesis has a more dynamic notion.

The dominance of Industrial Organization (IO) assumptions are (stable and existing) oligopolistic settings, given the observed stark concentration of the total market share within the hands of relatively few competitors and accordingly suggest the use of SPC concepts to address the market. However, this "observed" degree of concentration differs very widely both across regulatory environments (e.g. U.S. versus European cases) as well as across fund product types. Despite the dominance of large players, the survival rate of products per incumbent is extremely low (on average below 5 years) and new product launches as well as de novo entry of new boutique firms dominate the field. Thus, from a competition point of view, an SCP analysis does not seem the right choice to describe the mutual fund market. We therefore focus here on the dynamic perspective offered by the efficiency hypothesis. As there is not yet an accepted integrated framework, the SCP-based approach initiated by Barney (1986) will be used with the necessary care, but viewed through the dynamic lenses of efficiency changes along the financial intermediation process that determines the financial service industry architecture (Matthews and Thompson, 2005). We have shown that from a basic structure-conduct perspective, the mutual fund industry is indeed dominated by large and integrated players as the notion of scale is a key characteristic of fund firm profitability and value is appropriated dominantly at the customer interface, i.e. the distribution function.

When addressing the firm differences and shifts in firm organization from a fund industry perspective, the role of interdependence of market growth, the firm's transaction volume and the firms choice in setting up new products have not been covered in deep by previous research. This interaction of firm level structure, intra- and inter-firm relations and the resulting boundaries of organization can be summarized under the term "industrial architecture". The industry architecture consists of a description of all the involved actors, their roles, as well as of potential advantages and disadvantages with respect to the actors' ability to generate cash flows in a given environment (Jacobides, Knudsen and Augier, 2006). Industry architectures itself emerge either when firms win momentum on the basis of superior capabilities or in terms of technical efficiency that allows reconfiguring organizational transactions of processes to be more efficiently (Jacobides and Winter, 2005). Another lever can be seen in legal innovation that allows to alter established processes and relations along vertical or horizontal firm boundaries, or, under technological innovation that redefines variable costs involved in the production process (Jacobides et al., 2006) and alters transaction or information cost.

Currently, when addressing issues from the management literature's point of view, many studies still based on the (sometimes even exclusive) observation that the nature and character of the competitive conditions facing a firm determines a firm's strategy (BARNEY, 1986) – a perspective that corresponds clearly to the basic SCP assumption. However, the concept of competition is not as unambiguous as its use in rather statistic microeconomic models might imply. With respect to mutual fund industries, ambiguity is especially relevant, e.g. when IO theory is used to describe competition at the industry (or sometimes the firm) level, but Chamberlinean monopolistic competition prevails in product markets (CHORDIA, 1996; SHY AND STENBACKA, 2003). This somehow urges the discussion on mutual funds to move towards a perspective of industry dynamics and market evolution, traditionally linked to Schumpeterian concepts. A focussed discussion of drivers for change not only for financial service firms, but in the distinct mutual fund context therefore becomes important and should be analyzed from an equally dynamic perspective in terms of theory building and measurement.

Challenging existing industry architectural structures along the building blocks

Drivers for change at the firm and industry level emerge from efficiency arguments within the dominant configuration of the industry architecture. Industry architecture thereby is ultimately bounded by the basic processes of financial intermediation.

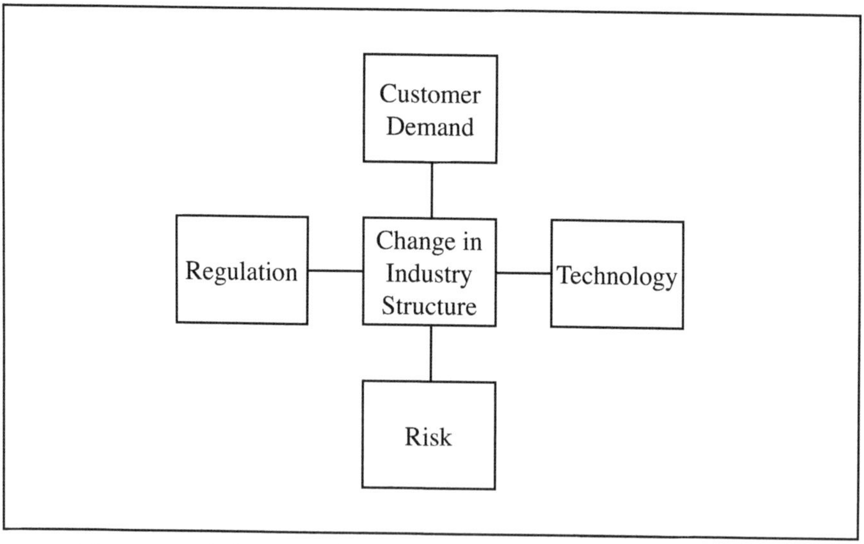

Illustration 4: Drivers of Change in the Financial Service Industry

The agenda of financial intermediation orients itself along four determinants of change (Bernet, 2006): Regulation, transparency, demand (compounding performance and risk management issues) and technology. These are the elements that allow the financial architecture (respectively its four functionalities) to be reshaped (Freixas and Rochet, 1997). For the special case of mutual funds, regulation and technology can be seen as the prime drivers of change, since other factors (i.e. risk, demand and transparency) mainly center at the features of the different products that are offered.

On the technological side, the strong impact of innovations on the industry structure and business models could be observed in a prominent case along the introduction of the internet. This innovation has not only shifted information (and hence transparency) standards, but it has also reshuffled distribution structures and trading modes as new entries (e.g. Internet-discount-brokers). Increased competition and new institutions (e.g. fund supermarkets) have started to redesign the costs and benefits of vertically integrated market participants. The main effect of the new technology has been its enabling of economies of scale due to globally (or regionally) pooled investment flows and straight-through-processing (Benner, 2007). However, the large scale application of the technology remains largely constrained by regulation issues up to now.

On the regulatory side, the potential abolition of these constraints could result in a second consolidation wave, as minimal scales are to be redefined. With respect to these regulation issues, the discussion focuses on the two (still) dominant regions, the U.S. and Europe. Whilst the U.S. industry has long been able to work in a relatively stable regulatory environment, mutual fund groups are facing tighter reporting standards with respect to three – sometimes integrated – large projects: Basel, Sarbanes-Oxley (SOX) and International Financial Reporting Standards (IFRS) (KPMG, 2007b). For the European market, the regulatory challenge goes even beyond that. European regulation standards are in a state of flux as a result of the drafting of new regulations (UCITS) that should finally allow the economies of scale and scope to be taken advantage of (Fisher and Harindranath, 2004; KPMG, 2007a; Otten and Bams, 2002). On the other hand, the influence of SOX on European players is still very much limited.

Finally, *on the demand side*, real innovations are extremely scarce in the financial industry; most product innovations are either adoption of concepts already successfully implemented in other firm divisions or geographical regions (Matthews and Thompson, 2005). However, one (potential) innovation could be seen in the (albeit regulatory driven) introduction of master-funds that allow the pooling of previously illiquid investment products that are brought together from different competing asset managers (FISCHER AND DENOTTER, 2007). This innovation is interesting from a financial market perspective, as it leads to increased liquidity in certain securities and to a higher degree of international risk sharing across the financial system (DELL'ARICCIA, IGAN AND LAEVEN, 2008; MAYHEW, 2002). From an industry or fund firm perspective, it simply represents a broadening of the product portfolio in a high margin segment (rivaling the more traditional vehicles).

Regulatory shifts, new technologies and new demand structures or revised assessments of involved the counterparty and product risks are seen as the key determinants of market evolution (BERNET, 2003, 2006). Thus, it makes sense to analyze the mutual fund industry in detail with respect to the underlying economic dynamics and evolving new (sub) markets that are bound to define the complexities of the outlined strategic environment and eventually find evidence for fields of corporate strategy action. Different sectors of financial systems are thereby affected differently by the dynamics of market shifts in terms of:

(i) the underlying environmental and regulatory determinants;

(ii) the financial infrastructure and services that need to be provided (i.e. market information, financial research, financial rating services and portfolio diagnostics on the one hand, and trading, payments, securities clearance and settlement, and custody services on the other);

(iii) the generic information, interpretation and transaction cost advantages that the strategy literature refers to as "capabilities" (JACOBIDES AND WINTER, 2005). These capabilities are needed to add value and to profit from any flow-of-fund linkages. From a financial intermediation point of view, firm heterogeneity in the industry also can occur along demand structures (as they can be met more accurately or more cheaply) and risk transformation.

The ultimate boundaries for positioning alternatives are twofold: The first boundary is defined by the emerged *process organization*, and efficiency gains through improved organization and technology. The second boundary is set by the way mutual funds "create" value in an intermediation system by tailoring new products to meet demands more accurately, or to capture liquidity and risk sharing inefficiencies across existing single product sources (e.g. in fund-of-fund constructions), ultimately representing the motive behind customer's product choice.

Clearly, however, these boundaries only temporarily restrict positioning discussions. Both types can be influenced by new entrants, redesigning the process flows or by new product launches, fitting better the customer needs and shifting demand from an intermediation point of view.

Consequently, *the distribution capacity* equals the amount of money provided by its clients and the financial reserves that are pooled in mutual funds (closed and open-end) or pension plans. In the pooling process, clients are advised by private bankers or financial advisors to take the basic decision of fund or pension plan investment as well as in which form of mutual fund the money should be invested best. The funds allotted to pension plans are accounted for under pension regulations and entrusted to asset managers that engage in the actual portfolio management.

New entrants tap the markets from a process perspective mostly as support servicers that only engage in selected parts of the value chain that can be addressed by vertical diversification of their existing processes (e.g. an e-broker that also uses its systems to distribute mutual fund products and hence substitutes one (part) of an integrated bank's distribution channels) (KNUUTILA, PUTTONEN AND SMYTHE, 2006). When such an entry occurs, incumbents have to change their cost structure, as the new entrants either eradicate certain steps in the value chain or compete at marginal cost of capacity utilization in the case of related diversification, the same mechanism can also be observed in purely industrial cases, e.g. the automotive industry (BRESSER, ESCHEN AND MILLONING, 2001; CARROLL, BIGELOW, SEIDEL AND TSA, 1996). The (process) organization of the market is thus defined by fund-sponsor centricity, and firm heterogeneity evolves along the sponsor's value proposition and results in an efficiency oriented, commission based or routine oriented set-up of the firms in the market. New entrants are easily making their way on to the stage with both standard type products and meta-fund constructions – such as fund-of-fund constructs that try to add value by bringing together different categories of (often small and not liquid) third party funds in a new product in terms of risk-performance, but also cost characteristics. Incumbents react by spreading their product variety and tapping all kind of new trends, ranging from "mega trends", new emerging regions (emerging countries) or asset classes (collateralized debts to natural resources). The distinctions along these features generally are following a risk-performance dimension. This spread can be observed along fund families or platforms (sharing similarities in asset style) or along classes (that enable the use of different fee and tax structures for identical investment strategies).

This may lead to the expansion of different classes (i.e. distribution segments; generally tax focused) or risk types (i.e. portfolio adjustments in terms of shifts in weights of the securities in one "basket") without a requirement for distinct capabilities as they are available at the family level. Additionally, new products can be launched at relatively low marginal cost, once the basic regulatory approval per fund family is permitted (FISCHER AND DENOTTER, 2007). Therefore, firm heterogeneity from a product perspective results from different commitment and capability development in terms of research skills, risk assessment and branding, or marketing power from a fund firm perspective, and the result of (changing) customer demands and firms ability to adjust in terms of risk and performance characteristics of the offered products from a clients perspective respectively. Thus, the general notion of risk and demand being two separate drivers for change is somewhat combined when taking a product stance. Linkages between the process view and the product view exist throughout the entire value chain, but they can be assumed to be most dominant in product distribution, and the distribution of custom-tailored vehicles.

Summing up the process and the product view from an intermediation perspective shows the connection between structure efficiency and product tailoring to industry dynamics and differentiation at the firm level. Firm heterogeneity (or drivers of change) can thus be attributed to regulation and technology responsiveness under the process perspective, or to the ability of superior transformation of risk, respectively the superior adaptation to customer demands from the financial intermediation and product perspective. These drivers correspond to some extent to product and process innovations in the mutual fund complex. Heterogeneity in one or more of these drivers enables new entry (or lack of adaptation facilitates failure). Consequently, the notion of market evolution can be broadly linked as depicted in Illustration 5. The interesting questions in this context focus on the dynamics of adaptation and the swiftness of building firm heterogeneity or creating and destroying industry value in this mutual fund complex. WALTER (1998) structured these efficiency issues in a comprehensive way and from a financial intermediation optic. Illustration 5 depicts the structure for the specific case of mutual funds and places the general overview into the context of the market evolution discussion. The drivers of market evolution (technology, risk-adjusted demand and regulation) shift barriers to entry and allow firms that are more efficient in terms of information processing, transaction costs, research or branding capabilities to penetrate markets more deeply, or even to enter entirely new markets. Accordingly, there are two levers of entry or market evolution:

First, process efficiency is sketched as a function of existing resources, i.e. capacity of the firm and its competitors, and the degree of capacity utilization. Infrastructure and technology are the main variables here. Thus, the perspective of the fund sponsors must also be dominated by a notion of "efficiency", resulting in initiatives towards increased "straight-through-processing" and standardization of products and distribution channels vis-à-vis a heterogeneous customer group. Second, information efficiency and product innovation defines a capability development and know-how base framed competition field that has more of a "commission-fee" (i.e. cost-performance ratios of products) attitude towards the fund sponsors. Both levers are strategically dependent on path-dependency with respect to resources and capabilities, as well as the ability and the commitment towards further investment in one (or both) of them.

The different advantages and dynamics that flow from resource and capability commitments show up in the positioning or in the functional dynamics of the intermediation process, where securities are tailored to meet fund sponsors and capital market needs most efficiently. Consequently, resource based as well as capability based explanations are relevant in describing existing patterns and future strategies in the field. Independent of the chosen strategy, competition centers on relative advantages generated by superior information, interpretation ability of the information and transaction costs when settling the deals. These eventually firm' specific advantages are reflected in different approaches towards the risk-return transformation of financial assets under a collective investment agreement. The capability background and the cost base to perform this transformation process yields specific advantages in either product origination, asset management (brokerage and trading) or distribution. Additionally, a broad set of support activities such as accounting, or legal and compliance services forms a key part of the "industrial" production chain of mutual funds, but it does not have a direct function in the financial disintermediation process. Nevertheless, especially these support functions play a particularly important role as they are affected first, once change in industrial design gets started, simply because they are generally seen as the "least" strategic or competitive advantage by most firms.

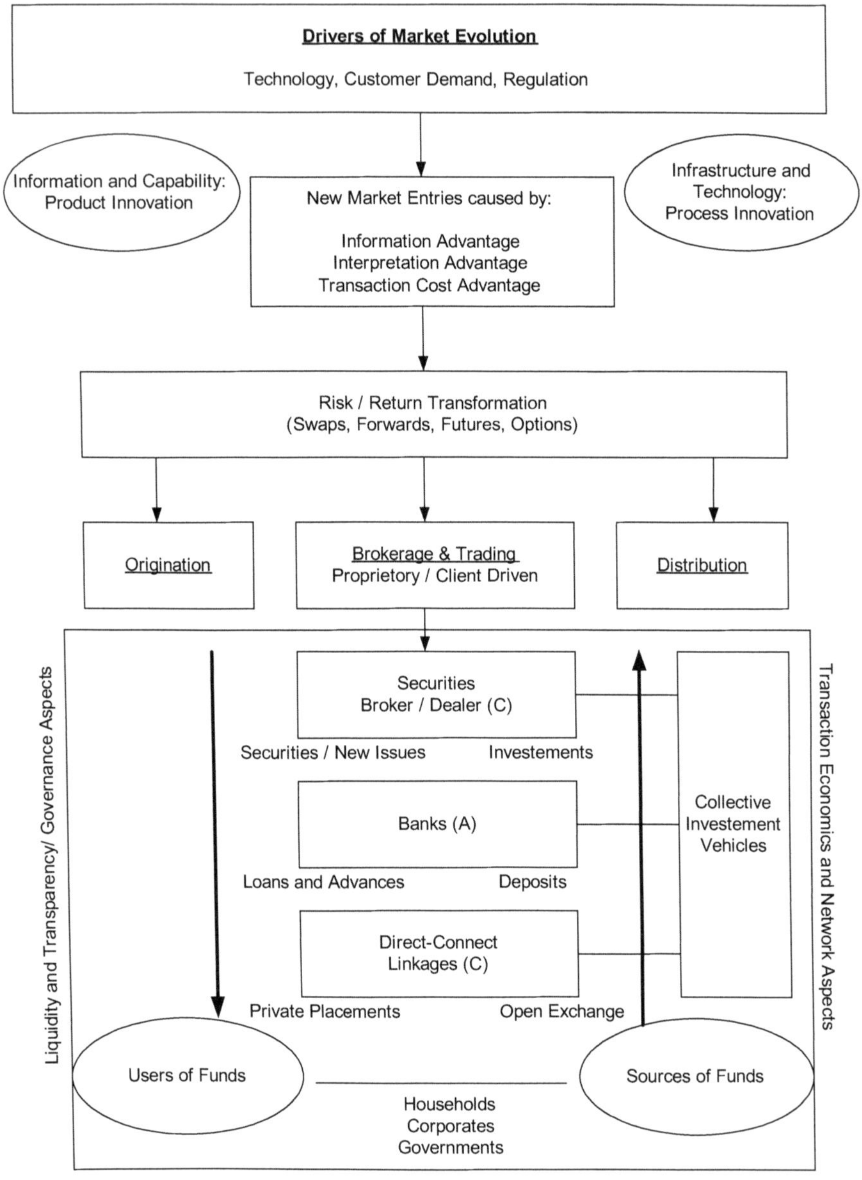

Illustration 5: Market Evolution and the Mutual Fund Structures – An extended version of the basic Intermediation Perspective proposed by WALTER *(1998)*

Drivers of Change in the Mutual Fund Industry – The current state of discussion in the literature

When discussing industry dynamics and drivers of change, the most traditional paths are carved by (neo-)institutional economic theory, and within this context more specifically by transaction cost arguments. More recent approaches build on the early works of Schumpeter and link this discussion towards an industrial dynamics perspective and the role of capabilities as discussed in the capability-based theory of the firm (EISENHARDT AND MARTIN, 2000). Evolutionary economic concepts and the economics of market entry are thereby the corresponding concepts to measure these effects in large samples.

With special focus on the mutual fund industry, (neo-)institutionalism is only indirectly introduced into the discussion. The main focus of the literature lies on those drivers that directly affect the financial intermediation process performed by the vehicles, or on demand side aspects that have had a strong influence on the earlier discussion. At this stage, the discourse has been restricted to demand issues and consequently resulted in product innovations that adjust more smoothly to these trends. WALTER (1998, p. 8) outlined the main demand-side drivers for change in the mutual fund industry:

1. A continues broad-based trend toward professional management of discretionary household assets in the form of mutual funds or unit trusts, and other types of collective investment vehicles.

2. The recognition that most government-sponsored pension systems, many of which were created wholly or partially on a pay-as-you go basis, have become fundamentally untenable under demographic projections that appear virtually certain to materialize, and must be progressively replaced by asset pools that will provide the kinds of returns necessary to meet the needs of growing numbers of longer-living retirees.

3. Partial displacement of traditional defined-benefit public and private sector pension programs backed by assets contributed by employers and working individuals – under the pressure of the evolving demographics, rising administrative costs, and shifts in risk-allocation by a variety of defined contribution schemes.

4. Reallocation of portfolios that have – for regulatory, tax or institutional reasons – been overweight domestic financial instruments toward a greater role for non-domestic asset classes, which not only promise higher returns but also may reduce the beneficiaries' exposure to risk due to portfolio diversification across both asset classes and economic and financial environments that are less than perfectly correlated in terms of total investment returns.

The growth implied by the first three of these factors, combined with the asset allocation shifts implied by the fourth factor clearly shape the dynamics and competitive structure of the global institutional asset management industry. However, we sense that the restriction on these demand side shifts and the resulting product specific answers might be too narrow. As outlined, we see a motivation for a more comprehensive attempt, taking also technological (including process innovations) and regulatory redefinitions of the markets into account. Consequently, this industry and its competitive environment are, from an academic perspective, a very promising laboratory for innovation and industry dynamics. We address the multitude of affecting factors by focusing on the node of sensitivity to market evolution: Shifts in barriers to entries that enable new competitors to test new products and service processes frame incumbents' responsiveness and display the logic and dynamics of the competitive environment underlying the single firm's corporate strategic actions. In order to maintain the comprehensive nature of the contribution, we address the drivers of evolution that (re)define barriers to entry very generally as "innovations", independent on their product or process relatedness or their endogenous (e.g. learning, new product ventures) or exogenous (a competitor's behavior or regulatory action) nature. This theoretical set-up also allows one to divert from the established paths of the strategy literature to some extent, as product or process answers are seen as two forms of firm reaction that do not exist independently of each other. Vertical and horizontal diversification can – despite the literature tradition in management – be observed as two potential answers to one identical "input" problem.

From a traditional perspective on market dynamics, there are two explanations for this problem: First, the transaction cost argument and second, asymmetric information (ALLEN AND SANTOMERO, 1998). Overcoming one of these elements reduces friction in intermediation and yields benefits for the customer or the market participants (based on the degree of competition in the respective sub-market. Thereby, regulation and technology are one pillar (generally associated with transaction cost) in the argument, information asymmetry is a second, whilst the third, "market evolvement and capability development" is completely different. The transaction cost features are addressed by FISHER AND HARINDRANATH (2004), who provide a good overview with distinct focus on electronic distribution of fund products across Europe. Transaction economic arguments for industry structure outcomes as well as for firm boundaries within a specific industry structure setting represent a whole string of literature, building upon the seminal works of COASE AND WILLIAMSON (COASE, 1937; WILLIAMSON, 1985, 1991, 1999) or the critique on transaction arguments by GHOSHAL AND MORAN (1996). Generally,transaction cost arguments are – with respect to the mutual fund industry – split into two subsegments: Distribution and exchange processes, i.e. the buying and redeeming of mutual fund shares of an investor versus the corresponding cost of trading for the mutual fund provider. Considerable literature has been devoted to this problem by presenting evidence for the information cost aspects and for the industry structure's influence on these costs (ABIRU, NAHATA, RAYCHAUDHURI AND WATERSON, 1998; ADMATI AND PFLEIDERER, 1990) or by outlining the trading cost aspects (BERGSTRESSER, CHALMERS AND TUFANO, 2004; KOPPENHAVER, 1999).

Most attention, however, has been given to the disruption of business models that have affected distribution channels, e.g. most recently the introduction of internet based sales and its influence on organizational boundaries. Based on the theories of CHRISTENSEN (CHRISTENSEN, 1997; CHRISTENSEN, JOHNSON AND RIGBY, 2002; CHRISTENSEN, VERLINDEN AND WESTERMAN, 2002), a number of case studies, very often for Scandinavian countries have been published (BRESSER ET AL., 2001; GOEKE AND GERSCH, 2007; KNUUTILA ET AL., 2006; KORPELA AND PUTTONEN, 2006; QUÉLIN AND CLAUDE-GAUDILLAT, 2005). Certainly, transaction costs and technology issues are a dominant topic for the assessment of the individual mutual fund firm. Equally, the shifts in trading costs and information transparency may well exert a strong influence on performance, as it was commonly assumed that (all) mutual funds can trade at significantly lower cost (than individuals) and can therefore achieve diversification goals much more cost efficiently (DEUTSCHE BANK, 2007). Given this explanation, it might be expected that where an individual's trading costs for direct investments are lowered, the share of ownership of mutual funds would fall in parallel (ALLEN AND SANTOMERO, 1998). However, such a consumer behavior cannot be observed, despite strong evidence for gradually decreasing trading costs of both institutional as well as retail investors compared to a mutual fund firm's expenses (ICI, 2008) at industry level.

The other dominant explanation for mutual fund industry structure that exists beside transaction cost arguments, was developed by LAKONISHOK ET AL. (LAKONISHOK, SHLEIFER, VISHNY, HART AND PERRY, 1992) and focuses on information asymmetry approaches at the fund manager level. The authors thereby argue that, in money management, it is almost impossible to ascertain the future performance of any agent. This uncertainty leads into a segmentation of the industry into two business (or product) groups.

The first business group does – from an information asymmetry perspective – not face problems in the area of unobservable quality as the firms providing the services are large banks and insurance companies that provide fairly generic products (e.g. index funds immunized, dedicated-bond portfolios, guaranteed investment contracts and annuities). Hence, large firms offer standardized products that require fewer investment skills and thus inherently only yield average performances. It is sensible for market participants to buy these products from the large competitors as – given the equal risk-performance metrics of two competing products – their reputation makes up for eventual counterparty risks and thus wins an advantage over managers less focused on their reputation. This segment does not need to communicate frequently or directly with its sponsors (investors) and its cost structure shows rapidly declining average costs, allowing a small number of high-reputation banks to capture and keep a large share of the market.

It is another story for the second business group, which provides specialized rather than generic money management operations. Firms in this sector provide much more service and interaction to their sponsors or investors and engage in riskier exposures due to the necessary performance pressure that is linked to more information activity, but also in fewer liquid assets – as the continuous direct interaction with investors enables them to communicate and execute more sophisticated and more long-run investments. A similar result is also achieved for mutual funds by MAMAYSKY AND SPIEGEL (2002) and for vertical industries more generally by BONACCORSI AND GIURI (2001). From a managerial perspective, a corresponding process of capability development over time can be assumed to move towards the fit with the sponsor group. Such a capability building process was illustrated for the mutual fund provider "Vanguard" by SIGGELKOW (2002). However, interestingly enough, neither the separation along asymmetric information arguments and capabilities, nor the story of the diminishing incentive of collective investing as transparency is enhanced and exchange cost deteriorate, fits the observed industry challenge fully; and even more striking – the two arguments are somewhat contradicting with respect to optimal strategy advises. The second argument of asymmetric information gives a clue for more investments into capabilities and the fostering of specialized boutiques, whilst the prior argument with transaction costs supports well the cost focus of the discount brokers and ETFs. However, both these arguments also have a flip-side. Asymmetric information fosters not only boutiques, but also large banks that are "stuck-in-the-middle" and transaction cost does not really give a hint for why the firms should split up into the boutique-style and not keep their negotiation power vis-à-vis the exchanges as integrated firms.

3 Research Set Up

In chapter 2 we outlined the structure of the mutual fund industry. Thereby, it became quite obvious that the industry structure across countries varies widely. The first and most obvious distinction was made with respect to growth rates that can be explained to some part with macro figures, such as demographics, market opening or growth of local capital stock. The second difference refers to the variation in average assets under management per country and hence the potential economies of scale for the mutual fund firms. This difference might be more difficult to explain and arguably nests mostly in regulatory scope, size of the home market and logic of the mutual fund. All three of these effects are expected to be in the focus of future changes to the market, especially in Europe where the European Union attempts to deepen the cross-border market and joint regulatory standards with their directives known as Undertakings for Collective Investment in Transferable Securities (UCITS). Whilst in this context market size and regulatory scope have been analyzed well (e.g. OXERA 2006), the competitive logic of the market has not been looked in depths so far. But also here, the industry is expecting to meet challenges that might chain the underlying economic logic and affect the definition of boundaries of each firm. Table 7 summarized the main impacts expected by the sounding board of industry practitioners that accompanied the development process of this thesis.

Challenge	**Impact**	**Responses**
Move towards complex and structured products	Strong	3
Commoditization of Hedge-Fonds Strategies	Very Strong	5
Emergence of boutique-style firms	Medium	4
Outsourcing of core Asset Management	Medium	2
Outsourcing of back office services	Strong	4
Gradual opening of distribution channels	Strong	3
Open platforms	Low	2
Interviews:		6

Table 7: Challenges in the Mutual Fund Industry

Focal Issue and Guiding Research Questions

Given the outlined gaps in the literature and the practical challenges the mutual fund industry is confronted with, we choose an approach of exogenous change. A research policy to address the issues could follow three broad research questions:

(i) How can we understand, describe and influence market structures based on the economics of entry (i.e. market evolution) and the corresponding incumbent firm's reactions (market dynamics) in the mutual fund industry?

(ii) Do these reactions change when controlling for different types of a) ex-ante perceived or b) ex-post measured innovation impacts that cause the market evolution?

(iii) Once evolution occurred, how do firms adjust? I.e. what is the nature of these firms ex-ante and ex-post and what capabilities or what investment decisions in the resource based tradition have to be faced?

In order to structure these research questions more clearly, the research topic, the research object and the scientific objective are defined by a guiding central argument that ensures a comprehensive approach. For this the comprehensiveness shall be set by:

(i) One theoretical model to understand the market dynamics from a decision perspective (incorporating capability and resource investment decisions);

(ii) One measurement framework for empirical work to track the dynamics and;

(iii) One application framework for strategic discussions that emerge from the results.

Research Topic

The topic that frames this research policy is the asset management industry, and there, more specifically the mutual fund industry. The mutual fund industry is chosen as one type of investment vehicle that compound the management of a broad selection of securities for third parties. Albeit this thesis focuses on one type of collective investment structures, discussion sections and conclusions might be equally addressable from the perspective of other legal forms of investment instruments.

Research Object

Within the broad field of the mutual fund industry, we focus our attention on the economics of market entry and market evolution in the economic terms and its implications on strategic options. Thereby, we specially emphasize the role of disruptive versus gradual innovation environment on the market reactions.

The corresponding definitions for „disruptive" and „gradual" innovation are based on ABERNATHY AND UTTERBACK (ABERNATHY AND CLARK, 1985; ABERNATHY AND UTTERBACK, 1988). The application as driver for change follows CHRISTENSEN (CHRISTENSEN, 1997; CHRISTENSEN, VERLINDEN AND WESTERMAN, 2002) who transferred the observed disruptive and gradual changes in the business model to incremental and radical innovators in the industry. The theoretical model assumptions used to form an entry-based market evolution laboratory build on the work of SENGUPTA (2007) and KLEPPER (1996, 2002; KLEPPER AND THOMPSON, 2005). Finally, the strategic adaptation contributes to the wider literature on industry evolution and competitive dynamics in the tradition of NELSON AND WINTER (1974, 1982) and on the learning, capability and vertical (dis-)integration discussions that nests within this research tradition (DOSI, NELSON AND WINTER, 2001; JACOBIDES AND WINTER, 2005; NELSON AND WINTER, 1973). In accordance with those strands of research, *market evolution* is characterized by entry of new competitors or launch of new products and *industry dynamics* are characterized by the rate of financial product and process innovations through time. *Product innovations* usually involve creation of new financial instruments (e.g. caps, futures, options, swaps) along with the ability to replicate certain instruments by bundling existing ones (synthetic securities) or to highlight new financial attributes by re-bundling existing instruments (e.g. structured, derivative products). New approaches to contract-pricing or passive index-based portfolio investment techniques also fall under this rubric (GOETZMANN AND MASSA, 2002; MESA MANAGEMENT, 2008). *Process innovations* include contract design (e.g. cash settlement future contracts, methods of clearance, payments, custody, securities settlement and trading, and techniques for efficient margin calculation).

The aim is to position this proposal within the broader research policy of

(i) change in Financial service intermediation theory, represented by the mutual fund industry dynamics and evolutions

(ii) strategy Processes, i.e. "Development of Comprehensive models for strategy formation" and "the role of change management" on a first level and

(iii) competitive strategy issues such as "what role do resources and capabilities play in shaping firms and industries over time" on a second level.

Limitation to the scope of the research topic

Given this broad research topic, it is necessary to clearly state what's not in the focus of this project. Understanding the nature and consequences of the competitive dynamics among firms is a key objective of the strategic management field. Recent developments here have focused on six broad research streams: competitive action and response, first-mover advantages, co-opetition, multipoint competition, strategic groups and regional clusters (KETCHEN, SNOW AND HOOVER, 2004). The focus here is on multipoint competition aspects, or more explicitly on "entry and exit behavior" and "internal firm characteristics" (KETCHEN et al., 2004, pp. 788). Furthermore, the underlying notion of competition is efficient and not static as in Structure-Conduct-Performance models (SCP). Comparative SCP issues are not addressed within this framework diretcly, but used as an introduction into the dynamic literature.

Scientific Objective

Ultimately, we expect to observe, classify and analyze the reaction patterns of mutual fund firms to different types of market innovation and use these findings to extend the contingency framework to design business strategies in this special field of financial services. Thereby, we have three objectives:

(i) "Understanding": What is the industry structure in the mutual fund industry like? What are the drivers of competitive dynamics in the mutual fund industry?

(ii) "Explaining": How do firms react upon innovation under this kind of competitive dynamics? How does this interplay affect market evolution in the mutual fund industry? And how can observed industry structures (equilibria) be explained based on the presented theory?

(iii) "Influencing": What lessons can be learnt for strategy and policy formation? Both from a theoretical stance as well as for the distinct case of the mutual fund industry.

Methodology

"Understanding" an industry and its dynamics calls first for a descriptive overview of the research topic, and second for a thorough understanding of the "mechanics" of the industry. Following ATTESLANDER (2000) it is thereby not the usefulness or the accessibility of data that should guide research, but rather the pure logic of the outlined research objective and its inherent logical streams. Consequently, the descriptive perspective and the literature evidence that is presented in an introductionary section has to be condensed into a formal model of the fund market and its dynamics. This model shall reflect the responsiveness of market participants within the industry towards different innovation triggers under the conditions of a multistage game. This approach follows the method developed for market entry simulations in game theory (ANDERSON AND ENGERS, 2005; DUFFY AND HOPKINS, 2004). Here, the applied methodology is based on microeconomic models of the organization of firms (AGHION AND HOWITT, 1992, 1998; DREZE AND SHESHINSKI, 1984; KLEPPER, 1996; KLEPPER AND THOMPSON, 2005; SENGUPTA, 2007). Within this micro-structure of the mutual fund market, game theory (ANDERSON AND ENGERS, 2005; DUFFY AND HOPKINS, 2004) is in a second step used as an instrument to sketch decision outcomes under changing environments and thus highlight the (potential) dynamics of the industry and its responsiveness. The resulted equilibrium outcomes

are placed in the context of management theory in a third step (BARNEY, 1986, 1991; DIERICKX AND COOL, 1989; DIXIT, 1980; GEROSKI, 1991; HELFAT et al., 2007; JACOBIDES AND WINTER, 2005; JOHNSON AND HOOPES, 2003; MEHRA, 1996; NELSON AND WINTER, 1974) and shall in this combination contribute to the objective of "understanding".

The notion of *"explaining"* is supported by tracking the innovation that triggered change and dynamic response in theory empirically (DIEKMANN, 1995). Here, two idealized features shall be in the focus: disruptive and gradual innovation. The thesis will analyze the respective structural changes and their implication for market evolution. The first empirical project will be to observe effects of gradually emerging capability (routines), whilst the second looks at the shifts in structure (measured by bid-ask-spreads) and its impact on new trading and distribution modes after disruptive innovation. The task of "explaining" is based on empirical analysis, whereas the *"influencing"* objective builds on the derived results and on market observations. Empirical instruments to address product and capability as well as process and transaction costs are seen in evolutionary metrics of firm routines in the first case and in the evolution of trading spreads in the second case. A key point in the methodology is the introduction of a comprehensive base of analysis for the empirical work. This means an measurable construct that both can be used to track product related capabilities (for a horizontal perspective and gradual innovation effects) as well as to track a resource-related process perspective (for vertical perspectives and disruptive innovation effects), and ultimately to describe industry structures and dynamics. The dominant measurement approaches to be found in literature focus on industry structure only and result consequently in different concentration indices, e.g. Herfindahl-Indices (CETORELLI AND GAMBERA, 2001). These concentration indices are well suited when it comes to comparing different industries or one industry across different countries. The concepts, however, cannot track static and dynamic effects within an industry. For this, literature generally refers to comparing industry margins. We are to some extent following this attempt. Nevertheless, instead of margins focusing on trading spreads. Spreads are more flexible, and what's more important, specific to individual products, firms and firms value chain steps. For the spread-application, we assume constant demand patterns for a comparable good across competitors; spreads reflect directly the efficiency of the strategic position of an observed entity.

Based on this theoretical and empirical work, we will lay the grounds for the conceptual work (DIEKMANN, 1995) that is meant to *"influence"*. This third objective is enabled by the means of an adjusted strategic framework (JACOBIDES

AND BILLINGER, 2006) that builds upon the understanding of the market and the explanation of observed market effects.

The *implications* for strategic analysis from this lie in the power to discriminate between what is and is not controllable – and exogenous innovations are as a matter of fact not; thus management is constrained, as strategic choice is limited to endogenous (path dependent) structures on firm as well as on industry level. The capacity of evolutionary economics might serve as a foundation for both the positive and the normative research agendas of the strategy field in this respect and helps to form a framework that integrates management options when facing exogeneous change.

Central Argument

The central argument of the dissertation is that the underlying dynamics in the mutual fund industry are dominated by entry and exit of new competitors, launch and stop of product issuance and overall growing supply (of net new money inflows into the industry). These emerging shifts are influenced by changes in technology, regulation and financial intermediation demands as well as by the (tactical) response of incumbents to the corresponding entry-threats. These relationships can be understood with micro-economic and game theory models. The contribution of the strategic management literature lies in this context in the establishment and structuring of the concepts that drive these changes (e.g. different types of innovation and different resource endowments and capabilities for the involved firms). The depths of understanding can be tested when using the concepts to explain observed industry effects and draft policy or corporate strategy initiatives to actively influence the position of the individual firm in its industrial context.

4 Basic Thinking in Industrial Dynamics and Market Evolution

"What appears to be competitive advantage derived from innovation is frequently the return to a system of organizations capable of producing a series of innovations. This is an example of a second distinctive capability which I call architecture. Architecture is a system of relationships within the firm, or between the firm and its suppliers or customers, or both. Generally the system is a complex one and the content of the relationships implicit rather than explicit. The structure relies on continued mutual commitment to monitor and enforce its terms. A firm with distinctive architecture gains strength from the ability to transfer information which is specific to the firm, product or market within the organization and to its customers and suppliers. It can also respond quickly and flexibly to changing circumstances." (KAY, 1993, p. 14)

When looking at the mutual fund industry and its structure, in Chapter 2 we referred shortly to the Structure-Conduct-Performance Paradigm. This SCP perspective has been seen in the context of innovation and industrial organization as one of the key concepts. Especially when looking at innovation activity from a structure perspective, many of the underlying concepts work strongly on Schumpeter's conjecture that large monopolistic firms are the key source of innovation. This assumption is especially dominant in classical industrial organization perspectives. The focus in SCP approaches is – as defined by the very term – on industry structure. The key thereby is in the question on how industry structure influences firm performance.

When moving the economic underpinnings beyond this (early) Schumpeter notion, where firm size and market structure were at the heart of innovation activity and industrial change, a broader set of influencing factors and a more integrative perspective between economic and management literature is possible. Traditionally, management literature structures answers to these questions along the classification of resource based view (RBV) and capability based view (CBV) explanations when discussing heterogeneity of firms at industry level (RUMELT, 1984) and either diversification or vertical integration backgrounds when looking at the boundaries of organizations from a firm level perspective (BONACCORSI AND GIURI, 2001; CACCIATORI AND JACOBIDES, 2005).

A newly emerging field puts the structural approaches for identifying competition into the center of analysis, which allows ultimately describing how structures emerge, well ahead of explaining economic performance as a function of that emerged environment. A recent chapter in the Annals of the Academy of Management has been dedicated to this topic. Our overview follows partialy their literature review structure (Yue and Ingram, 2008). For this, multiple interacting levels of analysis have to be taken into account: Literature in this field assumes that competition between organizations and other actors emerges ultimately because of a shared reliance on one identical critical resource for all industry actors. With this background, organizational ecologists point to a condition of so-called "niche overlap" as the basis of competition (Hannan and Freeman, 1989), meaning simply that a set of organizations rely on some of the same resources for founding, growth and survival. The corresponding empirical strategy when having to identify competition derives from population biology. Here, the "Lotka-Volterra" equations have emerged as the starting point for measurement construction as these equations assume that the carrying capacity of a focal population (its number of members in equilibrium) is a negative function of the density of a competing population (the count of its members). When transferring this to the organizational environment, different types of actors do impact potential growth and rates of failures of other participants in a market. The relationship again is mediated by the industry distinct factors, e.g. the "density and founding growth" which corresponds basically to the minimal scales necessary to break even under a given setting. When transferring this construct onto dynamic competitive conditions, the argument is that competition within a population rises along the density, i.e. wherever more organizations pursue the same resources or an equal number of competitors require more resources to survive. Such shaped competition reduces founding of new entities, growth of existing firms and increases failure rates in the market (Carroll and Hannan, 2000). There are literally dozens of empirical findings that support the competition element of the theory of density dependence (Baum, 1996). This ecological notion of competition within organizations of a population is similar to the typical earlier practice in industrial economics, where competitors were seen as organizations in the same industry, or organizations that serve the same market (Scherer, 1980). Equally, empirical setting reflects recent trends in evolutionary economics. Generally, in all of these approaches an industry is regarded as more competitive if it is closer to the theoretical idea of perfect competition—a large number of firms, relatively homogenous products, low market concentration, and low entry and exit barriers. However, the dynamic element is not reduced to entry-and-exit of firms under changing population condition, as relationships on the sub-population and sub-industry groups are important intermediating factors.

At some point, the focus of analysis has to move beyond the obvious simplification of categorizing all organizations in one population e.g. in an industry, as discussed in the cases of industrial organization. Hereby, there exists a multitude of approaches to consider heterogeneity in competitive intensity for different organizations even though they still may share common industry or population labels. Literally, this gives credit to the fact that industries are made up of a variety of sub-groups. The basic premise, that organizations of the same type compete more intensely, has been applied to these sub-groups earlier (BORENSTEIN, 1989, 1992).

Sub-group research can be grouped along three basic strands of theory development: First, resource partitioning that argues that different sub-groups have distinct (and different) patterns of resource utilization (CARROLL, DOBREV AND SWAMINATHAN, 2002), which leads to asymmetries in intra-group competition. The second is the idea of centrality. "Centrist" concepts stress the idea that in every assembly of sub-groups there is a "center" which is occupied by dominant players (often incumbent firms) which control largely the resource distribution. These centers often emerge around consumer preferences or (exclusive) distribution channels. These organizations than may take advantage of economies of scale and offer products that appeal to the modal consumer. Finally, as "centrality emerges", peripherical sub-groups can emerge as well in niches. These "specialists" are often newly entering innovative firms who occupy less-central places in the resource distribution (as a consequence of their later entry), away from the center, and where the products offered by the generalists are less appealing. Theory assumes, however, that these peripherical firms cultivate a higher variety and may be responsible for innovation on top-industry level to a relatively large extent. Evidence for these ideas has been found in a number of industries, such as newspapers, breweries, wineries and automobile producers to mention just a few (CARROLL, 1985; CARROLL, BIGELOW, SEIDEL AND TSA, 1996; CARROLL et al., 2002).

Given these sub-group effects it can be interesting from an industry perspective to ask what is behind industry value creation and what defines the intra-industry division of created value (i.e. who engages where and to what extent in value appropriation)? Or how does this ability to create and appropriate value reflect in the heterogeneity of (regional) industry structures and ultimately firm performance? These questions stand at the heart of the theoretical body that drives the ongoing discussion on entry dynamics and market evolution. A term often used to summarize this theoretical body that has emerged around the issues of industry dynamics, innovation and growth is "Neo-Schumpeterian" (LEVINTHAL, 2006). This tradition is often judged difficult to classify under established economic schools. Clearly, the work builds on the early works of the Lausanne School, especially on Walrasian concepts of competitions towards which temporary equilibria (or rents) from monopolistic competition (Barney, 1991) are being eroded as change (innovation) destroys (creates) institutional arrangements (Andersen, 2006; Diamond, 2007). The dynamic of this process can be observed both for rents based on capabilities or on other (intangible) resources. However, based on previous investments and capabilities and ongoing change, industry dynamics follow a path of market evolution (Andersen, 1996). This notion stood at the beginning of the relatively new tradition of "evolutionary economics". Schumpeterian tradition carved a relatively unique path in economic theory that spread thematically into a number of research traditions: (Im-)perfect competition, uncertainty and information at first sight. Network concepts and game theory are seen thereby often as the most important instruments to address emerging issues (Andersen, 1991, 2006). The observation of these dynamics let literature contribute concepts that produced a strong counterpart to the ideas of "costly and bounded rationality" and the "economics of managing". This line of thinking can be summarized based on five broad "headings": (1) The equilibrium and dynamics, (2) working, managing and entrepreneurship, (3) costly rationality and decentralization, (4) incentives and (5) bounded rationality (Radner, 2006). For the purpose of this thesis, the focus shall be on the ideas of equilibrium and dynamics in markets at different levels of observation within firms, their linkages and the impacts of these equilibria, dynamics and linkages on a (changing) industry structure.

In the management literature derived from economics, the approach to represent competitors by sub-industry groups has been embraced by the strategic group literature. This field builds on the general assumption that organizations are constrained by mobility barriers. Consequently, those in the same industry face comparable barriers and hence adopt the same or similar strategies, ultimately forming strategic groups (Helfat et al., 2007; Hoskisson, Hitt, Wan and Yiu, 1999). In this way, industry is no longer viewed as a homogeneous unit, but an agglomeration of diverse strategic groups. When combining competing entities into sub-units that are so similar and that share many and often close relations, the idea of moving from mere competition towards cooperation might be near and is often summarized by the notion of "no business is an island" (Hakansson and Snehota, 1989) – this certainly holds even the more for closely interacting strategic groups. As Hoskisson et. al (1999) argued in this context, "the fundamental question is [not whether there are close relations, but rather] whether firms are actually aware of this mutual dependence within their particular groups" (p. 427). Once relations and dependence are shifting into the focus of attention, network analysis offers yet another approach to push the discussion one step further. Network analysis (methodically) can be seen as a tool for identifying structural similarity, or (conceptually) as a basis for explain competition and cooperation with the concept of structural equivalence. Structurally equivalent actors are those that are the same or similar in terms of relations to others. This can be illustrated by two actors that occupy an identical network position and therefore have access to the same resources from the network, which does not only offer ample room for cooperation due to "closeness", but may make them first of all prime competitors for that very resource. This idea is the foundation of network theories of competitive advantage, which emphasize that unique structural positions are privileged and sheltered from competition (BURT, 1992). Literature on these kinds of settings is wide. A classical work is for example the research into semi-conductor industries by PODOLNY, STUART AND HANNAN (1996). This approach was followed later by INGRAM, ROBINSON AND BUSCH (2005) who use structural equivalence in interstate networks and by BOTHNER (2003) who operationalizes competition in the computer industry using structural equivalence of firms through sales channels. The very same structural-equivalence concepts are often used to measure competition in network industries such as electricity grids or airlines (BORENSTEIN, 1989, 1992). Often, these approaches – when involving multiple population levels – are labeled multi-segment models.

Irrespective of management literature or economic modeling one can find a joint perspective here which defines broadly the field of industrial dynamics. In short, industrial dynamics refers to concepts that do not center on structure as the impetus for competitive settings, but that see industry and sub-industry group interaction and their dynamic as a common idea where competition derives from shared dependence on the same (critical) resources. The basis of competition between different organizations with an overlap in the resources they require, can be broadly defined in terms of customers, employees, endorsements, physical space, knowledge inputs, or anything else necessary for their founding, growth, or survival.

The approaches to cope with this shared understanding can be by defining industry groups the focal unit of analysis, by looking at partitioning, and at central or peripheral environments or by studying the network and relation effects that hold the industry together, respectively that transmit the impetus of change. Before the background of these contributions, research on industrial dynamics is moving forwards to capture not only the theoretical underpinnings of emerging competition and new industry structures or markets, but also the shift in value appropriation that ex-ante and ex-post industry architecture comparison unveils. This value perspective goes along with a more management literature driven question of how to position oneself in such a multi-level changing and interacting environment, respectively which resources to control and which capabilities to grow. This perspectives are often referred to in the context to the works of ANITA MCGAHAN (2004) or MICHAEL JACOBIDES (JACOBIDES, 2005; JACOBIDES, KNUDSEN AND AUGIER, 2006). The early lines of research in this more management oriented view of industrial dynamics can clearly be described as economically motivated and empirically driven: Contributions were made for instance by CARLISS BALDWIN (2008), who collected data on "vertical stacks" in three industries, allowing to investigate questions, such as whether there are patterns of profit migration from one vertical segment to the next or whether these changes reflect in market capitalization and in revenues. The objective here was to examine sectors whose structure has changed (PCs, semiconductors, and automobiles), largely shifting from integration to disintegration, and to examine the impacts of these changes on different parts of the value chain. In this literature stresses the importance for theory that links rules, routines and processes (JACOBIDES, 2008).

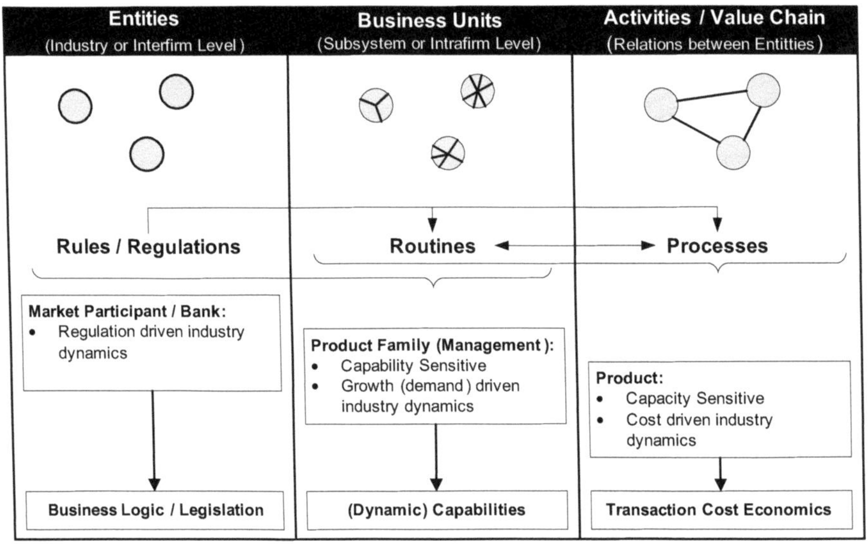

Illustration 6: From Organizational Economics towards Organizational Capabilities – An integrative Perspective, HOFFMANN AND MATTIG (2009)

This perspective to some extent loosens the importance of "pure" resource arguments. This might be significant as the multiple level approaches indicated that there is not only spillover and learning within the sub-groups, but that the environment and variety of these capability-growing sub-groups only can flourish within the boundaries of a process and or resource based environmental niche. Literature considers in this context how capabilities and knowledge bases drive scope and how scope affects capabilities and strategic dynamics. The management literature on capabilities and dynamic capabilities is sometimes extended by work on evolutionary economics that focuses explicitly on vertical scope and on industry architectures. The notion of industrial architecture can in this context be followed as stable or evolving ways in which labor and profit is divided in a sector. At the level of the organization, firms set their boundaries and link to markets along their value chain, examining how this affects their capabilities, however, the interaction with processes and resources that limit total capacity often gets lost (JACOBIDES et al., 2006). These interactions may nevertheless be a key element in understanding why certain parts of a value chain or certain sub-population relations are more sensitive to change than others (PISANIAS AND JACOBIDES, 2006). Illustration 6 gives a basic overview on these relations between rules, routines and processes at the different levels of analysis and how they relate to the corresponding theories such as transaction cost economics or dynamic capability views.

Building on this the interaction of capability and resources, respectively process literature an integrated framework (HOFFMANN AND MATTIG, 2009) cannot only be used as a rough orientation, but may also pinpoint how the different theories interact, respectively how the different layers of analysis reflects altered sensitivity for transaction cost, capability and business logic. This perspective allows for insights that are often lost when examining "one transaction at a time", as is often done in the related fields of New Institutional and Transaction Cost Economics (CACCIATORI AND JACOBIDES, 2005). We refer to this therefore in this thesis as a framework for how and on which level industrial dynamics affect and change market architecture.

Industrial Dynamics in the Mutual Fund Industry

Already when presenting the basic features of mutual funds, i.e. the components of the fund complex and the concept of multiple sub-products (sometimes often identical among each other) point to the suitability of applying industrial dynamic methods when discussing mutual funds just as well as the dominance of one joint resource for which all funds are competing, namely new money and/or new investors. Furthermore, the observation of high value appropriation at the distribution function points towards a setting that can be well explained with the "centralized" theories from population analysis. Despite these first observations, literature on mutual fund structure and competition is so far relatively limited, especially when comparing it against the importance of the sector its sheer volume (RAMOS, 2009). So far, methodologies applied to analyze the structures have focused on one layer of analysis and neglected interaction effects (Illustration 6).

Perspective	Theoretical Background	Unit of Analysis	Observed Characteristics	Authors
Economic	Industrial Organization	Fund Industry	Industry Structure and Fund Flows	Syverson, Hortacsu (2004)
Economic	Industrial Organization	Fund Industry	Industry Structure and Fund Flows	Mamayski/Spiegel (2002)
Economic	Finance	Product	Capital Market Efficiency / Information Cost	Berk, Green (2004)/ Sirri, Tufano (1998)/ Ippolito (1989)
Economic	Finance	Product	Capital Market Efficiency / Liquidity Premium	Nanda et al. (2000)
Economic	Finance	Management	Performance, Risk-Return	Wermers (2000)
Economic	Finance	Product	Persistence of Money Management Performance	Carhart (1997)/Grinblatt (1992)
Economic	Finance	Management	Incentives and Performance and Risk Taking	Chevalier, Elsion (1997)/ Jensen (1968)
Management	Banking	Fund Firms	Industry Size and Properties	Walter, 1999/ Ramos 2006; 2009
Management	Banking	Fund Firms	Organization and Product Performance	Lakonishok (1992)/ Shleifer, Vishny, Hart (1996)
Management	Banking	Fund Firms	The Role of Mutual Funds in Financial Intermediation	Walter, Chalmers, Edelen, Kadlec (2002)
Management	Banking	Management	Incentives and Fund Flows	Getmansky (2003)
Management	Strategy	Resources	Firm Heterogeneity and Comparative Advantages	Ramos (2007; 2009)
Management	Strategy	Capabilties	Firm Heterogeneity, Routines and (Co-)Evolution of Capabilties	Levinthal, Myatt (1994)
Management	Business Engineering	Processes and Services	Technological Standardization, Modularization and Structure	Zera, Madura (2001)

Table 8: A Selection of Mutual Fund Literature

There are, however two notable exceptions: First, the work of by SIGGELKOW (2002) who tracked the evolution of one particular fund firm (Vanguard) in its competitive environment and second, the study by LEVINTHAL AND MYATT (1994) who use the mutual fund to illustrate the co-evolution of capabilities. However, we argue that there is more in industrial dynamic theory and measurement approaches yet to be found: Some of the most obvious parts could be the "Concept of a centrist field of incumbents that control (established) distribution channels, a "high variety of peripheral and innovating firms who bring a notion of constant / gradual innovation into the strategic decision making processes of the incumbents" or over time and along with the constant threat of gradual innovation, "an increasing likelihood of disruptive innovation that might challenge the very notion of centrality, i.e. the distribution network".

In the following chapters we build upon the industrial dynamic literature in the mutual fund context. In order to have a joint trigger for change and to analyze various reactions and perspectives of changes from a more or less homogenous angle, we focus on established market players. These incumbent firms are challenged by an innovative event (e.g. a new entrant, a new technology or a new trend in demand). That innovation can be gradual, i.e. building on the path of previous ongoing developments or it may be in the early Schumpeterian view disruptive, leading to a sudden upheaval in markets and market participant's relations. In this, we rely on the basic notion of industry architecture as a nexus of interactions, respectively a nexus of multiple (temporary) equilibria. We see mutual funds are centrist markets. This means that we see assume a relatively oligopolistic setting at the stage of the distribution channel. At the same time, the environment gets increasingly contestable (BAUMOL, PANZAR AND WILLING, 1982) meaning that despite the small number of competitors controlling the network, pricing is not monopolistic, because entry and exit (at the product side of the value chain) is relatively easy. The overall environment can be thought of as a subsequent set of (temporary) "equilibrium" conditions, where industrial architecture and firm positioning is stable.

If one inserts a stimulus of change (and assumes uncertainty on the nature of this change) into this environments, the sequence of temporary equilibrium outcomes must move towards a "Nash type equilibrium" which is the result of any so-called dynamic or stochastic game (RADNER, 1991). The distinction links back to the assumptions of general equilibrium theory that postulate equilibria as outcomes of "rational expectation" (JORDAN AND RADNER, 1982) that is static (and optimal) in terms of static environments and stable but not necessarily optimal in a changing environment. Equilibriums of the game theory or Nash type thus are stable with respect to all potential decisions (but not under exogenous innovation). Under general equilibrium assumptions, however, no innovation (exogenous and endogenous) has a rebalancing effect on rational decision making, as competitors would immediately capitalizes on arising opportunities in a value appropriation sense. Such a thought experiment may show where the break-lines of the industrial architecture (i.e. the variance in sensitivity to processes or capabilities) is most fragile, leading to changing industrial architectures. Positioning and strategic decisions can be faced along these break-lines.

As a trigger, we introduce a non-specified type of exogenous innovation (as modeled in the next chapter). Innovations are bound to be endogenous (i.e. developed by an incumbent firm) or exogenous (i.e. brought into the system by new entrants or regulatory change). Literature groups such innovation effects into gradual and disruptive events, whereby research focuses on undisruptive events mostly.

Environmental change experienced by organizations in the study	**Authors' description of environmental change**	**Classification**	**Authors**
Loosening of regulatory constraints in California's saving and loan industry	"abrupt discontinuity;" "quasi experiment" (p. 28)	Shock/ Disruptive Innovation	Haverman (1993)
Deregulation in the US health maintenance organization (HMO) industry: change in their not-for-profit status	"radical change;" "radical environmental shift" (p. 445)	Specific shock/ Disruptive Innovation	Ginsberg and Bucholtz (1990)
Demand changes in the enrollment to US liberal arts colleges during the 1970s and 1980s	"profound environmental change" (p. 633) "environmental turbulence" (p. 632)	Disruptive change/ Disruptive Innovation	Kraatz and Zajac (2001)
Market changes and evolution around Vanguard mutual funds, 1974–1997	No specific description	Regular change/ Gradual Innovation	Siggelkow (2002)
Deregulation in the US airline and trucking industries	"discontinuous environmental change" (p. 842); "radical environmental change" (p. 837)	Specific shock/ Disruptive Innovation	Audia et al. (2000)

Table 9: Selected Literature on Innovation Events

The firms in the industry are endowed with different learning and adaptation capabilities and accordingly compete and response to the industry dynamics. The pressure to respond to dynamics thereby is mediated by the overall growth or decline of the industry (ANDERSEN, 1996). Depending on responses, adaptation and industry growth, overall value is generated or destroyed on an industry level (AGARWAL, AUDRETSCH AND SARKAR, 2008). Contributions in this strand have emphasized the role of entry and industry evolution, but also the intertwining of innovation effects at industry and firm level. Thereby, learning is the single most important unit of analysis that describes the diffusion of process and product knowhow, as it drives not only endogenous change, but also the industry reaction to exogenous events in terms of responsiveness.

New entry is attracted by the value creation or destruction on firm level and the dynamics of the industry. This attempt is based on SUTTON (1998) and corresponds clearly to resource based theories of strategic advantages. SENGUPTA (2007) presented a somewhat contradicting range of formal models to conceptualize entry induced market evolution and thus build the base for an introduction of measurement instruments that are tailor made with respect to the competitive dynamics of multiple sub units within an industry. With such measures, heterogeneity in competitive dynamics could be analyzed and applied to academic as well as to practically relevant problems, e.g. of corporate strategy. However, both strategy and economic literature are not ignoring capability based arguments and hence provide valuable footholds for linking these theoretical concepts, especially when digging a little bit deeper into the at-first glance resource based conclusions from economies of entry: The evolution of industries under the model of SENGUPTA (2007) depends on a discrete or continuous selection mechanism. This selection mechanism is on the industry level formed by the process of entry and exits of firms or on an organizational level by the different factors influencing the entry-exit decisions, respectively. The basic concepts to explain and track these evolutionary effects are shifts in barriers-to-entry and overall market growth by demand expansion or endogenous innovation. The first affects the distribution of the value within one market, whereas the second extends the overall achievable market value. One of the major determinants of the market entry process is the existence of potential and actual barriers. The pioneering work by BAIN (1956) argued that firms can earn profits above the competitive level in the medium and the long term if they are protected by entry barriers. He identified four types of entry barriers, for example economies of scale, product differentiation advantages, absolute cost advantages and large capital stock requirements. To this list, one might add two more: innovations efficiency in the timing and know-how of new investments (D'Aveni, 1999) and "creating strongholds for excluding competitors from their market segments" (Sengupta, 2007, p. 118). Once, these strongholds are formed, the role of innovation spreads to displaying industry level effects. Here, Klepper (1996) and others show that such innovation-based strongholds lead to increased concentration. Along this concentration process the minimal efficient scales (MES) of production grow more rapidly than demand and innovator's rise towards market dominance for the respective product segments. With this disequilibrium of MES and demand growth as key driver, the new radical-innovative entrant on a vertical level, respectively the new incrementally-innovative product on a horizontal level of competition provokes an adjustment process. Dreze and Sheshinski (1984) have considered the *industrial dynamics* of such an adjustment processes in the Walrasian tradition. Thereby they refer to an industrial example, assuming that new plants of a given type are built (scrapped) whenever their expected profits are positive (negative). The table of strategic options corresponds to this discussion.

The *market evolution* effect of the new entrant is than displayed with some time lag as the emerging oligopolistic structure shifts entry barriers for the followers, resulting in stable Cournot-Nash equilibria. Suzumura (1995) has analyzed this aspects and developed a general framework for entry dynamics that causes a period of an increasing number of firms proportional to the excess profits above the Cournot-Nash equilibrium. Thus, there is considerable evidence for a shift in the market structure of mutual-fund-industry like settings into two strategic groups: One group consisting of non-oligopolistic firms remaining in the market, and another of oligopolistic firms. The first engages in Walrasian competition and the second adopts in a form of monopolistic-competition in the Chamberlinan (Barney, 1986, 1989) tradition.

Such outcomes are especially interesting from two perspectives: From a value-creation concept of the market it means that a small group of firms at the top share a growing proportion of the surplus-rents generated by innovations, whereas a large and very volatile group of firms competes for a decreasing share of the diminishing market – in an overall growing industry! Whilst this chapter gave a broad overview about the nature and ideas behind industrial dynamics as a concept that is applied to the mutual fund industry, the following chapters will introduce a short note on literature that links to the distinct research questions addressed.

5 Theoretical Model: Industrial Dynamics and Organizational Responsiveness

"While much progress has been made in how organizations shape and are shaped by their institutional contexts, we still seem to lack a coherent theory of how actions aggregate into organizational outcomes. [...] our theory provides little information on how individuals decide and learn in a context with which they are interdependent". DRUID Fundamental 2008

When observing market structures that have emerged over time, it often seems hard to argue why in certain industries market architectures have developed so differently from their counterparts in other countries. In most cases, historical pathways and regulatory frameworks are held responsible for these differences. This article attempts to set up a basic formal framework in which to discuss different actions on multiple levels and their interaction with the environment (in this case exogenous innovation), industry structure and organizational response sets. To live up to this objective, this paper builds on industrial organization theory and market evolution models to develop a theoretical foundation that links two issues: (i) The boundaries of the firm (i.e. what should the firm do, how large should it be, and what businesses it should be in) and (ii) industry dynamics. The literature on industry dynamics reflects on how the firm should position itself to compete successfully under changing competitive environments. In this respect, the discussion of the (shifting) boundaries of the firm can to some extent be seen as a response to changing industry dynamics. We look into that somewhat causal relationship for the case of the mutual fund market. In order not to build theoretical considerations based on only one industry, we first mold the mechanism of the mutual fund market into a general competitive system, which is designated as multi-segment industry. Multi-segment industry has already been discussed as a concept in earlier works, e.g. (PANZAR AND WILLIG, 1977; STEINFIELD, MARKUS AND WIGAND, 2005; VANWEGBERG, 1992). After outlining the basic properties of multi-segment industries, we build a specific model to observe the sensitivity of that particular industry to two different triggers for change. We use that model to formulate basic propositions regarding the responsiveness of incumbent firms in multi-segment markets. The outlined model can be used as basic building block in the discussion of empirical observations in the mutual fund industry that follows in the next chapters, as well as in the discussion of potential market evolution.

We firmly believe that the analytical perspective must be clarified from the organizational point of view and analyzed accordingly before analyzing individual factors. First, company boundaries and competition are traditionally observed in isolated market segments, be they product-, geography- or industry-specific. However, as early as 1995, van Witteloostuijn (1995) promoted an increased focus on linkages and specifically on multi-segment competition analysis. In his 1992 article "Capacity as a Commitment Instrument in Multi-segment Competition, van Wegberg (1992) defines this multi-segment competition as an environment in which "firms engage in parallel in multiple product markets or multiple locations and multiple vertical business lines". The companies handle each of their markets separately when responding to industrial dynamics. From a cost point of view, however, the "youngest" markets benefit from artificially reduced marginal costs, due to the sunken costs accumulated by their peers earlier on. Second, in the literature the leading company's responsiveness to innovation is normally differentiated according to either gradual (Consoli, 2005; Ivkovich, 2001) or disruptive (Schumpeterian) innovation (Geroski and Masson, 1987; Goetzmann and Massa, 2002; Massa, 2003). The resulting entry dynamics reflect the difference in evolved market structures in the United States and in Europe.

The central underlying argument of this article is that strategic room for maneuvering follows the basic traits of industry dynamics. This is seen as especially true for incumbents who have to defend their market positions rather than find new ways to win their shares. Hence, strategic reactions such as reshaping company boundaries on a vertical perspective, or diversification on a horizontal line, follow the changing landscape as printed by underlying break-lines of industrial dynamics. An example can be given with securities trading: relaxed regulatory boundaries for alternative stock exchanges permits pooling of large block trades beyond the established players' platforms. The "remaining" trade volume is more opaque and more costly to trade. This may put pressure on trading firms' transaction costs and may provoke a break-line in their established business models. In response, both traditional stock exchanges and securities traders will have to adjust. Under previous conditions, securities dealers optimized their structure by building capacity and attracting volume. Now, response could also mean redefining company boundaries to improve the transaction cost structure in the changed environment (e.g. buying their block-trades like wholesalers on the alternative markets and specialization in less liquid assets on a smaller technological backbone), just as by diversifying, e.g. into independent research in greater depth, in order to offer more value per trade.

In order to discuss such movements more systematically, one needs to sketch market shifts and related responses as generically as possible. We therefore take an unspecified impetus of change as the basic trigger for dynamics and differentiate only between gradual and disruptive change that starts a (re-)adjustment process. The trigger is defined by an exogenous innovation "shock" that allows a new entrant to challenge the existing market structure. For the model, it is not relevant whether this innovation affects industry architecture on a relational, transactional or routine level.

The contribution of this article is therefore a basic model used to analyze and describe the general dynamics of industries and to sketch the basic response options that must be expected. The paper focuses on the reactions and configurations of incumbent market leaders in a multi-segment market as defined in WITTELOSSTUIJN (1995). For these market conditions, we propose first that the dynamic effect of change is significantly different for disruptive and gradual changes in innovation patterns. We propose that large incumbents will expand vertically in the case of disruptive innovation and respond by offering a potential substitute product portfolio in the case of gradual innovation.

The remainder of this chapter is organized as follows: first, we show why mutual fund markets may be a case for multi-segment industries. Next, we discuss the background for the theory building – that is the tradition of the multi-segment market analysis in economics and industrial organizations. Third, we build a basic model to sketch innovation effects onto a multi-segment industry, before concluding with the resulting proposition and likely response options.

Dynamic Properties of the Mutual Fund Market

The provision of a mutual fund involves six basic functions: investment management, distribution, custody and fund accounting, and transfer agency or shareholding services. While all of these activities underlie the provision of a mutual fund, the fund itself is not required to perform all these services itself, but it often opts for buying parts of these vertical value steps from other market participants (LEVINTHAL AND MYATT, 1994). Most firms that do so focus on investment management product development. Developed fund products can thereby be grouped into families with related product properties and on the product level itself into different classes of an equal product, generally offering different models for paying the accrued fund charges. Management decisions are made primarily on two levels: the overall corporate structure that is responsible for the corporate strategy and the investment management level that guides the product portfolio and the product or asset management strategy (Otten and Bams, 2002). Hence, the money managing industry is characterized by a strong organizational feature linking both product and capacity aspects in the economics of strategies, representing the first property for modeling the industry.

Second, most of the mutual funds build a transaction and distribution backbone and build at least the ability to launch new products continuously on the market at low cost, should there be a corresponding demand. The second special feature is that all fund firms are forced by law to distribute substantially all net income from dividends, interests and capital gains directly to their investors. This leads to an implicit control for otherwise often disruptive decision factors such as ownership or, more broadly, corporate governance issues.

Third, competition in the financial service industry in general has always been strongly regulated. In response, scholars began to agree that the pace of consolidation and market dynamics in the industry will be strongly determined by changes in economic environments that alter the constraints faced by financial service firms on a macro level (Raff, 2001). Several decades of regulatory changes have erased merely legal constraints upon strategy and success from competitive landscapes.

The three factors of a tradition of vertical integration, technology relatedness and regulatory easing can be quoted when indicating the reasons behind the burst of new product innovation that has continued for approximately twenty years now and that has significantly altered the product space for the industry itself. The common acceptance of new technology and the radical changes this suggests as to the size and location of potential customer bases also casts into doubt established ways of making money and the attractiveness of established strategic plans. In this environment, the optimal definition of the company's boundaries becomes a key factor for success (Jacobides and Billinger, 2006).

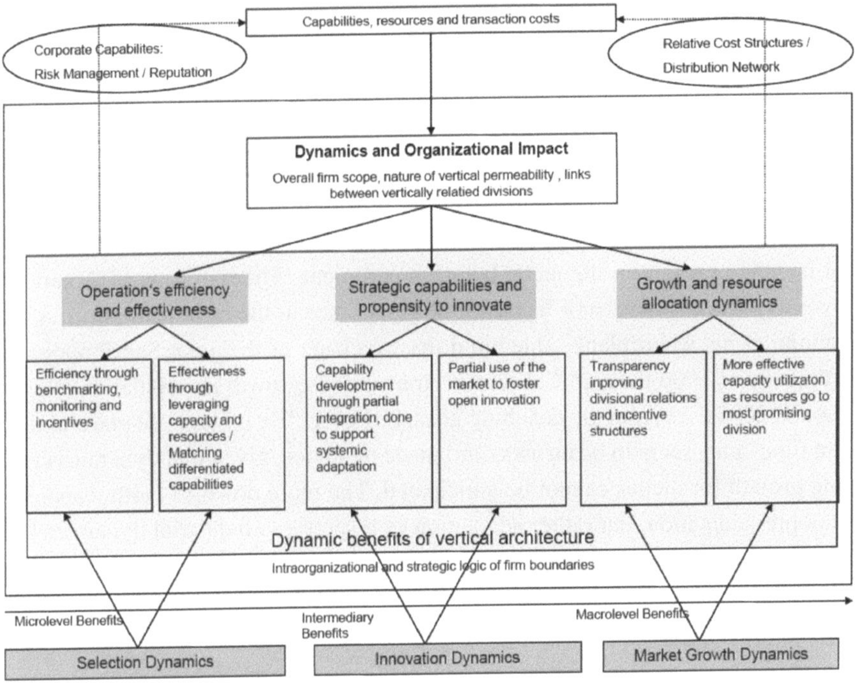

Illustration 7: Extended Jacobides-Billinger Framework 2006

This concept can also be applied to changing features in other segments of the financial service industry. Illustration 7 depicts an extended version of the Jacobides-Billinger framework, linking organizational features (i.e. the propensity to innovate, the operational efficiency and/or technological base and environmental change (i.e. growth and resource allocation dynamics) to the dynamic benefits of the traditional vertical architecture that still continues to dominate industry logic. The stability of this logic is closely connected to selective, innovative and demand-side dynamics that affect capability-building routines as well as transaction processes across multiple levels. When observing banks and bank strategies in particular, the differences in these levels (BERGER, DEMSETZ AND STRAHAN, 1999) and the analysis of different submarkets such as the credit and lending business (CLAESSEN AND LAEVEN, 2004) are quoted as important driving forces. Thus, when looking at one of these sub-segments – the mutual fund industry, the basic assumption is that along these factors of industry dynamics, new markets may evolve eventually, which have the potential to alter the distribution of value generated across the industry players. In other words, once these dynamics start to bolster heterogeneity sufficiently within the industry, new niches will evolve. And once a given set of niches comes into being, the way to earn profits lies in occupying and dominating them (at a reasonable cost, of course).

The great question of strategy in the context of industrial dynamics is therefore how to be able to anticipate niches with future growth potential or, more simply, your competitors' strategies. The simple answer to this is pre-adaptation, that is, being present in the niche before it is a niche. The old Bank of America serves as a good example of being in the right place at the right time, from A.P. Giannini at his wood plank table amid the wreckage of the great San Francisco earthquake of 1906 through California's tremendous growth in population (WINCHESTER, 2005). As strategic coaching goes, however, "Be in the right place at the right time" may seem to be an awkward piece of advice, given that dynamics creating growth for niches cannot be anticipated. The more down-to-earth response is not pre-adaptation, but rather adaptation or response to industrial dynamics by adjusting organizational structures. Wherever incumbents engage in this type of adjustment process, industrial organization is bound to re-shape; a process generally known as either integration or disintegration.

When rethinking the logic behind the Jacobides-Billinger framework for the case of the mutual fund industry, one can depict the various inter-linkages that form the nodes for vertical benefit as well as the dynamic break-lines as in Illustration 8. On the top level, fund firms compete with each other for volume. They thereby rely on technologies, dubbed transaction type A or type B, to mimic alternative platforms. On this technological backbone, fund products are developed, based on distinct capabilities of the fund firms. In this layer, products share their dominant characteristics (i.e. the risk-return relations) not only across, but also within competing fund firms. Market growth therefore has two equal levels: total growth of the mutual fund market and a growth rate for a certain risk-return combination. The different mutual funds are divided into capability-dependent groups again (SIGGELKOW, 2003). These group boundaries can be drawn along asset types or fund families, e.g. equity or fixed income products. Each fund family includes a wide variety of products and can launch additional funds of the same type without incurring a significantly increased fix cost burden as it rests upon one transaction platform, one legal fund sponsor and equal resources for research and management. Here each new product coming into the market out of an existing fund family can take off at lower marginal costs than its peers that are already in the market. KEMPF AND RUENZI (2004) analyze the decision of launching new products from an intra-family tournament point of view, while ZHAO (2001) points out different capabilities required for different products. Both studies found that basic economic property. Overall, this setting leads to four potential break-lines: survival of fund firms (1), choice of transaction platforms (2), fund family size as successful risk-return combinations attract monies (3) and fund size, as competitive products in winning fund families scale up (4). Competition in such a setting takes place on multiple levels and multiple segments. Industries that follow such logic have been labeled multi-segment markets in industrial organization theory (VANWEGBERG, 1992).

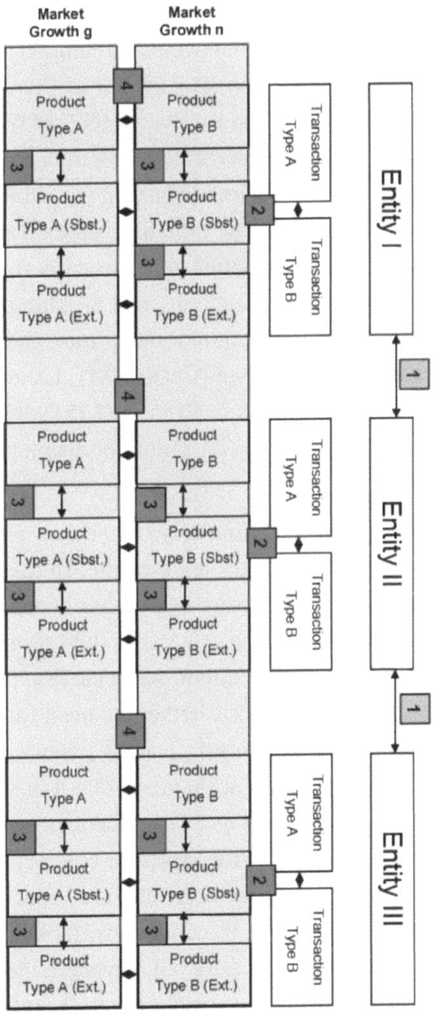

Illustration 8: Multi-sub-market Dynamics in Bank Competition

Literature and Background

Generally, we see competitive dynamics as shifts in industrial structure on the macro layer of these multiple sub-markets. These shifts are driven by exogenous or endogenous motivation factors (Claessen and Laeven, 2004). The set of such drivers for change can be organized along shifts in (customer) demand, technology, regulation and risk (Bernet, 2003, 2006).

When focusing on these driving forces, we find that economic literature has primarily focused on these drivers on the macro level by describing how new markets evolve, how existing barriers to entry emerge and existing barriers are eroded over time, thereby influencing the overall structure of an observed industry as measurable by market concentration (Baldwin and Gorecki, 1989), competitiveness, respectively erosion of margins (Burt, 1992; Mayhew, 2002) and new entry dynamics (Sengupta, 2007). Management literature on the other hand takes a more firmly centrist position, effectively combing two strands of research: first, literature that focuses, like the economic literature, on industry patterns (Barney, 1991), and second, management literature that observes reactions of the single firms, following structure-conduct paradigms and arguing on this ground about the extent of or the need for diversification or integration and about specialization and disintegration on an aggregate level (Chen, 2005; Langlois and Robertson, 1995). An exception to this is the work of Stigler (1951), who suggested that the size of a market limits the extent of specialization (or disintegration on an industry level).

The existing literature focused primarily on the four above-mentioned (potential) break lines for existing industry architecture. In this regard, research on process and technology effects on transaction cost has been the first, the literature on capability the second key element in research. When starting with nodes 3 and 4, both economic and management literature see scale as a primary driving force for industry shifts. Here, it is irrelevant whether the need for scale arises through technological or exogenous absolute cost changes given constant and inelastic demand curves, whether the need for scale arises due to a single company's advantageous cost structures, the adoption of best practices or finally the alignment to emerging industry standards under the structure-conduct paradigm. However, from an economist's standpoint, it has been observed that despite ample room for specialization and scale building in economics, these do not always occur (Jacobides, 2005). Thus, scale is generally not considered to be a good explanation of disintegration or other industry level effects (Langlois and Robertson, 1995). There are almost no systematic studies of the emergence of integration or disintegration, despite substantial research on the social institutions of market exchange in general (FLIGSTEIN, 2001), new research on vertical scope (JACOBIDES AND WINTER, 2005) or economic models for market evolution (SENGUPTA, 2007). The main reason for the relative dearth of knowledge is seen in the fact that the literature, particularly in transaction economics (WILLIAMSON, 1985, 1999), has largely focused on company decisions to "make versus buy" in given transactions. Such analysis is conducted at a sub-company level in that the units of observations are particular choices made "on the margin" by individual firms (JACOBIDES, 2005) and not by industry groups based on full costs. It therefore does not look at entire industries by examining, for example, how markets emerge to create new markets, vertical disintegration to foster scale through specialization or horizontal integration to increase scale in executing functions and scope through improved allocation mechanisms or more efficient internal markets for the different products.

A key constraint that explains the current literature focus is the difficulty involved in measuring shifts and testing hypotheses with competitive dynamic backgrounds. Traditionally, the strong reliance upon transaction cost theory led to a relatively static observation standard. Existing studies measure industry effects by changes in concentration rates (Boon or Herfindahl indices), by scales influenced by the Gini coefficient comparing market share and margins of market leaders to those of followers (BERGER et al., 1999), or by calculating proxy variables for relative entry dynamics and new entrants' relative strength (by which they mimic the shape of market barriers, e.g. (KING AND TUCCI, 2002)). All these factors are static and can be measured only after the fact, but hardly modeled or simulated for ex-ante decision making. The long-standing theory of industrial organization has shown that the competitiveness of an industry cannot be measured by market structure indicators alone, such as numbers of institutions, or Herfindahl and other concentration indexes (BAUMOL, PANZAR AND WILLING, 1982). Previously, research often has coped with the problems discussed here by building on case-based empirical collection.

In this tradition, KHORANA AND SERVAES (1999, 2000) look at the specific determinants of mutual fund launches or on takeovers and mergers within the mutual fund industry. They thereby find that corporate actions are driven primarily by factors such as intra-product competition or the potential for additional economies of scale. Their results are thus in line with classical market structure research that handily explain performance outcomes of the companies, but do not do so adequately for the emerging structure itself (MASSA, 2003).

A second strand of literature focuses on the innovative pattern of fund launches and thus on the impact on the markets (mainly the stock market) and a decrease in oligopolistic structures therein. From this point of view, there are two potential channels through which mutual funds may influence the market. The first relies on the information dimension and builds on the earlier results of ADMATI AND PFLEIDERER (1990). The introduction of a mutual fund, just like any financial innovation, should increase the informational completeness of the market. The second channel relies on market frictions such as the limits of arbitrage and inelasticity, e.g. as a consequence of transaction cost (PETAJISTO, 2003). The interactions between products or fund families and the upstream integrated services have recently attracted additional research: KEMPF AND RUENZI (2004) analyze the decision to launch new products from an intra-fund-family tournament point of view, while ZHAO (2001) points out different corporate capabilities required to maintain a portfolio of different products.

Organization and the industry structure of the mutual fund industry are strongly intertwined. The mutual fund industry is generally considered a highly competitive market with product substitution within and between the competing companies, whereby the leading firms are embedded in large diversified banks (LEVINTHAL, 2006). The company's organizational setup includes a transaction and processing organization, a variety of product families as well as a distribution function (WALTER AND SISLI, 2006), whereby the leading firms can count on synergies with their corporate parents' structures in terms of initial capacity utilization. The product families represent a set of funds launched and managed by a joint sales, research and trading team that shares certain fund strategy-specific capabilities, and that learns and gains additional experience over time. Within its family boundaries the team can launch various products with slightly different risk-return properties, or different classes of a product (e.g. class A, B, C shares) that allow customized structuring of the associated fees on a discretionary basis and are dependent on the regulatory expectations of potential investors (GHEMAWATT, LEVINTHAL, 2000). Thus, each new product coming into the market takes off at lower marginal costs than its peers already in the market. As a consequence, the industry leaders act in an environment that is both highly competitive on the product side, but scale-sensitive and potentially oligopolistic on the distribution and processing side. Economic theory coined the term multi-segment markets for this type of company structure that is interlinked vertically and product-wise (VANWITTELOOSTUIJN, 1995). These multi-segment markets can be characterized with respect to the product segment as highly salient potential intra-firm rivals as pointed out by ANDREWS (1949), LYDALL (1955), HINES (1957) and BRUNNER

(1961), which would suggest that each firm minimizes the number of funds in the market. From an inter-company standpoint, however, the relative cost required for the set-up of a new product or product class is company-specific rather than product-specific. A firm may use its capacity to supply a technically slightly different product to a new product market, to foster related diversification, or to start serving another country market at marginal cost. It thereby bypasses entry barriers that seem insurmountable to other potential rivals such as new firms (e.g. BRUNNER 1961). Thus, building barriers to entry becomes a critical factor for the success also of a mutual fund company.

When we extend the literature's focus from the narrow perspective of the observed industry towards general theory, BRANDER AND KRUGMAN (1983) or CAIRNS AND MAHABIR (1988) showed that the use of the multi-segment concepts can be a powerful tool with respect to industrial organization analysis. This strength lies in the multi-segment organization's inherent distinction between product market competition and integrated production capacity oligopolies. This feature is reflected in the fact that the marginal prices on the product markets vary based on the upstream capital investments in capacity (VAN WEGBERG 1992); multi-segment research has shown primarily that a difference in marginal cost between the traditional products and (newly) launched products were based on a complete market separation in the response of a firm. This market separation rests on two assumptions: (i) constant returns to scale and (ii) the segmented market's assumption that prices between the markets may differ in the absence of arbitrage trade (BRANDER AND KRUGMAN, 1983). From the point of view of strategic response, this separation of analysis meant that what counts is not just competitive strategy (i.e. how to compete – which is the essential question in inner-market competition) but also corporate strategy, i.e., where to compete geographically and product-wise.

With respect to the organization and strategy discussions, SHY AND STENBACKA (2003) raise the idea of multi-level interaction leading to industry structure outcomes when characterizing a systemic relationship between the diversification incentives and the market structure of the mutual fund industry based on the investors' attitudes towards risk. They find that with sufficiently low competition the sub-game results in perfect equilibrium and a small number of rival products. This research strand finds valuable support and complements in the scarcely discussed topic of vertically integrated markets and (strategic) company reactions. In this area, BANERJEE AND LIN (2003) show that downstream oligopolists may invest more in cost-reducing R&D than a downstream monopolist. Intuitively, the result follows from the output-enhancing effect of R&D, which allows the upstream firm to increase its input price, thus raising the rival's costs. In the fund context,

R&D investment can be seen as a parallel to research cost and development of new capabilities or of building a brand name. In line with these findings, BROCAS (2003) studied a setting where downstream companies face costs for switching technologies licensed by innovating upstream firms in order to give strategic advice. He found that the prices of licenses vary with the level of switching costs: easily substitutable technologies are licensed at low prices, whereas innovative technologies with high switching costs command high prices. In such a setting, both upstream and downstream companies may find it profitable to integrate vertically. Thus, there is a strong hint that vertical integration is a valuable answer to innovation and disruptive features in the market.

One common feature in all attempts to mold these theory streams into a dynamic perspective is the fact that evolution unfolds over time and hence, company reaction must be studied in subsequent game configurations. In this, BUEHLER AND SCHMUTZLER (2008) highlight the role of intimidating actions associated with vertical integration and downstream investments and their impact on strategic response and industry structures in dynamic multi-stage games. As the model set up will show, this feature might be an influential aspect in technological or capability capacity building in the observed markets.

A Model for Response in Dynamic Multi-Segment Markets

Preliminary Assumptions

The basic assumption here is that two extreme case scenarios exist: gradual or disruptive change. Both of these scenarios trigger different reactions or responses by incumbent firms, when anticipated. The model builds strongly on the Schumpeterian model of dynamic entry as introduced in (SENGUPTA, 2007, p. 83). For ease of reading, the variable specification is depicted below prior to the model debate.

a	Number of products (funds) on the sub-population level
C	Cost, specified by indexes
F	Barrier to entry (cost to access open platforms, e.g. in distribution)
i	Number of potential product scope (i.e. fund families or platforms)
K	Maximum capacity of a firm to launch new funds (measured by the MES/ average scales of a fund firm
k	Relative capacity utilization, measured by the average fund size
m	Mark-up between value chains in integrated architectures
n	Number of units (steps in the value chain)
P	Product-specific factor (i.e. margin per fund)
Q	Demand, specified by indexes
r	Discount rate
S / s	(Marginal) compensation per additional unit (value chain step)
x	Output (fees generated at different value chain steps)
Z	Capability stock
z	Capability spill over among different related funds on sub-population level
π	Cash flow
β / δ	Proxy Variables, dependent of market structure

Multi-segment Economics

The laboratory in which we model responses is an industry that follows basic multi-segment properties. The main properties are a capacity-sensitive integrated production set-up and a non-complementary multi-product base. The system is integrated across different levels of analysis, as discussed earlier.

In the tradition of earlier studies (JOHNSON AND HOOPES, 2003; KESSIDES, 1986; SUTTON, 1991; VANWEGBERG, 1992), we assume that the company decides over time to invest in capacity and thereby accumulates sunkness which supports barriers to entry compared to later entering competitors. Management here can decide on all or some of BAIN's (1956) sources for later barriers to entry: absolute cost advantage, product differentiation and scale economy to invest in. The literature generally defines multi-segment competition as product differentiation (e.g. advertising investments) on the product dimension and capacity-based economies of scale on the corporate function as the critical forms (VAN WEGBERG, 1992).

On the dimension of vertical corporate structure, capacity is the sensitive variable driving the industry structures. Capacity which is measured in terms of output has a cost s per unit and the incumbent's cost function is assumed to be of the form

$$C\,(x,K) = nx + sK + F;\ \text{for } x \neq K \qquad 1.1$$

$$C\,(x,K) = (n + s)x + F;\ \text{for } x = K \qquad 1.2$$

where x is output and F a reversible entry barrier building fixed cost and n the scope of vertical production steps or the marginal cost incurred when producing services. The potential entrant has no sunk cost like the incumbent and hence it would have a cost function of the form

$$C(x) = (n + s)x + F \qquad 1.3$$

Profit maximization on this dimension follows the idea of minimizing the cost of each of the outlined vertical cost components, by either accumulating sunkness over a long time or by increasing the product volume x. This is the first functionality as introduced by DIXIT (1981) to support BAIN's (1956) structural view of economies of scale as a barrier to entry under Cournot conditions. The capacity dimension is strongly cost-motivated and cost calculation is carried out as under monopolistic conditions; capacity expansion is governed by a standard demand curve for product (P)

$$P(Q) = a-Q; \text{ with } Q = q_1 + q_2 \text{ and } a>0 \tag{2.1}$$

Profit functions for multi-segment companies are set by the amount of products given demand for segment 1 q_1 and demand for segment 2 q_2. Product expansion is thereby limited only by the marginal cost base and challenged only by shifts in demand structures. Each incumbent firm on the product dimension is a price taker and therefore minimizes the initial present value of long-run costs in order to stay in the industry indefinitely. At any time $t > 0$ the incumbent firm's average cost is thus given by the conditional cost of the prior period's capacity per product unit and the corresponding variable costs. Thus, on the product market's track, firms face more of a demand-(Q)-driven decision space. Q refers to a mean price elastic demand structure in a Walrasian environment. Under these circumstances, the more commoditized an offered product, the more public information is made available and the fewer company-specific negative externalities are shouldered. Thus, the relative development cost decreases with increasing public information in sufficiently large and commoditized markets, whereas in specific niche markets, there would be positive externalities from proprietary research. We can expect to see specialization patterns along capabilities in proprietary research for specialized submarkets and releases of new funds to the point where the marginal benefit of in-house externalities (scales and spill-overs) match with the nearest competitor's relative cost of dilution. In such a framework, a large company has a clear advantage over a small one given its superior ability to utilize complementary effects (if they are available) of its proprietary skills, which again have economies of scale due to indivisibilities. Note that the incentive to innovate for the industry with the more elastic demand curve is greater for the large companies and hence any innovation-induced price reductions yield a greater expansion in output for more elastic markets.

The intersection of capacity- and product-dominated organizational economics is indicated by the vertical structure-product node. For ease of exposition at this vertical product node, we introduce a consulting firm that will perform only the final "assembly" function of advising a customer on its optimal portfolio.

Let C_a denote the variable cost of assembling one unit of the final products (e.g. one equity fund), and F_a be the fixed cost of assembling approximately n units of the final product, i.e. the consulting function, where n is the assembly run size of the final product. As no manufacturing steps other than assembly are performed by the "advisor", a firm will purchase from outside vendors all of the parts and components needed. Let C_p denote total variable cost of ordering and purchasing all components needed to assemble one unit of the final product, and let F_p denote the fixed cost of purchasing and ordering all the components needed to produce approximately n units of the final product. The firm's cash flow from the focused advisor approach would be discounted over time at rate (1+r) and interdependent of the demand (Q) and Product (P) specifics. This cash flow function follows the basic form introduced by SENGUPTA (2007, p. 84) and incorporates equations (1)-(2).

$$\pi_f = P\frac{1}{(1+r)} - [C_a + C_p]n - [F_a + F_p] + Sn - Q(1+r); \text{ if } Q(1+r) < n \qquad 3$$

We use a very simplistic cash flow function for a mutual fund. The function's components are a margin or fee for the product with a discount factor for year-end payment. From these fees, the fund pays for variable (C) and fixed (F) cost both on sub-population and firm level. At step Sn, the fund firm is compensated for non-core functions, best illustrated by a kick-back he gets from a second fund who uses its distribution network. Comparable to a demand elasticity constraint in traditional economics, we complemented the cash flow function by a "demand capacity" constraint (i.e. a maximum for additional resource utilization, which follows the definition developed in SENGUPTA (2007). In other words, this cash flow (and its potential) is restricted by the demand elasticity, which can be calculated as marginal cost per product times number of units (elasticity trigger) minus total demand potential. The reason behind this module is that the willingness to pay move linearly along the cost base only as long as the number of products that are issued does not have an adverse effect on margins that can be attained through these products.

The relative cost of assembling a distinct portfolio of products from the incumbent remains dependent on his marginal benefit from his vertical integration, best illustrated by straight-through processes and reduced transaction costs for the case of the mutual fund industry. The innovation in terms of marketing and sales or product quality that is offered by the new entering firm has to overcome these scale arguments to become profitable. Thus, the profit function of a multi-segment market firm can be described along the vertical integrated corporate dimension and the product dimension. The corporate dimension is the sum of all inter-value chain mark-ups m_i minus the expenditure for the vertical expansion, equaling the marginal cost for acquiring the next up- or downstream vertical unit times the cost for the respective capacity K_i and the variable costs for production per output-unit x, C_x. The product market is ruled by the cost on the corporate level, initial cost base for each product category and the conditional marginal cost given the existing degree of vertical integration for each product class added to this portfolio.

The design of the thought experiment: triggering organizational responses

In order to trigger changes across the potential break-lines for industrial dynamics, we build a thought experiment where a new competitor enters the market as a new niche emerges based on distinct capability demand first and based on a new technological environment second. The first entry is assumed to depend upon gradual innovation (e.g. learning or improvement in research or product development, whereas the second corresponds to a disruptive innovation for the industry in focus.

Multi-segment economics under innovation

Market evolution is basically driven forward through innovation and the resulting shift in previously accumulated entry barriers. This ultimately coincides with the entry of new firms (Bain, 1956). In this respect, it is irrelevant whether the barriers erode exogenously as the consequence of a disruptive shock and the resulting "de-valuation" of the barriers or due to gradual innovations of new niche firms that become effective in terms of new capabilities which better meet customer demands. However, the difference in innovation type can affect the incumbent responsiveness and thus influence the dynamics of the evolutionary pattern observed (Sengupta, 2007). This variance in dynamic evolution and its economic features are discussed by Kamien and Schwarz (1982) or Aghian and Howitt (1992) as a basically positive relationship between innovation and the degree of concentration. Where concentration turns towards near-monopoly, it may yield excess or above-normal profits.

Competitive adjustments in the Walrasian framework, on the other hand, assume free entry with no barriers. Long-run entry occurs only when prices vary absolutely or innovation shifts barriers with respect to absolute prices in the corporate structure or to relative prices with respect to specific capabilities (Sengupta, 2007). Thus, the potentially large companies expand their (potential maximum of) achievable externalities when facing threats by innovative competitors. It must be noted that if there is sufficient excess capacity (i.e. $K>x$) prior to the innovation event, the incumbent's marginal production cost is only n, whereas the entrant's marginal production cost advantage helps to deter entry in equilibrium. However, innovation effects in this context often lead to instabilities in the competitive adjustment process. Three important sources of instability must be mentioned with respect to multi-segment cases. The first arises when there is an adjustment lag or delay, e.g. as a consequence of regulatory approval mechanisms. The second arises in the dual adjustment process where there are increasing returns to scale and third, where entry-exit dynamics affect the discounted value of future expected profits with an exogenous discount rate, e.g. following a disruptive shock (JANSEN, 2003).

Response Options in Multi-segment Competition under Innovation

We assume that each management will engage in entry-deterring behavior when facing innovative shocks (BUEHLER AND SCHMUTZLER, 2008). Thus, a firm's response has in every case a dynamic post-innovation effect, even though the overall structure will not shift. However, in order for this assumption to be stable, we have to model with an infinite game; say that the firms compete with each other over time, again and again. This also implies that competitive moves that might have short-run benefits may hurt the company in the longer run. Once its competitors have had time to make countermoves of their own, the reaction might be assessed differently and possibly less positively. Bearing this in mind, entry-deterring strategies are worthwhile only if two conditions are met: the incumbents earn higher profits as a near-monopolist than they do as a duopolists, and the strategy changes the entrants' expectations about the nature of post-entry competition. Although contestability theory shows how the mere threat of entry can keep (quasi-)monopolists from raising prices, results for long-term contestable markets are difficult to find (BORENSTEIN, 1989). Assuming that the incumbent monopolist's market is not perfectly contestable, it may expect to reap additional profits if it can keep out entrants. In practice, three forms of deterrence strategy have emerged: limit pricing, predatory pricing and capacity expansion (BESANKO, DRANOVE, SHANLEY AND SCHAEFER, 2003). The management will decide on its specific deterrence strategy based on its team's particular capabilities and its experience. We expect that each management has experience with gradual innovation, but not with disruptive innovation. Here, managers are faced with decisions under uncertainty as well as with sudden re-valuation of their corporate resources.

This process affects the marginal costs c_i of all downstream firms in the last stage. Solving the profit maximization problem for given levels of marginal costs yields an (Cournot) output q_i, mark-ups m_i, and profits Δ_i for all vertical dimensions of the decision process (KREPS AND SCHEINKMAN, 1983).

The strategic reactions of the involved management teams are that the large incumbents will expand vertically in the case of disruptive innovation and respond by offering a potential substitute product portfolio in the case of gradual innovation. These reactions influence the market structure, the competitive dynamics and ultimately the boundaries of the company. We argue that both product variety expansion for gradual innovation and capacity expansion for disruptive innovation generate what we call an "intimidation" effect for potential followers of the innovative firms. That is, in the case of vertical integration, the incumbent's capacity and efficiency are expanded above the ex-ante rational equilibrium. At the same time, this reduces the rationale for cost-reducing investment by competitors. Similarly, in the case of product range expansion, the competitors' expected returns from launching their new innovative products are eroded due to substitution effects.

This results in a basic strategic motive for vertical integration and portfolio expansion even beyond deterrence that has gone unnoticed in the previous literature.

The Response to Innovation

Management acts within the outlined framework based on the assembling of two separate optimization problems. Both problems are conditionally linked and the solutions are based on path dependency (number of products) and value chain integration as well as on the company's specific capabilities.

Illustration 8 depicts the basic idea of the theory. Based on the theory and a the notion of a constant cash-flow-based environment, the reactions to different types of innovation yield different structural boundaries for the incumbent firm (and are faced at different levels of management).

In order to illustrate the interaction mechanisms at the "assembly node" and to permit expansion of the theoretical assumptions, LUKACH et al. (2005) have developed a dynamic duopoly model in the Cournot-Nash framework where one firm is bigger in the sense that its marginal cost of production is lower. This model is applied to an intra-firm interaction. We assume that the response function for all firms facing multiple dimensions (e.g. two) are taken under no intra-firm competition and that the two dimensions are not equally important for the firm.

This model uses a linear inverse demand curve in normalized units as

$$P_t = 1 - X_t;\ X_t = \text{total output} \quad 4.1$$

with cost comprising two components: production costs (4.2) and costs for enhancing the firm's set of capabilities (4.3) as

$$C_i = (a_i + k_{it} + \beta k_{jt})x_{it};\ i, j = 1, 2;\ i \neq j \quad 4.2$$

where a represents a constant for a research and management team, k the product-specific costs per value chain step.

$$C_j = a_j \frac{z_{it}^2}{2};\ i, j = 1, 2 \quad 4.3$$

where a again represents the existing resources and z denotes the capability externalities.

The dynamic evolution for each marginal part of the vertical value chain is of the form

$$k_{it} = (1 - \delta)k_{it-1} + z_{it} \quad 4.4$$

This means that there is room for scale increase on the vertical axis wherever there is marginal capacity utilization potential (i.e. the platform is not yet fully used and each additional dollar generated on that platform has a positive effect) plus (as a consequence of additional experience) capability spillovers z are expanded.

In such a setting, one assumes automatically that the large incumbents have an advantage, e.g. via brand name a (sunken advertisement expenses) or production cost b (marginal cost for launching a new fund) over the new entering products, that is $a_1 < a_2$ and $b_1 < b_2$.

We expand this basic model in order to incorporate the different elements that are possible under the introduced innovation scenarios: We are considering a two or multistage game. In the second stage, each firm maximizes its total profit function as

$$\mathrm{Max}_{(it)} = \sum_{t=o}^{t} (1+r)^{-t} [1 - x_t) x_{it} - (a_j k_{it} - \beta_{it}) x_{it} - \beta_i \frac{z_{it}^2}{2}] \qquad 4.5$$

Subject to equations (4.1)-(4.5) we can compute optimal solutions.

Thus in the first stage each firm chooses its organizational set-up based on a maximization of its marginal capacity utilization in a constant value chain design. Capacity endownment z can not be acitvely influenced.

The impact of controlling additional vertical value chain steps and the cost thereof can be expressed by a derivative of equation 4.5 when holding output x constant:

$$k_{it}^{'} = \frac{2a_i - a_j + \sqrt{(2a_j^2 + 4a_i a_j + a_j^2 + 24x - 12\beta x)}}{4 - 2\beta} \qquad 4.6$$

Alternatively,

the impact of additional vertical scope, e.g. through related products can be based on a maximization of output (by number of products offered on a modular fund family platform), which is expressed by a derivative of x:

$$x_{it}^{'} = \frac{1}{3}[(1 - 2a_i + a_j) + (2 - \beta) k_{it} + (2\beta - 1) z k_{it}] \qquad 4.7$$

This leads to an optimal cash flow function of the form:

$$\mathrm{Max}_{(it)} = \sum_{t=o}^{t} (1+r)^{-t} [1 - x_t) x_{it} - (a_j k_{it} - \beta_{it}) x_{it} - \beta_i \frac{z_{it}^2}{2}]$$

This function corresponds to the optimization problem under Schumpeterian entry in SENGUPTA (2007). Since these are both standard linear quadratic control problems, the optimal solution, if it exists, must be written as a feedback rule (4.8). Hence the impact of vertical versus horizontal response can be expressed as a feedback to existing capability spillover and existing capacity relative to the cost structure when the utilization rate marginally increases or decreases. Formally this can be expressed as:

$$z_t^* = H_t k_t + h_t \qquad 4.8$$

With

$$z_t = \binom{z_{1t}}{z_{2t}}; k_t = \binom{k_{1t}}{k_{2t}}$$

H_t, h_t depend on all the parameters. Several implications of the optimal response rule and the capability investment trajectories are illustrated both theoretically and numerically. First of all, the management of the more efficient company (i.e. the bigger firm with lower marginal cost) invests more in capability building and broadens the product offering more rigorously than the less efficient one. In the beginning of the planning horizon the capability investments for each firm rise over time, but at a decreasing rate. Therefore the bigger incumbent with more ability to internalize the capability spillover effects tends to invest more in capability-enhancing resources than the smaller entrant. Thus, in case of $n > 2$, the higher the industry concentration, the greater the incentive to invest in capabilities. Investment in capability building would peak in oligopolistic settings, given market clearing capacity in place already.

On the other hand, when observing the problem set from a product perspective, increasing scope – although adding to Walrasian competition – also benefits the company-specific ability to capitalize on internal spillovers z. In this case $p > 2$ adversely affects concentration but pushes the feedback loop positively as benefits increase and relative cost per new product decrease. Hence over investment in capacity might be a consequence. These results are clearly in line with the model and empirical findings presented in LEVINTHAL, MYATT (1994). These authors saw certain functions in the mutual fund industry (transfer agency or custody operations) as scale-intensive businesses. But independent of this scale intensity, they could show that feedback loops based on experimental learning were able to overcome the capacity elements on a product scale. However, although the role of capabilities could be shown, LEVINTHAL AND MYATT (1994) did not link product capabilities and capacity-scale arguments theoretically, nor did they explicitly address this problem (as this was not required in their empirical setting).

However, from an active decision-making point of view, the two intertwining feedback loops must be addressed. In practice, to solve this problem, management is forced to keep one of the two dimensions constant, structuring the hierarchy within the organization not as a matrix organization, but with one dimension having a clear lead over the others (OTTEN AND BAMS, 2002). This organizational control leads to stable outcomes, but also to management decisions backed with one of the two dimensions calculated upon on a marginal basis, whereas the other is kept at absolute cost. The stable feedback loops thus can be written as either

$$Z_t = \binom{Z_{1t}}{Z_{2t}}; k_t = \binom{k_{1t}}{k_{2t}} \quad 4.9$$

$$z_t = \binom{z_{1t}}{z_{2t}}; K_t = \binom{K_{1t}}{K_{2t}}$$

Given our previous discussions, company management results are now enforced by the various feedback rules, regardless of whether they emphasize vertical integration (in the case of disruptive innovation) or whether they expect gradual innovation, whereby their response is absolutely less costly and consists only of a portfolio expansion.

Implications and Discussion

Based on these basic functionalities, a mutual fund uses different approaches to define its strategy. Companies build entry barriers both on the product dimension as well as on the corporate dimension. Absolute cost advantages are achieved by leveraging the capital structure, i.e. through the thereby generated marginal cost effect when launching new products within an existing fund family. At this point, each firm is restricted to a certain amount of minimum capital, but, once it knocks down this barrier, it can expand its product scope (normally through new classes of funds denoted A, B or C) without limitations. Equally, it can increase the funds managed through one fund or one class as long as customer demand remains attentive.

The second type of barrier is created at both single fund management and group management level: each additional year that a company is present in the market, its funds – though they perform successfully – increase the brand awareness of a product. This effect might even have an exponential pattern, given an expanding bunch of funds per family. Finally, on the group management level, there is a classical scale and capacity pattern on an overall firm level. The more fund families of an issuer in the market, the better its capacity utilization and the higher the potential to leverage its vertical backbone such as standardized transaction and reporting functions for a variety of products. While the marginal capital effect fades over time, it is mostly brand awareness and capital utilization that prevail over time and increase barriers to entry in favor of the incumbents. Thus, we observe in the fund industry – parallel to BAIN's (1956) three types of barriers to entry – three levels of decision-making that all react sensitively to time in the market, but not all with the same time horizon. Only the group management that decides on capacity expansion has a full fixed-cost perspective, while fund family management in particular assesses its situation based on marginal costs.

However, decisions on pricing and the launch of new product classes are faced at a fund-family management level and based on customer demand relative to market share and marginal costs of product launches (MASSA, 2003; SHY AND STENBACKA, 2003). To this end, a simple linear model in the tradition of SALINGER (1988) is applied, which was modified to include both endogenous integration and investment decisions. That is, vertical integration serves as the dominant strategy (FUDENBERG AND TIROLE, 1984) geared towards tapering the competitor's cost-reducing investments. Importantly, this effect does not rely on the existence of strategic substitutes in the product market, even though we are working in a Cournot framework.

Based on observations in the literature, the mutual fund firm is a price taker on the product market (CHORDIA, 1996). CHORDIA (1996) analyzed a broad set of fund charge structures, thereby showed that after risk adjustments fund firms are pure price taker. In these settings, the companies have two basic dimensions for strategic movement: the product portfolio and the corporate structure. Following the multi-segment structure outlined above, in equilibrium the economics on the product side can be described as a cost-minimization function, given the existing boundaries of the company. This can be written as

$$\text{Min } C(x_i; K) = \text{Min} \sum_{K=1}^{x} \binom{z_1}{z_2} x^K a^{n-k} \qquad 5.1$$

Parallel to this, each firm maximizes the volume of funds processed based upon its corporate capacity, which is

$$\text{Max } \pi(n_n; Z) = \sum_{Z=1}^{n} \binom{k_1}{k_2} n^Z a^{n-z} + \sum m_{ij} \qquad 5.2$$

Functions 5.1 and 5.2 can theoretically be combined only within a min-max problem set when holding the relative feedback determinants constant.

$$\pi^*(n_j; Z, K) = \sum_{K=1}^{x_i} \sum_{Z=1}^{x_j} [\binom{z_1}{z_2} \binom{k_1}{k_2} x^z a^{n-k} + \sum m_{ij}]$$

The resulting company-specific saddle function corresponds to multiple paths and cannot be solved with a finite solution. When holding one of the dimensions constant, sub-game Nash equilibrium results can be derived. Each time the process is re-run (in a multiple game), the results tend to move more towards extreme values in the directions „capability improvement“ and „capacity utilization“ and the corresponding response strategies „(related) diversification“ and vertical (re-)integration. Key variables that affect outcome are thereby not only the path-dependent endowment with specific capability and capacity, but also the value of mark-ups across ex-ante vertical integration.

In a more constant environment and given a gradual development of capabilities, companies have little incentive to alter the industry architecture fundamentally, and it takes time until break lines in the set-up become visible. However, where disruptive innovation affects market (exchange) prices and mark-ups deteriorate with sudden drops, e.g. in bid-ask spreads charged, industry architecture may change fast and responses are more viable along the capacity dimension.

Hence, when looking for likely responses in this economic setting, one can first assume a gradual innovation with cost per new product and opportunity cost due to lost market shares subject to the absence of deterring product launches. This corresponds to setting a > x (i.e. a constant expansion of output at cost of scale) in the model and constant mark-ups m on the vertical axis. In this setting, the larger the distance between the two variables z and k, the stronger the feedback loop function and the more likely the deterring product launch becomes subject to potential capability-based entry of new competitors.

When calculating for response to disruptive innovations, old capacity gets devalued, i.e., $k = 0$. The solution to this leads to the loss in competitive advantage which must be contested either by further integration, as long as the cost of doing so is less than the opportunity losses on the volume through un-restricted entry of new products (or else a move to the market), and is reflected by a sudden change in the (achievable) value m. Eventually, market solutions will become a cheaper form of transaction.

This argumentation can be illustrated. Assume that a company has a certain amount of experience in gold-based funds. Its marginal cost for launching an additional gold fund or a new class of the same gold fund are almost zero as it can draw on existing management teams, expertise and infrastructure. The cost for launching a new related product, for instance a silver fund, are marginal to the extent that the firm can again draw on most of the existing fixed-cost resources, but might need to add additional management resources at variable cost. Furthermore, the more related the new product, the higher the learning effects and knowledge spillovers (z) for the managing team. This leads to an optimal strategic path characterized by high volume per fund product, a focused fund product portfolio of near-related products and a concentration on specific processing functions along the value chain that optimally caters to the specific capacity of the company's product portfolio. Despite the existence of such an optimal path from a macro perspective, decisions on the product dimensions will be made based on fixed-cost considerations along the capacity dimension and on marginal cost assessments on the product dimension. Accordingly, entry deterrence will be pursued by expanding the product portfolio with self-substituting and related offerings. The perception of entry threat is that of a demand model, despite being a price taker. In contrast to this, decisions on the corporate dimension are based on marginal capacity costs and absolute product costs. The perception of entrants is that of a cost model comparable to an oligopolistic environment.

The choice for deterring along product markets or corporate firm boundaries is made based on management expectations for the perceived innovation impact. This innovation impact is relative to the company‘s existing capability base and relative to its vertical integration status. A high relative innovation impact leads to a high willingness to pay for deterrence strategies. Accordingly, again, expensive vertical strategies are pursued if the threat is massive. These strategies were discussed earlier, e.g. with respect to Internet-based innovations of business models (Consoli, 2005). The relative cost of the fixed capacity lost value for the incumbents, so that they reacted by investing in increasing efficiency in their jeopardized distribution channels. This meant either leaving the market, expanding upstream into shared platforms and trading systems or integrating downstream towards additional distribution channels such as online banking and telephone banking (Consoli, 2005). Dixit (1980) summarized this concept by stating that "a capacity investment transforms variable costs into sunk costs, and thus reduces marginal costs". However, this deterring influence is restricted to capital-intensive industries. Yet multi-segment settings undermine this view. Given low capital and a highly labor- or expertise-intensive sub-market, it might still be the vertically upstream market's capacity that defines the ability to compete successfully. The upfront capacity commitments set the relative bounded marginal costs plus a mark-up that corresponds to the efficiency of production on the sub-market level. The vertical corporate structure represents accumulated investments that resulted in barriers to entry (F). With respect to the fund market case, these can be distribution and transaction capacity or marketing and branding investments. Given the character of sunkness of these investments, management decisions on the corporate dimension are made based on marginal cost per additional step in the vertical production chain (k). Economies of scale are high and consecutive. Thus, a firm that already has high excess capacity per production step can expand its capacity further at marginal cost, since its decreasing cost for transaction volume per value chain step attract continuously new volume and products are assessed based on absolute costs. Achievable scales drive the structure on this dimension towards an oligopoly and the decision function accordingly depends on the marginal cost for increased excess capacity, but absolute cost per new product. Furthermore, the high existing volumes processed also drive the cost of vertical expansion marginally down, compared to less vertically integrated firms. Thus, on a corporate dimension each firm moves continuously up the integration ladder as potential entry dynamics increase. The willingness to pay under constant cash flow conditions went above the fixed cost investment that guaranteed market stability in ex-ante stage.

Product portfolios in contrast are relatively easily shifted. The company thereby ignores the conditionality of vertical boundaries on the micro-level, with potentially disastrous consequences: Under the condition of capability-driven market evolution, new and specialized firms can still enter the market along the production dimension. In this case companies have only their specialized products and need to cover their development costs as well as the distribution costs. The incumbent reacts by copying the niche product in terms of risk-return characteristics and marketing expenditures, thus by expanding its product portfolio to deter the entrant, or at least to stay in the market with a substitute product that can be sold and produced through the existing value chain. Take a recent development in the fund industry: a couple of years ago, a set of firms were perceived to be the incumbent leaders in the market for fixed-income fund products. When new firms recently entered this space successfully by offering new products based on structured fixed-income cash flows, the incumbents perceived a high impact on their established submarket's structure and ventured into the new product array at marginal prices beyond what would have been rational on a macro-level.

Regardless of the accuracy of guesses about the entry dynamics, all firms deviate from the optimal path towards a second-best solution. Depending on the company's organization, however, final decisions are made either on a fund family or product dimension or on a corporate vertical structure dimension. Thus it is organization that determines how the firms deviate and internal knowledge spillovers and learning effects (z) that determine the underlying feedback rules and thus the pace of adjustment, i.e. response. Given differences in organization and management culture or regulatory effects such as Chinese walls that prevent certain knowledge spillovers, market structures will adjust differently in different geographic settings. This might also link to discussed aspects in industry structure (Walter, 1999), such as the perception of the disruptive power of the Internet at management levels, leading to the assumption of high Schumpeterian economics in the U.S., the set-up of fund exchanges and increased vertical expansion with reduced product offerings. Today most vertically integrated fund service firms are operating without products and the product-offering firms are managing higher volumes within the same fund product.

In the meantime, in Europe the Internet was embraced more intensively as an efficient way to communicate and distribute externalities, leading to an expanding number of products per company. European mutual funds offer more substitute products with less volume per product and vertical integration is less prevalent. At the same time, there is no evidence of eroded barriers to entry (e.g. by functioning large-scale fund supermarkets). Finally, despite the differences in market structure configuration, both decisions deviated from the optimal path. We thus summarize the arguments in the following propositions:

Proposition 1

Management's perception frames the willingness to deter entry, both by setting the responsibility for actions organizationally, as well as by defining the willingness to pay for deterring strategies.

Proposition 1 can be backed by the calculation of the two entry mechanisms and accompanying instability in competitive adjustments.

Proposition 2

When deciding on the basis of capability and capacity endowment, it is a viable strategy for fund firms to react to entry based on gradual capability innovation by expanding the product offering on an existing platform

Proposition 3

When deciding on the basis of capability and capacity endowment, it is a viable strategy for fund firms to react to entry based on disruptive process innovation by vertically integrating in order to ensure control over the industrial bottleneck, in this case the necessary transaction capacity.

Proposition 4

The dynamics of both solutions are enforced by positive feedback loops, stemming from the above-mentioned capability or capacity endowments. These endowments are often intertwined with organizational tendencies and increase the run towards extreme positions in terms of (i) small niches, (ii) large funds per fund type and (iii) vertical structure. This is supported by the positive feedback loop argument as introduced in (4.9).

Summing up Propositions 1–4, it is the interaction of management teams with its environment (i.e. anticipated entry dynamics and thus local competition) that leads to capability dependent micro-level strategies. Given different capabilities and sunken investments in a market, funds confronted with the same innovation impact will choose inherently different solutions. We thus argue that winners of these games are specialized innovators that can enter the market, large conglomerates that can accept cross-subsidizing some products, and modular firms that can adjust their cost base at variable fund volumes. The propositions and the sketched models are in line with the market structure and market structure adjustments of a number of vertically related industries documented in the literature, including the oil industry (Bindemann, 1999), the beer industry in the UK (Slade, 1998), and the US cable television industry (Chipty, 2001).

Conclusion

The mutual fund industry is characterized by a classical multi-segment segmentation with two dimensions for strategic response: The product dimension and the production and distribution structure. Its sensitive to innovation and market dynamics is formed. The paper addressed this by taking two extreme scenarios into account: gradual and disruptive innovation. Thereby, the willingness to pay for deterrence strategies increases along the gravity of the (expected) impact of innovation on entry (and thus market evolution) dynamics. With this background, we analyzed the decision functions and their determinants based on a multi-step game micro-economic and industrial organization line of argumentation. We found initial evidence that in the individual interaction layer, it is of key importance whether the decision-maker has a more product-oriented or more company-oriented perspective. This perspective is developed along the boundaries of a firm's organizational features. Second, the economics of the decision process, when separated along these dimensions, is driven by a biased assessment of marginal and absolute costs under the threat of entry. So gradual and perceivably low impact innovations are counteracted by an expansion of the product offerings based on marginal product and absolute capacity cost considerations, while for strong impact disruptive innovation, the dominant strategy is based on marginal cost of building excess capacity and absolute product costs to fuel this increase in fixed assets.

In practice, however, the product dimension is not independent of the capacity dimension and vice versa. Given an existing transaction base, the cost for issuing and distributing existing and new products may vary depending on the level of assets that are considered sunk on the corporate dimension and that are internally attributed to the product cost. The same is true along the vertical line of the corporate dimension. The more investments that are sunken, the lower the mark-up calculated at each step of the value chain. This is reflected in differences with respect to bid-ask spreads when trading own versus third party products over an existing platform. In this context, the bid-ask spreads represent a measurable indicator for mark-ups at the specific node of process-to-distribution along a vertically diversified fund firm. Equally, the capacity dimension depends on the volume of existing products. In this respect, the individual micro-level decision-making structures deviate from optimal macro-level measured outcomes. An optimal cost-minimizing function would mean that each firm maximizes its assets or transaction volume per standardized product and that it minimizes the variety of products (standards) within its overall structures.

The separation of decision functions and their differences in assessing options when deterring entries are one important reason for differences in directions. The fact that these differences are – within one market – not mediated towards a "middle way", but tend towards extreme points can be traced back to positive feedback loops in decision processes.

The main contribution of this paper is to outline the underlying economic logic of the industry and its main parameters in dependence of basic industry dynamic driving forces. We make no pretense of formulating "the" model for mutual funds or to explain fully mutual fund market decisions or even multi-segment market reactions in general, but wish only to outline a basic formal framework as a foundation for theoretical and empirical work in the sector as presented in the following chapters.

Previous literature has already shown the importance of capabilities (z) and their spillovers on strategies and structure outcomes (LEVINTHAL AND MYATT, 1994; SIGGELKOW, 2003), and the similar loop for capacity spillovers k has been highlighted by the consequences of the work by KOGUT AND ZANDER (1992). However, to the best of our knowledge a linking framework was missing. This paper complements the literature with such a potential framework and lays the ground for formalizations. Based on this argumentation, we showed that when two decision layers interact on the micro-level, incumbent decisions reflect only the dynamics of one of these dimensions. This, in connection with an "endless game", leads to a stable "whole-game" equilibrium on the respective segment's sub-game decision patterns and thus is in line with recent evidence from BUEHLER AND SCHMUTZLER (2005, 2008) for general organizational outcomes when analyzing the sub-game-perfect Nash equilibrium under entry deterrence assumptions.

The framework basically forms a platform or parameterization for future research, e.g. with respect to the logic of the industry, on how different regional organizations for one industry emerge or to outline the movement of bottlenecks in the architecture (more precisely defined as the migration in value appropriated. In the following chapters, we use this basic parameterization in order to dig deeper into the consequences of gradual and disruptive exogenous innovation on the mutual fund market's industry architecture.

6 Gradual Innovation Perspective: Measuring Industrial Dynamics in Mutual Fund Markets

Scholars who are involved with economic processes in industrial economies have long been concerned with the dynamics of companies' adaptation to new circumstances (Mathews, 2006/2001). Building on the findings in this research tradition, in 2001 and in an update in 2006 Matthews developed a conceptual framework within which industrial dynamics and competitive inter-company interactions could be analyzed in terms of adaptive responses to changes in the complex system of which the companies are a part. He introduced a new perspective compared to the established angle of anomalies and exceptions such as the "market failures" and "externalities" favored in many of the more classical approaches in microeconomics. The integrative nature of his concept resulted in a structure that positioned companies to play the central role as actors, whereby their resources, routines and relations with each other in fact generate the complex structures such as networks, consortia, and development blocks which mediate and shape the strategic responses made by companies. The approach thereby draws heavily on insights from four current business perspectives, namely the dynamic capabilities perspective on the company (incorporating the resource-based view) as developed in the literature on strategic management; the markets-as-networks view of inter-company coordination within industrial markets; the evolutionary economic view that seeks to account for changes in companies' competitive performance in terms of variation in their underlying organizational routines, and the entrepreneurial discovery perspective of Schumpeter.

The mutual fund market is one such example, in which competitive dynamics flow from the complex interaction of multiple layers across the inter-company and intra-company interaction of processes and routines. The market forms part of the wider asset management industry that is populated by a large number of de-facto substitute products. As has been discussed in earlier chapters, investors allocate their money based on their risk-taking attitude, and/or invest from a theoretical perspective in products based solely on risk-return characteristics. However, information on correct risk-return characteristics is costly and many (retail) investors prefer to eliminate these information costs by assuming risk-return homogeneity between the banks with which they do business and alternative distributors competing for the same commodity, which has been shown in a number of empirical studies, e.g. (Matthews and Thompson, 2005; Vives, 2001; Zera and Madura, 2001). This gives incumbent companies, especially where they own a proprietary distribution network, a clear competitive advantage under the assumption of stable industry architecture. In contrast, distribution owners are initially confronted with the high fixed costs of maintaining a sales or brokerage network giving the mutual fund market a notion of stability.

Despite this notion of stability, the market is shaped by a constantly high number of new competitors that enter the market primarily with new product innovations. The reason for this market characteristic is mostly tied to demand and capacity arguments. For new entrants, just as for the incumbents, capacity expansion is costly and the incentive to bear such costs low. Hence, new entrants may favor the option of investing in superior skills and in developing routines that enable them to capture niche product markets where they can sell their products through the incumbent's distribution network at marginal prices instead of investing in proprietary channels at full cost. Such innovators build on their distinct capabilities to produce superior returns for customers that allow for a higher price and hence the potential to compensate the distribution owners for selling their products. In addition to capacity, customer demand may be a motivating factor for exactly the same process. Increasingly, customers are becoming aware of banks' conflicts of interest when they have to decide between well-incentivized cross-selling and consulting for "best-in-class-products" from internal and third party providers, especially in markets where products are far from unique in terms of labeled risk-return characteristics which are marginal.

A hybrid version of the same story can be observed wherever new entrants develop some additional capabilities, but link their processes tightly to large incumbents who decide to increase their capacity utilization rate by either trading additional products through their system, or to service such additional products, e.g. through a "white-labeling" scheme. However, regardless of the motive, some incumbents have an incentive to support new start-ups. Combined with low regulatory barriers to entry, this leads to large numbers of small-scale producers frequently entering and exiting markets, and a small number of oligopolistic network owners.

This paper addresses precisely this nexus of business perspectives. Our main argument in this article is that dynamics of multi-level companies can not only be observed according to exclusive process, resource or capability perspectives, but must be examined in an integrated framework that reflects the various interdependencies in explaining the performance or competitiveness of companies and products. In our example, when looking at drivers of success behind the idiosyncratic elements of the mutual fund industry, it can be observed that despite an overall long-term perspective, the life span of single products is generally limited to 3-5 years, after which the products are replaced (i.e., they are subjected to a change in the asset allocation strategy and are rebranded), terminated or merged into related investment vehicles. Furthermore, the survival of funds is ensured either by being able to attract new money inflows constantly over time in order to justify the cost of maintaining a product, or by producing sufficient knowledge spillovers to allow a small universe of slight variation to spring up constantly. These variations are sufficiently related to the focal platform fund and build on short-term trends, which facilitate the steady attraction of new money that is merged into the dominant platform after a certain period. However, this second survival strategy is more capability-sensitive, inflicts a different, higher cost structure and requires standardized rules and processes within a given platform to become successful. Hence performance and competitiveness must be examined across time and the hierarchies of a fund's reporting years.

In a first step, this paper adds an industry case to the challenge of an integrated framework of multi-level interaction among processes, routines and regulations. Second, the article proposes a model for the formal measurement and breakdown of the competitive interdependencies encountered in theory. Based on this model, hypotheses are generated to detect and examine the fragile components of the mutual fund market's industry architecture even in the absence of large-scale disruptions. The results provide a good indication of market dynamics and sources for competitive action over time.

Background

The underlying constructs in theories of multi-level entities include close interaction of intra-company processes and evolving routines that are standardized and efficiency-oriented. These enable a company to thrive and create new value based on the environment, which is basically formed by customer demand, regulation and most certainly inter-company competition. The tightly-meshed interaction of all these factors defines the basic foundation of any industry architecture. In turn, industry architecture spurs the dominant processes of any sector. Based on the existing capacity in the market, ex-ante distribution of market shares and the variable cost of production shape the boundaries of the company and thus the intra-industry division of labor. Ultimately, it provides the framework for the logic of competition, i.e., the share of value each party involved can appropriate throughout the production process. Economic literature and especially business literature have contributed to these issues substantially. However, they focus mostly on single aspects such as industry structure and performance, resource intensity, capability formation and/or processes and transaction costs within companies and across markets. The evolution of change or industry dynamics evidently could only have been shown along one of those aspects framing the competitive system under analysis. Classical statistics and mostly (neo-)classical economic growth models were used for the reliable measurement of these effects. However, like macroeconomically oriented growth theory, endogenous growth models either could not capture the causal factor for growth (although they model the effects of growth well), or they got stuck in micro-modeling of a non-generalizable problem set. This type of analysis provides a certain contrast to many traditional economic approaches. Especially in neo-classical models, there are economic features to which such a fundamental role is not attributed, despite the fact that they are often considered quite important in practice. The first to mention here is the category of market. Rather than assume that markets exist, as is often done, dynamic perspectives must take into account that markets emerge as a result of the exchange relations between actors.

This thinking reflects a Schumpeterian approach (Mathews, 2001), and is closely related to the "markets-as-networks" view developed more recently. The Schumpeterian relationship can thereby be traced to the notions of "market process as discovery" (Kirzner, 1985), whereas the network concept roots are reflected in the concept of the "markets as networks" school, as set forth by (Forsgren, Hagg, Hakansson, Johanson and Mattson, 1995; Hakansson and Snehota, 1989; Johanson and Mattson, 1994). One key difference here is that the more interactions become multi-layered, e.g. in networks, the more emphasis is placed on actual exchanges in networks, leading to models with indefinite and sequential properties (Powell, 1990).

The integrated model of the economy as presented by Matthews described probably for the first time economic dynamics in terms quite different from those used in conventional neoclassical analysis. The main difference can be seen in the object of analysis forming the focus of empirical work: classical work focuses mostly on the features of a company's activities such as cost, price, and bottom line on the business side, or in the economic context, on the existence of market-clearing prices in given settings, as pursued in general equilibrium theory. The challenge these approaches may face is inherent to their design and reflected in their label: general equilibrium theory is designed to replicate models for a comparative statics setting, and not for a scenario of dynamic interaction.

Dynamic approaches, on the other hand, are concerned with path-dependent trajectories followed by sets of companies as they adapt to external circumstances in terms of their constitutive resources, routines and relations. In these scenarios the focus shifts towards the adaptive behavior of the companies themselves, individually and in interacting groups (networks) as the complexity of the system evolves. Consequently, it is the resources which are available to companies and the routines the companies design to nurture capabilities as well as the networks they create through their relational interactions that become the prime focus of interest, not only in a static sense but as pathways of development. The dynamics through which companies acquire and utilize resources and the processes through which new resources are produced within an economy – in short the resource dynamics of the economy – thus acquire a significance which is almost totally suppressed in conventional microeconomics.

Technology and standardization, or more broadly, processes within companies have been one of the factors attracting research with the objective of explaining the degree of freedom a system has internally to dedicate to innovation and the degree of cost advantage it can obtain through stringent and efficient execution. However, the literature also links processes directly to the other factors in industry architecture, most notably capability development through competence accumulation. Driven by co-evolutionary strategic behavior that is inherently incorporated in stringent processes, processes may change competencies and environments as suggested by Dosi et al. (1994). However, such observations are often based on case studies; so far it has not been possible to reproduce them dynamically, which may explain the lack of focus on process to some extent. But, as Santos and Eisenhardt (2005, p. 504) put it: "Process research can more readily uncover the causal mechanisms shaping boundary formation [...]. This may allow the field to move away from simple contingencies to a deeper understanding of the complex and evolutionary role of boundaries in organizations." Intra-company processes therefore can influence not only company intra-company-level positions and inter-company standards, but also influence theories of industry structure design.

Based on Santos and Eisenhardt's (2005) notion of the influence of processes, resources and routines move into focus. When accumulating strategic factors through processes (which are superior or optimally environmentally adapted), the focus is on resources and capabilities. While the classical interpretation of strategic assets (Rumelt, 1984; Wernerfeldt, 1984) is still frequently oriented towards distinct resources, the focus has been on capabilities more recently, especially in largely commoditized aspects of the financial service industries (Raff, 2001). As they have so far kept their somewhat static flavor in the context of structure performance concepts (Barney, 1991b; Barney and Ouchi, 1986), the role of resources in the type of setting being studied is mainly that of an input factor to which processes as well as capability management may provide more direct links.

Thus, in this context sources of distinctiveness that generate competitive advantages are found mostly in routines and in a company's capabilities as well as in processes. The underlying theories were developed primarily by Teece, Pisano and Shuen (1997), who contributed much of the of language and terminology used today. In particular, the dynamic capabilities perspective is seen as a concept that facilitates differentiation precisely from the somewhat static approach taken in conventional resource-based theory. Thus, dynamic capabilities focus above all on how companies' capabilities are fashioned and adapted to changing economic circumstances. Basic descriptions of dynamic theory are thereby provided by Teece, Pisano and Shuen (1997) and later Dosi, Nelson and Winter (2001) who added an updated summary with applications. In all these arguments, the underlying idea is that companies' dynamic capabilities may be developed from a combination of their resources, routines and relations. Neither of these frameworks has had a significant impact on the wider economic literature yet, despite the fact that the general concepts of evolutionary economics are moving rapidly towards the mainstream. This may be somewhat surprising, given that the seminal text of evolutionary economics written by Nelson and Winter (1982) explicitly formulated an approach to evolutionary dynamics grounded in companies and in the organizational routines they develop. Nelson and Winter (1982) insisted that companies do not make instantaneous responses to the environment, e.g. (securities) price signals, as in the traditional notion of market-price-company interaction, but in fact make "satisfying" responses mediated through their "sticky" routines. It is variation in these routines and the resultant changes in selection pressures felt by companies (positive or negative) that account for competitive dynamics from an evolutionary perspective (Gupta, Knott and Hoopes, 2005). This deviates clearly from traditional economic theorizing about companies (in terms of production functions, instantaneous transmission of information and perfect information concerning technological possibilities) and shifts the focus towards serious engagement with the internal dynamics of companies' capabilities development. In this context, it is most straightforward from a dynamic perspective to put the consideration of how these elemental categories make varying contributions to the creation of companies' capabilities as they grow at the center of scientific observation. Such observation thus spans the evolution of capabilities and processes over time and contrasts the adaptive strategizing and industry formation with company performance and company survival. One such "process or capabilities life cycle" approach is the "industrial market system" theory from Matthews to which we refer as an integrative starting point for this project (Mathews, 2001, 2003).

A holistic market system approach is not only a nice tool with which to integrate theoretical strings. The real strength and key reason to rely on that framework in this paper are revealed when the specificity of resources, routines and relations in functional settings is considered (e.g. the resources and routines needed for new product development). In the original context of the "industrial market system" this is described in the sense that a company's position and its processes are not given for all time, but constitute a base from which the company may make adjustments as it seeks to adapt its operations to changing circumstances. Different real options chosen, or pathways followed by the company, can be captured in terms of the variation in corresponding resources, relations and routines. Independent of the decision reached in the end, such options and pathways can be traced as trajectories in a "resource space" or "routine space" where different strategic priorities and different starting points will lead to different trajectories (Matthews' terms).

The interdependencies between the processes of competence accumulation and the external environment have mutual impacts upon each other, as expressed in the words of Henderson and Mitchell, who state that "companies develop capabilities, either through choice or selection, that then shape the environment which, in turn, further shapes capabilities" (HENDERSON AND MITCHELL, 1997, p. 12). The thus shaped environment and more directly the dynamics of shaping that environment drive the companies to explore the new opportunities constantly arising, e.g. in the technological toolset, and turn them into a competitive advantage. In this context, "a firm's true competitive advantage for coping with turbulence is not in its current distinctive competencies, but in those that it can grow tomorrow. A firm's organizational ability to leverage and strengthen existing competencies is important, but it must be aware that it is restricted by process and capability bases just as much as these bases allow building new scope (KARIM AND MITCHELL, 2000; RUMELT, SCHENDEL AND TEECE, 1991). It can be assumed that any analysis of competence accumulation must include not only the external environment, but also the dynamic interactions which shape the competence patterns over time and across existing factor endowments. This point in the relationship between the external dynamics and the internal dynamics creates persistent differences across companies over time. Such persistent differences are a major concern in many financial service markets, for example in the mutual fund market (CARHART, 1997; GRINBLATT AND TITMAN, 1992). From a strategic point of view, the same persistence problem can also be seen from a more positivist angle: "The [...] perspective opens the conceptual lens of strategy to admit a more dynamic view of competition in which differences in idiosyncratic company capabilities matter greatly and are the basis for much of the competitive advantage a company may enjoy in its product markets in the long run" (SANCHEZ, 1996, p. 3).

Increasingly, level interaction between and within companies, regardless of whether it is based on rules or routine shifts, is becoming more and more common throughout industry, and even more important, is constantly accelerated by the rapid changes in technology (Kogut and Zander, 1992; Rosenblom and Christensen, 1994). Especially in the short term, the introduction of such dynamics into the competence notion implies that the temporary states of the competence base may act as a platform for new developments. This notion of platform seems important in a positivist strategic sense when discussing dynamic multi-layer entities, as change that expands or diminishes these platforms becomes vital for company behavior and for company success.

More recently, the discussion of infraction on intra-company levels has also led to an increased focus on the theoretical underpinnings of processes, routines and capabilities even beyond the question of how they interrelate and depend on each other. This perspective links again to the very basics of theory development, namely to McCardle, Barney, Lippman or Rumelt who take the resource (value) view as a starting point for the question of value appropriation within company units across industry value chains (Barney, 1989, 1991a; Lippman, McCardle and Rumelt, 1991). This level of individual action and strategic interaction is once again a topic of debate when it comes to explaining why inertia (Kaplan and Henderson, 2005), market dynamics from factor market intelligence and asymmetric information distribution (Makadok and Barney, 2001) and finally company heterogeneity (e.g. one industry across countries) (Felin and Hesterley, 2007; Gavetti, 2005; Gavetti and Levinthal, 2004) can persist in rational liquid markets. To illustrate these issues, Jacobides (2008b) refers to the distinctions in value appropriation across different historic traditions in the bottling industries, namely the Bordeaux versus Porto industry architecture differences. Whereas in the first case the producer manages to capture the most of the value, the distributor does so in the second case. This heterogeneity does not arise from differing capabilities but from different historic pathways of process and value chain development across countries, such as the "chateau" versus "English merchant" history of market makers for the two beverages, respectively. This is just one example of how the same strategic resources lead to very different outcomes, beyond just referring to some broad (and variously defined) capability, but as a result of what is today often referred to as "the micro-foundations of capabilities" (Abell, Felin and Foss, 2008), or the complex interaction of processes, rules and routines over time in multi-level environments (Jacobides, 2008a; Wolter and Veloso, 2008).

With regard to moving from theory building with these emerging topics towards doing empirical research beyond case-study approaches, there is so far no established measurement technique that would give sufficient credit to the complexity and evolutionary properties of the involved trajectories. A reliable method for doing so would have to be embedded in the evolutionary metric designs themselves. In this respect FISHER (1999) and PRICE (1972, 1995) provided early work by showing that change is based upon variations in properties and that it can be measured accordingly. In particular, Price's partitioning therein included not only the effect of selection but also the effect of causes that increase variation (ANDERSEN, 2004a, 2004c; KNUDSEN, 2004). PRICE (1972) demonstrates that this equation is an identity that may be used for the breakdown of any kind of evolutionary change. With respect to these metrics, we see a research gap in the applicability of the measurement of evolution and the breakdown of evolutionary aspects into positive theory. Selection and innovation effects can be counted as a percentage of total evolutionary aspects; however, theory stops at this point. It is not possible to make estimates of future industry trends given the measured effects, nor is it possible to link the observed effects to economic theory when it comes to traditional industry measurements (such as a Herfindahl Index) or to competitive strategy literature. This second stream of literature in particular gives greater weight to routines, rules and capability when assessing industry change and company adaptation to this change.

Inquiries structured in this manner therefore focus on the process of economic transformation itself. In the following section, we explore the idea that it is transformation which enables growth and that the process of economic transformation is an evolutionary process. Like all evolutionary processes it can be broken down into three elements: variety or micro-diversity of agent behaviors; selection processes that transform that diversity into patterns of economic change; and, development processes that generate and regenerate that behavioral variation (METCALFE, 2001). It is the manner of interdependence among these three elements that defines any particular process of economic transformation. The challenge is to measure the elements correctly and to the match measurement approaches with the complex systems to be measured. This calls for a rigorous definition of key constructs aligned to the chosen methodology.

Methodology and Definition of Key Constructs

When observing research methodologies used so far, there is no standard track with which to formalize industry dynamics. In the past, a variety of methods including graph theoretical methods using simulation in terms of intelligent agents, Markov processes, or models of fitness landscapes have been applied (see JACOBIDES' studies on the IT industry (PISANIAS AND JACOBIDES, 2006). However, in the context of financial markets and financial market product complexes, we must rely on an approach that emphasizes the interplay at different levels with varying cost structures rather than the vertical shifts over time, as for instance in biotech or

IT. Therefore, we build partly on the definitions introduced in MATTHEWS' market model (MATHEWS, 2003, 2006/2001) and supplement the concepts where links to the survival-based evolutionary economics theory call for amendments.

Companies. Companies, or more broadly "market participants", are the basic driving entities in changing industrial patterns and consequently form the focus of research. The interest in companies stems from their designation as the prime actors in the observed landscape; they exist to carry out activities in ways that are both effective and efficient. They legally control the resources needed for activities; they develop the routines through which resources are utilized; and they establish relations with each other. They make choices about all these things in terms of their goals, values or "fitness function."

Resources. In the distinct tradition of BARNEY (1991), resources stand for the productive assets of companies, the means through which activities are accomplished and the stock of input that frames (to some extent) static industry structure and performance levels. The basic insight that separates the resource-based view of the company and the concepts of evolutionary economics from neoclassical models and industrial organization analysis is that here, resources are seen as lending distinctiveness to companies, i.e. they generate heterogeneity directly and are a mere measure for the effects of some other processes. In this sense, there is no "representative" company from a dynamic point of view. On the contrary, the point in this case is to model companies in all their heterogeneity, starting with their different resource endowments and moving on to the dynamics of the processes through which these resource endowments may be changed (extended, contracted) through the development of routines and the interrelations between companies (MATHEWS, 2001). Market participants' resources set limits to what the company can do. This is very much in the tradition of RUMELT (1984) who was among the first to link not only strategic positioning, but strategic direction with resources when he argued that the company's strategic significance is "characterized by a bundle of linked and idiosyncratic resources and resource conversion activities" (RUMELT, 1984, p. 561). In this context, resources include all tangible factors, such as production systems, technologies, machinery, as well as intangibles such as brands or property rights and patents. For these types of resources, TEECE, PISANO AND SHUEN (1997, p. 521) employ the term "specific assets", whereby they emphasize the idea of "specialness" of things that are difficult to trade.

As pointed out by WERNERFELT (1984), products (activities) and resources are two sides of the same coin. WERNERFELT (1984, p. 171) explicitly commented, "Most products require the services of several resources and most resources can be used in several products. By specifying the size of the firm's activity in different product markets, it is possible to infer the minimum necessary resource commitments. Conversely, by specifying a resource profile for a firm, it is possible to find the optimal product-market activities." Resources are utilized in the company's activities to convert inputs into outputs; the inputs themselves are not counted as resources. The distinction between services provided by resources, which enable the company to accomplish its activities, and the stock of resources itself is derived precisely from this definition. The explicit aspect of this distinction is important since services and resource perspectives are sometimes treated differently, even within the resource-based view of the company, and even more so when discussed against the background of network models. For example, PENROSE (1995), just to mention one of the early contributors, included raw materials and work in progress in her list of resources. In the present account these are seen as inputs (or outputs) to companies' activities, not the resources utilized in production activities. From a network perspective, JOHANSON AND MATTSSON (1994) spell out a formal model involving actors, activities and resources, but it is unclear whether they are making the distinction defined here. JARILLO (1988) uses similar constructs. Both articles later argue that "actors use certain resources to change other resources in various ways", thus leaving open the interpretation that resources might refer to production inputs as well as to technology and equipment.

The interesting aspects of the resource-based view with respect to multi-level industry dynamics lie within the company or the acting unit itself, as it is in control of its own resources. This is complemented by an approach in which companies are able to access further resources by virtue of their relations with other companies, e.g. through their cooperation with competitors or through membership in complementary networks. Above all, these relational perspectives represent access to a range of resources and expand the strategic options available to companies. In parallel, the resource dependence of companies on other actors with which they are interlinked may also be interpreted as a constraint on strategic initiative. An initial exploration along these lines is provided by DYER AND SINGH (1998).

Routines. The resource aspects in interaction stress the important role of inter-company relations. At the intra-company level, a similar role is assigned to routines and processes or standard operating procedures. Distinguishing processes and organizational routines may be difficult and varies from almost synonymous wording to a separation of organizational and technological context, as can be seen in the early works of CYERT AND MARCH (1992) on standard operating procedures, for example. In particular, the enormous volume of literature of the 1990s on "business process re-engineering" reflects the importance of business processes as opposed to routines (LEE AND DALE, 1998; ZAIRI, 1997). As outlined above, we thereby distinguish between factors: in much of the resource-based literature, a distinction is maintained between resources (assets) and capabilities by AMIT AND SCHOEMAKER (1993) and TEECE, PISANO AND SHUEN (1997). One might impute a sense of the company's capabilities to the breadth and depth of the routines which it is able to call upon as its operating circumstances change.

Capabilities. The emphasize of company capabilities in that context is based on the idea that capabilities can be derived from the way that companies choose and activate their resources, from their development of routines and from their choice of linkages with other companies, i.e. relations.

With respect to industrial dynamics, routines are once again one of the key constructs, as they are an underlying component in the effectiveness and efficiency of companies as instruments of action. For instance, companies purchase resources such as capital equipment through routines such as capital asset budgeting procedures and investment evaluation routines. Companies have routines for conducting their activities. CYERT AND MARCH (1992), respectively referring to their earlier work of 1963 introduced the concept of standard operating procedures and made them the basis for a behavioral theory of the company, seeing them as "sticky" attributes which are difficult to change. NELSON AND WINTER (1982) added an important evolutionary and purposive dimension to the concept, calling them routines that form the basic foundation for strategic capabilities. Their value lies precisely in their being able to function repetitively, giving stability to the company's operations (MATHEWS, 2003). However, this repetitive character means that companies can be "stuck" in behavioral patterns that may also become maladaptive as circumstances change. Hence, variation in routines can generate selective dynamics in companies and thus an evolutionary process, but may also hamper timely adaptation once shocks have been experienced.

Relations. Relations are tightly linked to the famous notion of "No business is an island" (HAKANSSON AND SNEHOTA, 1989). With regard to markets and industry interaction, companies certainly exist, but they gain much of their information and their potential from developing an identity based on the relations they build with other companies. In these relations they may act either directly as suppliers or customers or indirectly as collaborators or competitors in a network.

From a dynamic perspective, acting market participants (see comments in the resource section) must be treated not only as atomistic entities making all their decisions for themselves only, but as interconnected units in large or small, tight or diffuse networks (FORSGREN et al., 1995; POWELL, 1990). The dynamics of companies' relations – the creation of linkages, the modification or rupture of these linkages and the patterns formed – thus become a central focus of interest, not only limited to the network view. Therefore, from a positivist perspective, management of these dynamics can become a factor in companies' success and explain heterogeneity in performance (MATHEWS, 2006/2001). However, relations, like resources and routines, can be changed only slowly. Thus companies can be caught in networks that represent a threat to survival if the network as a whole is losing competitiveness. Inter-company relations are brought into focus, without making the mistake of claiming that network structures are always advantageous.

Fitness functions. When using companies, resources, processes and routines as well as inter-company relations as the basic constituents of industry architecture and innovation as the prime reason for shifts in that very architecture, there needs to be one joint factor that can be relied upon as a means of reference in order to explain the success and failure of industry dynamics. This means of reference can be derived from the idea that companies are intelligent agents which assess their current choice of resources, routines and relations against the alternatives available, and against the performance of their activities relative to that of their competitors. Sometimes, the point of reference for the actors may just be a goal-setting function that provides the company's values, or it is the theory of their own efficacy (JACOBIDES, WINTER AND KASSBERGER, 2006). This function allows the company to make choices, or to discriminate between courses of action. Fitness function is all that, but in a purer fashion. Matthews sees fitness as "the function through which the company determines its activities and their intensity, and how it makes choices as to the resources, routines and relations needed to support these activities". In a slightly broader evolutionary context, fitness is the distinct driver of company characteristics that decides whether existing resource, rule, routine and relation configuration prove successful in a given (stable or changing) environment. Thus fitness criteria can be used as the joint point of reference for measuring the interaction of rules and routines across intra-and inter-company levels.

From a purely theoretical point of view, there is a relationship between competence accumulation and industrial dynamics, but the degree to which these dynamics (internal as well as external) interact and influence each other is still unclear. The first step is therefore to establish a joint perspective for resource accumulation, process and routine development and industry dynamics. As early as 1999, a conference paper by Mette Praest molded this problem into the question: "How can changes in the profile of competencies, i.e. the profile of competence dynamics, be measured for the single company?" (PRAEST, 1999, p. 6). In her case, this question was solved for the single company by the development of a typology of competence accumulation to identify the type of competence accumulation and explore the differences across companies in telecommunications, in the particular case cited. In a very similar way, we argue that it is possible to use inter-company relations and rules and combine them with interrelational process and routine types in order to measure them by the homogenous fitness factors that determine inter- and intra-industry success.

Measurement and model implications for shifting industry architecture during gradual exogenous innovation

When trying to quantify dynamic aspects, not specifically in pure networks, but much more generally in interrelated hierarchical or relation-driven multi-level structures, established tools used to compare structures and company-level performance reach their limits fast. As it is the dynamics of the companies' ability to vary their activities in terms of their underlying resources, and to engage in resource-sharing and resource-extending behavior through network dynamics that gives them enhanced competitive capacities, precisely these features must be partitioned over time, across companies and across company units at various levels to provide insight into the real engines of dynamic economic response to changing conditions.

In order to establish a quantitative toolset to address these questions, a joint measurement link is initially required. We see this link in the basic relationship that market participants build with capabilities through the use of resources, routines and the relations that bind them to other companies. In this context, processes are best described in terms of resource dynamics, i.e. as transfers or exchanges of resources between companies through different linkages. In the language of METCALFE this means that: "…markets are to be judged by their capacity to adapt to new opportunities and to facilitate the creation of new resources, and it is this openness to change which is the defining characteristic of market capitalism." (METCALFE, 1998, p. 7).

All resource-related dynamics are basically rooted in the creation of value: "Value is created by companies, usually through the recombination of existing resources, or by expanding existing capabilities towards new knowledge, so occasionally, through the very creation of something new" (MATHEWS, 2003, p. 10). An oft-cited example of such resource creation is the process of technological standardization, especially in IT-related literature (CLARK, ZMUD AND MCCRAY, 1995). A technological standard is a resource which enables producers to build or to broaden a market for a distinct product (HILL, 1997). The process of standardization, dubbed one of the most important facets of economic dynamics (MATHEWS, 2003), is best understood as a process of resource creation and diffusion. This requires a distinguishing factor for resource-accumulation-based capacity competition and capability-sensitive innovative activity. Once a standard is established, complementarities facilitate the generation of competitive advantages. An alternative source of resource dynamics is found in the formation of economies of scale through the creation of new segments, i.e. through modularization of production processes (BALDWIN, 2008; JACOBIDES, 2008b). Scales in this sense constitute two suppositions: first, companies with economies of scale cannot (fully) recover costs with marginal cost pricing. Second, when the production technology exhibits economies of scale over the full range of output, the industry structure with the lowest costs is monopoly. This was clearly demonstrated in the early works of PANZAR AND WILLIG (1977). In a formal approach, these suppositions are thought to follow from the standard definition of scale: There are economies of scale if a small proportional increase in the levels of all input factors can lead to more than proportional increases in the levels of outputs produced (MANSFIELD, 1970; MENGER, 1954). This leads, beyond other aspects, to an asymmetric incentive in opening up a proprietary network (e.g. distribution). The larger a company and the broader its capacity, the higher the willingness to attract third party access that allows increasing capacity utilization. We see in this the second aspect of resource value creation. This second aspect, however, is closely linked to the notion of underlying market growth as driver for scarcity and marginal capacity in an observed market (ANDERSEN, 2004c).

Discussion of new approaches to measuring these dynamics requires a joint factor, or measure that links the two different resource dynamics to comparable routine and capability dynamics. Furthermore, the creation or appropriation effects may be played out on multiple and interacting levels of a scientific object. For the latter, it is increasingly recognized that population thinking is a basic characteristic of that discipline (ANDERSEN, 2004c). There are several forms of population thinking. The most basic form is intra-population thinking for single populations, and this thinking easily extends to structured populations, where selection takes place at several levels (METCALFE, 2001). There are also many different mathematical approaches to the study of population thinking or more broadly natural selection: the most common are FISHER'S (1958) fundamental theorem for population genetics, ROBERTSON AND HILL'S (1966) covariance theorem for quantitative genetics, and HAMILTON'S (1964) rule for kin selection. All of these approaches are united by the second precondition for measurement – a joint factor that drives change or evolutionary processes. Such systems are seldom directly tied to the well-developed results from biology (ANDERSEN, 2004). One issue is that each mathematical approach tends to focus on a partial analysis of total change; another is the fact that genetic or biological models cannot be applied directly as outlines. Nevertheless, in economic settings as well, total change can be split into change-triggering factors. It is now common to start with

Price's equation (ANDERSEN, 2003; METCALFE, 2006) note on Price's equation for evolutionary economics: Deviation, interpretations, and simple applications, which is an exact, complete description of natural selection and its evolutionary consequences. When a regression model is fitted to a character using any arbitrary set of predictors, Price's equation describes the total change in the character by analyzing the predictor variables. (ANDERSEN, 2004). A natural partition follows between the two components mentioned above; frequently, a change in predictors is caused directly by natural selection and changes in the effects of each predictor after transmission. The natural selection component can itself be divided into distinct causes. This division is the familiar causal analysis of fitness using multiple regression (ARNOLD, 1983). This "fitness criterion", as a factor in theory (MATTHEWS, 2002) as well as in measurement literature (HAMILTON, ROBERTSON, FISHER, ANDERSEN, METCALFE), now constitutes a joint measure for all levels of interaction and for all types of value creation and appropriation – or innovation and selection, to use more biological terminology.

In this approach, we build upon Price's equation to link the related elements of Fisher's fundamental theorem, general multiple regression models of natural selection, and kin selection in competitive environments. We work with this little known equation as it provides a powerful instrument for dividing overall evolutionary change into a selection effect and what may be called an innovation effect (METCALFE, 1998). Explicitly, the strength of this method versus other competing approaches is that "[the Price-based] partitioning serves as a means of accounting for evolution and as a starting point for the explanation of evolution. The applications of Price's equation cover relatively short-term evolutionary change within individual industries as well as the study of more complexly structured populations of companies. It also, to some extent, helps to understand the effects of co-evolution between populations and the emergence of new populations" (ANDERSEN, 2004, p. 3).

Results can be expanded to arbitrary selective systems and types of inheritance. The expansion that we build upon in this article is a framework that allows incorporating contextual variables and multiple levels of analysis to explain the evolutionary change of characters. The contextual variables are not specified explicitly, but may include maternal effects, group-level traits, soft facts such as capabilities, and a wide array of other factors that can explain some of the variance in character values and fitness (GOODNIGHT, SCHWARTZ AND STEVEN, 1992; HEISLER AND DAMUTH, 1987).

To break down (evolutionary) change it is necessary to draw upon observations of individual members of a population for at least two periods of time. Variable values for the first period are therefore denoted with their ordinary names and variable values for the second period by adding primes. Along the timeline, information on four variables must be obtained for each member at each point in time:

The first is the characteristic value z_i. This in fact corresponds to the very same dominated z_i in the basic Nelson-Winter model, i.e. in their case the productivity of a company's capital stock. The second variable is the change of this productivity between two periods Δz_i. The third variable values the population share s_i. In the Nelson-Winter model, in which the underlying population may be said to consist of machines, this variable is a company's capital share s_i. The fourth variable is the reproduction coefficient w_i, which is simply one plus the growth rate of the population criterion critical for survival (METCALFE, 2007). In the relevant literature, this coefficient w is more often referred to as the "fitness factor". Given these basic definitions, we can calculate additional variables (as illustrated in Table 10).

What fitness means in evolutionary terms, however, has been disputed for decades now (ARIEW AND LEWONTIN, 2004; HAMILTON, 1964; HAMMOND, 2007; ROBERTSON AND HILL, 1966). The dispute frequently centers on the prima-facie problem that "fitness" has primarily tautological features, especially if contrasted with the characteristics influenced over time. Yet these tautological aspects are often very helpful in unpacking the content of multi-level theories of which variation cum selection-based evolutionary theory is one (METCALFE, 2007, p. 11). Generally, the literature agrees that fitness-tautology is not a problem, as long as the expression and measure of fitness are clearly distinguished from the causes of fitness. Thus, fund manager's ability to generate performance, or a sales force's ability to attract business may both have a positive impact on productivity or total transaction volume. However, the underlying cause for volume is not necessarily (only) market performance, but internal processes and capabilities.

Variable	Description	Definition
s_i	population share of entity i	
Z	mean value of characteristic	$\Sigma\, s_i z_i$
$Var(z_i)$	Variance of characteristics	$\Sigma\, s_i(z_i-z)^2$
W	Mean reproduction coefficient and characteristics	$\Sigma\, s_i w_i$
$Cov(w_i, z_i)$	Covariance of reproduction coefficients and characteristics	$\Sigma\, s_i(w_i-w)(z_i-z)$
$\beta(w_i, z_i)$	Regression of reproduction coefficient on characteristics	$Cov(w_i, z_i)/Var(z_i)$
$E(w_i \Delta z_i)$	Expected value of change in characteristics in the end population	$\Sigma\, s_i w_i D z_i$

Table 10: Core statistics / ANDERSEN (2004)

This becomes clearer when the link between fitness criterion and characteristics is drawn:

Let w_i be that fitness for an individual unit, w the mean fitness of the population and Δw the change in mean fitness and let $Var(w_i)$ be the total population's variance of fitness. Then the Fisher theorem says that

$$\Delta w = Var(w_i) \tag{1}$$

In order to study selection or innovation effects on the different levels, one must calculate the basic effects on total population level (e.g. among companies). It is important to see the distinct meaning of the mean reproduction coefficient as the central element in the calculus (as well as in the theoretical context derived from this type of analysis). When starting from the regression coefficient of reproduction for a particular characteristic, e.g. company productivity, once finds the degree to which selection exploits differential productivities across a company. Plainly speaking, this shows how well a company uses its most important economic driver to support its critical resource, independent of whether this is a resource or a capability. This can be expressed by the linear relationship

$$w_i = \alpha + \beta(w_i, z_i) z_i + \varepsilon$$

Given the above definitions, one derives to the two elements of Price's decomposition of evolutionary change. Mean change in the characteristic value thus is

$$\Delta z = \frac{Cov(w_i, z_i)}{w} + \frac{E(w_i \Delta z_i)}{w} = \frac{\beta(w_i, z_i) Var(z_i)}{w} + \frac{E(w_i \Delta z_i)}{w} \tag{2}$$

Equation (2) is an identity (ANDERSEN, 2003b), which means that it holds for any change in a characteristic. This property enables us to reformulate the equation to

$$w\Delta z = Cov(w_i, z_i) + E(w_i \Delta z_i)$$

where the first term corresponds to the „selection effect" and the second term to the „innovation effect". In other words, the left-hand side stands for the change in the characteristic weighted by the mean fitness coefficient of reproduction and the expected change of the characteristic based on its previous success in changing the competitive landscape. Hence, the short-term change in any competitive setting is defined by a selection impact that exploits the weighted variance of the key characteristics and an additional innovation effect. The additional notion of innovation for change can be easily seen, since if there is no change in the characteristics of a particular company, e.g. its productivity, the effect would add up to zero and competition would rest solely on size and market share to drive the selection effect.

The basic math of that illustrated population effect can now be easily expanded on different levels of an interdependent entity. Most basically, the expansion runs towards population, inter-population and intra-population separation of selection and innovation effects, ultimately capturing actors, processes, rules and routines as well as fitness factors mathematically and allowing for accounting for these theoretical elements in an empirical setting. In the broader concept, this means that one can effectively explore multi-level population analysis through a dynamic, perhaps even game-theoretical lens (HAMILTON, 1964) on an intra-population level first, and through a co-evolutionary perspective on inter-population level (SAVIOTTI, 1998, 2001, 2006) later. The corresponding math was developed by ANDERSEN (2004a, b, c) and by METCALFE (2001, 2007).We reprint in brief the main formulas that are necessary to build the test sample.

Level of analysis	Selection Process	Innovation Process
Inter-population level	$Cov(w_{ij}, z_{ij}) = s_i \Sigma [(w_i - w)(z_i - z)]^2$	$E(w_i \Delta z_i) = \Sigma s_i w_i \Delta z_i$
Intra-population level	$Cov(w_i, z_i) = s_i (w_i - w)(z_i - z)$	$E(Cov(w_i, \Delta z_i)) = w_i \Sigma(z_i)$
Capability spillover	n/a	R-Innovation = 0
Capacity expansion	n/a	K-Innovation = 0
System growth	g_c	g_e

Table 11: Basic Formulas for change decomposition

The total change and the individual effects may be denoted as follows:

$$\Delta w_i = \Delta_i^{selection} + \Delta w_i^{innovation}$$

To specify these two effects, one can easily form a general derivative of Price's equation (see appendix) of the form:

$$w_i \Delta z = Cov(w_{ij}, z_{ij}) + E(w_{ij}) + E(w_{ij}, z_{ij})$$

for the selection effects on inter- and intra-group levels, and

$$w_i \Delta w_i = Cov(w_i, w_i) + E(w_i) + E(w_i \Delta w_i)$$

for the joint innovation and selection effect on an inter-population level.

The basic concept followed in applying the mathematical framework is embodied in the idea that we are observing a short period of time of only gradual innovation. Disruptive innovation effects that would alter (in the sense of broad standardization) or expand the total capacity available and hence have a strong influence on the laxness of the fitness criterion are absent. In a later chapter, we will focus specifically on these kinds of disruptive innovations. A second argument potentially affecting results, which possibly requires the inclusion of more complex calculations, involves classical learning or spillover effects that do not have such an impact on short periods of observations. Longer periods generally refer to time spans of more than ten years, but there is some variation in terms of technological sensitivity reported in the literature (e.g. PODOLNY et al., 1996) find that in IT and semiconductor industries the required time span is 3-5 years, while for textiles it easily tops the indicated ten-year period (PODOLNY et al., 1996). We therefore set the corresponding "R" and "K" innovation factors in this project to zero. In a longer period of time, these factors could simply been integrated into the basic calculus, but with an exponential add-on to the innovation term of the equation.

Application of the measurement techniques to the mutual fund market

First, we applied the measurement technique to the mutual fund market to check for its suitability and to group mutual funds descriptively with regard to selection and innovation effects. For this, we used a sample of mutual funds from a joint regulatory space (Switzerland). We used a data set from the Swiss fund industry, consisting of assets-under-management or fund volume, fund type, fund management company, fund performance and commissions and other costs associated with the funds. We collected these data for all funds registered under Swiss law (i.e., no Luxembourg or Dublin funds sold in Switzerland) to control implicitly for regulatory dispersion. The basis for these data sets was formed by the list of accredited funds of the Swiss Banking Supervisory Authority (EBK/FINMA). In a second step, the data corresponding to the accredited funds were collected from their annual statements. We excluded special funds and fund-like entities for qualified investors only and derived at a regulatory homogenous sample of funds with Swiss domicile and Swiss accreditation for retail customers. Due to the very recently changed law on fund transparency, we have comparable performance data for the past few years (but not yet beyond). We calculated net new money inflows as we have annual fund reports with volume and performance data; hence inflow is defined as the remaining difference in year-to-year comparison. The sample size counts 171 homogenous entities and covers a time span between 2003 and 2008. Over this period of time we had no significant influence due to environmental, i.e. regulatory change or radical technological innovation.

The unit of analysis is the fund sponsor. The population share of each individual entity (e.g. UBS funds) corresponds to the number of products in the market. The main characteristic (z) of the fund product is defined as its volume (net asset value, NAV times outstanding shares). Under a gradual innovation scenario, the volume represents a good proxy for productivity of a fund from a sponsor's perspective, as it equals the "mass" that can be used to fuel the utilization rate of the total capacity on a fund company level. The change between two different levels of capacity utilization or volume is said to be the risk-adjusted performance after cost. This represents basically the fitness factor of each company, as it directly increases total existing capital stock and supports the attraction of new money inflows. This basic relationship can be illustrated with the tight correlation of performance and next-year volume and inflows (see correlation matrix in Table 13). Finally, the reproduction coefficient w is one plus growth rate (total money newly invested in mutual funds), which is reported by the central statistics of the Swiss Mutual Fund Association for each year. As indicated already, evolutionary thinking in economics is rooted in biological theory building and was successfully introduced into theory building, but less so into empirical work. Theory building with evolutionary elements began by describing relatively simple game-theoretical configurations and gradually moved on to shape the discussion in industrial dynamics literature with more complex multiple interactions.

The underlying principles for this transfer are the principle of variation, the principle of heredity and the principle of selection (Brandon, 1990; Lewontin, 1974). The variation principle states that all entities out of any given population have multiple characteristics and vary at least with respect to one potentially selecting characteristic that is observable and can be copied with more or less effort.

Accordingly, heredity as the second principle in evolutionary models guarantees that in any interacting system there exists a mechanism that enables copying, e.g. through learning effects. Thus, given changes in the environment, any system has components that adapt more easily and therefore grow faster than the industry average. However, over time these superior growth rates of the "lucky" entities are eroded through copying of the competitors, bringing the system back to stability with more or less equally distributed growth rates. However, in any adaptation process there are both among the "lucky" entities with the "right" characteristics, as well as within the copying and adapting competitors, some entities that have the ability to go faster through such a disruptive process. The principle that explains this inequality in adaptation rates is selection; in an economic setting, regardless of the ex-ante company-specific characteristics, selection is the reason for the pace of a market's reaction to disruption and also the principle that determines the winners and losers of change, regardless of the ex-ante characteristics (METCALFE, 2001). This means that not all markets react equally fast to disruptive shocks – i.e. technology-oriented markets are generally assumed to be faster than agriculture or, notably, banking. And within a market some companies are again more able or willing to adapt – i.e. entrepreneurially organized companies are perceived to embrace change better than hierarchically organized ones (I. CHEN, 2005; Y. CHEN, 2001).

From a methodological stance it is therefore important to analyze different markets differently and to give credit to selection-enabling resources (financial means, learning capability and learning opportunity (TEECE et al., 1997). Thus, evolutionary models focus on analyzing populations within markets and describe transformation patterns, entity characteristics and learning effects within these populations, whereby selection and innovation are generally the most important independent variables. When describing changes in an industry, for example, total change can become selection-dominated transformation, in which institutions with different characteristics enjoy different growth rates and variation, where open or hidden characteristics of the population entities allow for the formation of entirely new products or new sub-markets. Given these relationships, ANDERSEN (2004c) proposes a framework called "Evometrics" that builds upon these evolutionary mechanisms and facilitates the measurement of change effects, i.e., selection- or variation-based components of change. Methodologically, this measurement rests upon two mathematical concepts, Price's equation and Fisher's theorem. Fisher's theorem states that mean change (Δw) of a once identified fitness factor of any given population equals the variance of all items within this population.

We than calculated the fitness criterion w as (Sharpe ratio performance – Total expense ratio/TER). The Sharpe ratio is an established concept to express risk-adjusted returns of financial products and TER is the legally binding measure for all Swiss funds to express total cost directly related to the purchase of a fund product. In order to distinguish between "organic fund growth", i.e., the growth of the assets under management as stock market valuation increases and customer demand for fund products, i.e. the net new money in- or outflow of the products, we calculated the annual change in the reported fund volume and subtracted the yield of the reported fund performance. We thus obtained the change in the volume split into "organic", e.g., market-induced growth and net new inflows, representing the end-customer demand for a specific fund. We assumed that end customers make their decisions to buy funds primarily on the past reported Sharpe ratio-adjusted performance, meaning that c. p. those funds should attract mostly new money that reported the highest "organic" growth within their peer group. As we observed the funds after cost, bank-specific transaction costs should not matter and thus the issuer should not be of relevance for the decision. We used this assumption to test the measure for competition among banks at the corporate level under the label "inter-population effects".

Descriptive Statistics and Static Population Analysis

Group Statistics, Company Level and Strategic Focus Patterns

The population used as a test sample consists of a total of 171 mutual funds issued by 17 fund sponsors. The population covers eight broad investment strategies, namely money market, bond, strategic mix, equity, index, emerging markets, alternative investments and real estate, and add up to an overall volume of 93,306 million Swiss francs. In the sample, we used only companies that were consistent over time, i.e., existing prior to the start of the sampling period and not undergoing major changes in management and investment strategy over time. Hence, we are convinced that this is a stable group to represent incumbent companies over the discussed time frame.

Descriptive Statistics

	N	Minimum	Maximum	Mean	Std. Deviation
Volume 08	171.00	5.25	5,100.00	521.78	812.95
Performance [07-08]	171.00	-38.20%	2.10%	-4.98%	0.05
Volume 07	171.00	3.98	5,436.00	579.21	862.87
Performance [06-07]	171.00	-0.21%	18.31%	6.02%	0.02
Volume 06	171.00	7.00	5,362.00	579.50	857.38
Performance [05-06]	171.00	3.45%	17.93%	5.78%	0.01
Volume 05	171.00	4.50	5,360.00	503.58	800.68
Performance [04-05]	171.00	-6.12%	7.42%	3.02%	0.02
Volume 04	171.00	7.00	5,342.00	488.02	807.08
Performance [03-04]	171.00	3.18%	5.04%	4.21%	0.01
Volume 03	171.00	3.00	5,100.00	474.78	794.59
TER	171.00	0.25%	6.00%	1.44%	0.01
Valid N (listwise)	171.00				

Table 12: Descriptive Statistics for the Sample Population: Volume Performance, TER

While Table 12 gives a general overview of the main summary statistics, Table 13 depicts the correlations among these key statistics in greater depth. Explicitly, we state the correlation among performance, net new money inflow and volume development over time. As introduced earlier, performance is displayed as risk-adjusted Sharpe performance after cost (TER). There is evidence for a basic relationship of size (to a lesser extent) and past performance attracting new capital into the observed products. Performance seems to play a particular role as a reason to withdraw money; however, this could also be a distortion within a year of very high uncertainty as in 2007 – 2008. Generally, the relationship found (like the substantial randomness involved) is in line with expectations and rational market assumptions in mutual fund markets as observed in earlier market analysis (e.g. BERK/GREEN, 2004).

Table 13: Correlation of Key Statistics (see p. 124–127)

One factor of particular interest is whether distinct company or asset management strategies may play a central role in this total population. In order to resolve these questions, we grouped the population by "Issuer and Strategies", by the number of competing (substituting products) first and by managed volume second (Tables 14 and 15). We used chi-square tests of independence to clarify to what extent there is an underlying relationship between issuer, product size and product volume (e.g. as a consequence of a certain business strategy). We found no dependence in this respect, which is in line with comments made by mutual fund experts that reflect no such specialization of companies (e.g. in small volume, broad product portfolio etc.).

		Volume 2008	Volume 2007	Volume 2006	Volume 2005	Volume 2004	Volume 2003	Inlow 2007
Volume 2008	Pearson Correlation	1.00	.991**	.993**	.895**	.890**	.884**	(0.11
	Sig. (2-tailed)	.	.000	.000	.000	.000	.000	.14
Volume 2007	Pearson Correlation	.991**	1.00	.995**	.898**	.893**	.887**	-.209**
	Sig. (2-tailed)	0.00	.	0.00	0.00	0.00	0.00	0.01
Volume 2006	Pearson Correlation	.993**	.995**	1.00	.895**	.889**	.883**	-.203**
	Sig. (2-tailed)	0.00	0.00	.	0.00	0.00	0.00	0.01
Volume 2005	Pearson Correlation	.895**	.898**	.895**	1.00	.992**	.988**	(0.14
	Sig. (2-tailed)	.000	.000	.000	.	0.00	0.00	0.07
Volume 2004	Pearson Correlation	.890**	.893**	.889**	.992**	1.00	.994**	(0.13
	Sig. (2-tailed)	.000	.000	.000	.000	.	0.00	0.09
Volume 2003	Pearson Correlation	.884**	.887**	.883**	.988**	.994**	1.00	(0.14
	Sig. (2-tailed)	0.00	0.00	0.00	0.00	0.00	.	0.08
Inflow 2007	Pearson Correlation	(0.11)	-.209**	-.203**	(0.14)	(0.13)	(0.14)	1.00
	Sig. (2-tailed)	0.15	0.01	0.01	0.07	0.09	0.08	.
Inflow 2006	Pearson Correlation	-.389**	-.371**	-.384**	-.353**	-.342**	-.329**	0.07
	Sig. (2-tailed)	0.00	0.00	0.00	0.00	0.00	0.00	0.37
Inflow 2005	Pearson Correlation	0.09	0.09	0.10	(0.13)	(0.13)	(0.12)	(0.09)
	Sig. (2-tailed)	0.27	0.25	0.22	0.10	0.11	0.13	0.25
Inflow 2004	Pearson Correlation	-.316**	-.305**	-.307**	-.335**	-.404**	-.401**	(0.03)
	Sig. (2-tailed)	0.00	0.00	0.00	0.00	0.00	0.00	0.73

nflow 2006	Inlow 2005	Inflow 2004	Inlow 2003	Performance 07_08	Performance 06_07	Performance 05_06	Performance 04_05	Performance 03_04
-.389**	0.09	-.316**	-.309**	0.08	(0.14)	(0.11)	(0.10)	-.165*
.000	.267	.000	.000	.317	.068	.155	.188	.034
-.371**	0.09	-.305**	-0.294***	0.05	(0.14)	(0.09)	(0.09)	(0.14)
0.00	0.25	0.00	0.00	0.56	0.07	0.25	0.27	0.06
-.384**	0.10	-.307**	-.288**	0.05	(0.14)	(0.09)	(0.08)	(0.14)
0.00	0.22	0.00	0.00	0.51	0.06	0.24	0.30	0.07
-.353**	(0.13)	-.335**	-.355**	0.05	(0.14)	(0.13)	-.175*	-.247**
0.00	0.10	0.00	0.00	0.53	0.06	0.10	0.02	0.00
-.342**	(0.13)	-.404**	-.352**	0.06	-.180*	(0.14)	-.192*	-.261**
0.00	0.11	0.00	0.00	0.45	0.02	0.07	0.01	0.00
-.329**	(0.12)	-.401**	-.407**	0.05	-.186*	(0.14)	-.194*	-.259**
0.00	0.13	0.00	0.00	0.49	0.01	0.07	0.01	0.00
0.07	(0.09)	(0.03)	0.00	(0.00)	(0.03)	(0.11)	(0.15)	-.171*
0.37	0.25	0.73	0.97	0.99	0.69	0.15	0.05	0.03
1.00	(0.10)	(0.05)	.189*	-.237**	-.212**	0.02	(0.10)	(0.00)
	0.19	0.51	0.01	0.00	0.01	0.76	0.22	0.96
(0.10)	1.00	0.04	0.11	0.04	0.03	.158*	.160*	.160*
0.19 .		0.58	0.17	0.58	0.74	0.05	0.05	0.05
(0.05)	0.04	1.00	.411**	(0.06)	.322**	0.04	(0.01)	0.05
0.51	0.58 .		0.00	0.44	0.00	0.58	0.95	0.49

		Volume 2008	Volume 2007	Volume 2006	Volume 2005	Volume 2004	Volume 2003	Inlow 2007
Inflow 2003	Pearson Correlation	-.309**	-.294**	-.288**	-.355**	-.352**	-.407**	0.00
	Sig. (2-tailed)	0.00	0.00	0.00	0.00	0.00	0.00	0.97
Performance 07_08	Pearson Correlation	0.08	0.05	0.05	0.05	0.06	0.05	-.404**
	Sig. (2-tailed)	0.32	0.56	0.51	0.53	0.45	0.49	0.00
Performance 06_07	Pearson Correlation	(0.14)	(0.14)	(0.14)	(0.14)	-.180*	-.186*	-.180**
	Sig. (2-tailed)	0.07	0.07	0.06	0.06	0.02	0.01	0.00
Performance 05_06	Pearson Correlation	(0.11)	(0.09)	(0.09)	(0.13)	(0.14)	(0.14)	(0.11)
	Sig. (2-tailed)	0.15	0.25	0.24	0.10	0.07	0.07	0.15
Performance 04_05	Pearson Correlation	(0.10)	(0.09)	(0.08)	-.175*	-.192*	-.194*	-0.15*
	Sig. (2-tailed)	0.19	0.27	0.30	0.02	0.01	0.01	0.00
Performance 03_04	Pearson Correlation	-.165*	(0.14)	(0.14)	-.247**	-.261**	-.259**	-.171*
	Sig. (2-tailed)	0.03	0.06	0.07	0.00	0.00	0.00	0.03

Population: N 171

Table 13: Correlation of Key Statistics

flow 006	Inlow 2005	Inflow 2004	Inlow 2003	Performance 07_08	Performance 06_07	Performance 05_06	Performance 04_05	Performance 03_04
.189*	0.11	.411**	1.00	(0.03)	0.01	0.01	(0.06)	0.02
0.01	0.17	0.00	.	0.68	0.91	0.93	0.42	0.81
-.237**	0.04	(0.06)	(0.03)	1.00	(0.14)	-.212**	-.216**	-.220**
0.00	0.58	0.44	0.68	.	0.06	0.01	0.01	0.00
-.212**	0.03**	.322**	0.01	(0.14)	1.00	.275**	.309**	.299**
0.01	0.00	0.00	0.91	0.06	.	0.00	0.00	0.00
0.02	.158*	0.04	0.01	-.212**	.275**	1.00	.820**	.706**
0.76	0.05	0.58	0.93	0.01	0.00	.	0.00	0.00
(0.10)	.160*	(0.01)	(0.06)	-.216**	.309**	.820**	1.00	.943**
0.22	0.05	0.95	0.42	0.01	0.00	0.00	.	0.00
(0.00)	.160*	.189*	0.02	-.220**	.299**	.706**	.943**	1.00
0.96	0.05	0.49	0.81	0.00	0.00	0.00	0.00	.

Issuer and Strategies (Number of Substituting Products)

	Money Market	Bond	Strategy	Equit
BSI	0.00	4.00	1.00	4.00
Clariden	4.00	0.00	0.00	0.00
CS	0.00	7.00	2.00	12.00
Gottardo	0.00	4.00	2.00	3.00
Gutzwiller	0.00	0.00	2.00	0.00
LODH	1.00	0.00	1.00	5.00
MI	0.00	0.00	0.00	1.00
Pictet	3.00	1.00	0.00	3.00
Raiffeisen	1.00	2.00	0.00	2.00
Reichmuth	0.00	0.00	0.00	0.00
Swisslife	0.00	3.00	0.00	1.00
Swisscanto	0.00	3.00	4.00	11.00
UBS	0.00	8.00	6.00	16.00
Vontobel	0.00	0.00	0.00	2.00
Wegelin	0.00	1.00	0.00	3.00
XMTCH	0.00	0.00	0.00	0.00
ZKB	2.00	2.00	3.00	2.00
Number of Funds/Family	12.00	34.00	21.00	65.00

Table 14: Issuers and asset management strategies: product distribution

Index	Emerging Market	Alternatives	Real Estate	Funds managed
0.00	0.00	0.00	0.00	9.00
0.00	0.00	0.00	0.00	5.00
1.00	2.00	1.00	1.00	26.00
0.00	1.00	0.00	0.00	10.00
0.00	0.00	0.00	0.00	2.00
0.00	1.00	3.00	0.00	11.00
0.00	0.00	0.00	1.00	2.00
1.00	0.00	0.00	0.00	8.00
0.00	0.00	0.00	0.00	5.00
0.00	0.00	7.00	0.00	7.00
0.00	0.00	0.00	0.00	4.00
0.00	3.00	1.00	1.00	23.00
2.00	5.00	0.00	4.00	41.00
0.00	0.00	0.00	0.00	2.00
0.00	0.00	1.00	0.00	5.00
3.00	0.00	0.00	0.00	3.00
0.00	0.00	0.00	0.00	9.00
7.00	12.00	13.00	7.00	171.00

Issuer and Strategies (Number of Substituting Products)

	Money Market	Bond	Strategy	Equity
BSI	0.00	4.00	1.00	4.00
Clariden	4.00	0.00	0.00	0.00
CS	0.00	7.00	2.00	12.00
Gottardo	0.00	4.00	2.00	3.00
Gutzwiller	0.00	0.00	2.00	0.00
LODH	1.00	0.00	1.00	5.00
MI	0.00	0.00	0.00	1.00
Pictet	3.00	1.00	0.00	3.00
Raiffeisen	1.00	2.00	0.00	2.00
Reichmuth	0.00	0.00	0.00	0.00
Swisslife	0.00	3.00	0.00	1.00
Swisscanto	0.00	3.00	4.00	11.00
UBS	0.00	8.00	6.00	16.00
Vontobel	0.00	0.00	0.00	2.00
Wegelin	0.00	1.00	0.00	3.00
XMTCH	0.00	0.00	0.00	0.00
ZKB	2.00	2.00	3.00	2.00
Number of Funds/Family	12.00	34.00	21.00	65.00

Table 15: Issuer and asset management strategies: volume distribution

Index	Emerging Market	Alternatives	Real Estate	Funds managed
0.00	0.00	0.00	0.00	9.00
0.00	0.00	0.00	0.00	5.00
1.00	2.00	1.00	1.00	26.00
0.00	1.00	0.00	0.00	10.00
0.00	0.00	0.00	0.00	2.00
0.00	1.00	3.00	0.00	11.00
0.00	0.00	0.00	1.00	2.00
1.00	0.00	0.00	0.00	8.00
0.00	0.00	0.00	0.00	5.00
0.00	0.00	7.00	0.00	7.00
0.00	0.00	0.00	0.00	4.00
0.00	3.00	1.00	1.00	23.00
2.00	5.00	0.00	4.00	41.00
0.00	0.00	0.00	0.00	2.00
0.00	0.00	1.00	0.00	5.00
3.00	0.00	0.00	0.00	3.00
0.00	0.00	0.00	0.00	9.00
7.00	12.00	13.00	7.00	171.00

s(Nominal)	n	Volume t(0)	s(0)	Volume t(1)	(s1)	Volume t(2)
s(BSI)	9.00	2,841.00	0.04	3,094.00	0.04	2,856.00
s(Clariden)	3.00	1,473.00	0.02	1,837.00	0.02	1,792.00
s(Credit Suisse)	24.00	9,146.00	0.11	8,892.00	0.11	8,539.00
s(Gottardo)	10.00	2,181.00	0.03	2,226.00	0.03	2,118.00
s(Gutzwiller)	2.00	170.00	0.00	153.00	0.00	271.00
S(LODH)	11.00	2,771.00	0.03	2,877.00	0.03	3,060.00
s(MI)	2.00	197.00	0.00	199.00	0.00	210.00
s(Pictet)	10.00	8,924.00	0.11	9,580.00	0.11	10,047.00
s(Raiffeisen)	5.00	623.00	0.01	685.00	0.01	653.00
s(Reichmuth)	9.00	790.00	0.01	1,242.00	0.01	2,188.00
s(Swiss Life)	4.00	1,302.00	0.02	1,302.00	0.02	1,307.00
s(Swisscanto)	15.00	5,399.00	0.07	5,040.00	0.06	5,129.00
s(UBS)	51.00	32,892.00	0.41	33,947.00	0.41	35,300.00
s(Vontobel)	2.00	3,522.00	0.04	3,594.00	0.04	3,674.00
s(Wegelin)	3.00	2,924.00	0.04	2,898.00	0.03	2,884.00
s(XMTCH)	3.00	167.00	0.00	227.00	0.00	309.00
s(ZKB)	8.00	5,484.00	0.07	5,826.00	0.07	6,017.00
Total Volume	171.00	80806.00	1.00	83619.00	1.00	86354.00
Market Growth: Incumbents				3.48%		3.27%
Market Growth: Swiss Fund Market				3.78%		3.03%

Table 16: Swiss incumbent funds, data Morningstar 2009

s(2)	Volume t(3)	s(3)	Volume t(4)	s(4)	Volume t(5)	s(5)	Average Fund Size
0.03	3,098.00	0.03	3,159.96	0.03	3,175.75	0.03	337.49
0.02	1,859.00	0.02	1,896.18	0.02	1,905.66	0.02	597.94
0.10	8,785.00	0.09	8,960.70	0.09	9,005.51	0.09	370.33
0.02	2,348.00	0.02	2,394.96	0.02	2,406.93	0.02	227.91
0.00	276.00	0.00	281.52	0.00	282.93	0.00	119.54
0.04	3,698.00	0.04	3,771.96	0.04	3,790.82	0.04	302.56
0.00	283.90	0.00	289.58	0.00	291.03	0.00	122.54
0.12	10,696.00	0.11	10,909.92	0.11	10,964.49	0.11	1,018.69
0.01	862.00	0.01	879.24	0.01	883.64	0.01	152.86
0.03	1,537.00	0.02	1,567.74	0.02	1,575.57	0.02	164.82
0.02	1,302.00	0.01	1,328.04	0.01	1,334.68	0.01	328.16
0.06	9,352.00	0.09	9,539.04	0.09	9,586.73	0.10	489.40
0.41	41,389.00	0.42	42,192.30	0.42	41,700.04	0.42	743.20
0.04	3,908.00	0.04	3,986.16	0.04	4,006.09	0.04	1,890.85
0.03	2,891.00	0.03	2,982.48	0.03	2,997.39	0.03	976.49
0.00	285.00	0.00	290.70	0.00	292.15	0.00	87.27
0.07	6,089.00	0.06	6,210.78	0.06	6,241.83	0.06	747.26
1.00	98658.90	1.00	100641.26	1.00	100441.24	1.00	536.57
	4.25%		2.01%		-0.20%		
	7.12%		4.80%		n/a		

The group was then analyzed in a first (static) step with respect to the underlying distribution of products, companies and strategies. The main results with respect to sub-population shares per entity are shown in Table 16. The final descriptive perspective is in terms of market structure and links thereby first to the earlier one (more static structure-conduct theory), but also constitutes one of the required factors for dynamic analysis, the so called s-factor of entity weight as introduced in the method section).

When looking at the overall structure of the mutual fund market, the incumbent funds can be described as relatively stable entities over time. However, when comparing the structural distribution of market shares over time, and contrasting this with the total market growth in the observed period, we find that the position of the incumbents, measured by managed volume of the total market, decreased over time. This goes along with the observation that – if corrected for performance results – incumbent funds lose volume (by means of outflows) over time; they rarely manage to attract significant net new money inflows once they are established. This is somewhat contradictory, given that market comments often find that the age of a fund is a buying argument for investors and that (retail) investors generally pursue buy-and-hold strategies with respect to mutual funds (HORTACSU AND SYVERSON, 2004). We do not have sufficient depth of data to drill deeper into this puzzling observation. We assume that there might be two factors involved: first, a dilution due to institutional investors who dominate the market and often get fees waived, and second, something like an optimal "age" structure of funds, meaning that some (but few) very long-established and successful funds gain new money and new funds that engage in upcoming trends attract funds as well, whereas the large bulk of funds in the market has to make do with the funds that have been invested in early stages of its life cycle and gradual outflows when portfolios are liquidated. Occasional new investments apparently cannot equalize these effects and institutional money generally flows – if into one of the funds – into newly issued classes.

Management theory hints strongly at an advantage of proprietary distribution networks in selling products, or as in this example, attracting new inflows and increasing volume per fund. When looking at trends in the mutual fund industry, the pattern is fully comparable. Over many periods, the sale through proprietary networks even seemed to have increased. Reliable data for this process, however, are currently available only for the United States, where the respective industry association, the ICI (2008) reports an overall increase in bank network sales for the period 1991 – 1995. "Proprietary sales through the bank channel increased from 1,100 at year-end 1991 to 2,329 at year-end 1995. Proprietary funds accounted for 47.9 percent of offered funds, [...] up from 31.5 percent in 1991" (ICI, 1996, 2007). This pattern has slightly increased and remained stable at just under 60% since that time (ICI, 2007). Hence, the availability of a proprietary network is a key (intermediating) variable to take into account when discussing the fitness of fund companies and the room for selection- or innovation-based process and capability separation.

The ownership of a proprietary network can have a strong impact on structure and distinct characteristics, such as the volume invested in a fund. We therefore observed this externality weight of branch networks for the company level for the Swiss funds under analysis. We used descriptive statistics for the percentage of funds (out of the total sample) attributed to an integrated player, then regressed the volume with a dummy variable for an externality weight factor that should roughly correspond to the influence of a branch network. However, this is not a precise figure, as we had to set the standard error term to zero in this process. Based on the externality weight factor and the total volume in the funds, we calculate an indexed impact figure that can be used as a proxy for the influence that a proprietary network has on new money attraction by mutual funds (when holding risk-return patterns stable). In other words, the weight factor can be seen as that proportion of mutual fund money attraction that is not attributable to risk-return properties per fund type, whereas the indexed impact also controls for implicit size effects and thus can be used as an intermediating variable for network effects in the fund's success and/or as a dilutor of direct fitness.

The consequences of the network factor calculations are very much in line with expectations. The results are reported in Table 17 and shed light on a very high variance in the importance of networks between the different companies: whereas the weight explains almost 28% of UBS fund volume, and 11 and 10 respectively for the other two large network players Credit Suisse (CS) and the joint Swiss Cantonal Banks, the role is astonishing for companies such as the Raiffeisen group and Migros bank, two other players traditionally focused on retail. Unsurprisingly, the influence is less staggering for classical private banks such as Pictet, LODH or Vontobel. The third group could be "specialist fund providers", namely XMTCH, a unit of Credit Suisse that focuses on standardized low-cost products, and Reichmuth, who made its name with innovative products. The mean indexed values of the different groups are clearly different from each other, which suffices to differentiate distribution channels in the analysis and to assume distinct patterns that allow the non-network companies to stay and survive in a competitive market, beyond mere sales power. An interesting point of discussion that emerges from this (indexed) network perspective is that given identical funds characteristics, network owners maintain a comparative advantage, even though they include (to some extent) third-party products in their offered portfolio in the sense of third-party access or best advice for customers.

	Volume	Network	Funds Distributed	Indexed	Externaliti Weight
BSI	6,010.20	0	6.44%	2.43	4.87
Clariden	11,806.02	0	12.65%	4.78	9.56
CS	10,757.26	1	11.53%	4.36	10.71
Gottardo	1,276.54	1	1.37%	0.52	3.03
Gutzwiller	1,086.34	0	1.16%	0.44	0.88
LODH	2,150.09	0	2.30%	0.87	1.74
MI	3,498.00	1	3.75%	1.42	4.83
Pictet	9,928.35	0	10.64%	4.02	8.04
Raiffeisen	345.00	1	0.37%	0.14	2.28
Reichmuth	2,001.09	0	2.14%	0.81	1.62
Swisslife	1,627.00	1	1.74%	s	3.32
Swisscanto	6,588.99	1	7.06%		11.34
UBS	32,125.62	1	34.43%	13.01	28.01
Vontobel	454.00	0	0.49%	0.18	0.37
Wegelin	128.00	0	0.14%	0.05	0.54
XMTCH	2,810.00	1	3.01%	1.14	2.28
ZKB	713.55	1	0.76%	0.29	6.58
Total	**93,306.04**		100%		100.00

Table 17 shows the network aspects of the mutual fund population

In order to differentiate the population sample further, i.e. not only by strategy, size and network inclusion, but – as is the core of this methodological approach – by intra- and inter-population characteristics, we summarized the corresponding results in Tables 18a and 18b. We calculated selection and innovation Effects on the intra-population level for issuers or fund sponsors according to the formulas described above. In an additional step, we standardized the effects for mutual fund size in order to gain a measure of control. The same procedure applied to the intra-population level with the sorting variable strategies. We used this internal perspective as a last step to ensure data stability and to ask the first question of whether customer demand (i.e. net new money inflow) reflected preferences for certain issuers (network-adjusted) or certain strategies, and whether the reported selection and innovation effects were independent of adjoint issuers (e.g. brand or network) and favored strategies. In this respect, we asked the question of whether there was an issuer-specific effect of selection or innovation bias (although product scope and volume are independent of issuers as shown earlier). We therefore tested for equality of mean innovation versus equality of mean selection on an issuer-group basis and on an asset management strategy basis (Table 18a and 18b). Should there be equalities across issuer, or across strategy, the differentiation could – to some extent – be linked to process (for selection) or capability (for innovation) focus, as argued in the literature. However, this is only a stability test for the following analysis, as the number of investment strategies does not suffice to provide robust results in any case.

Total change per unit is the direct sum of the two effects; the standardized values represent size adjusted changes.

Intra-Population: Strategien

Intrapopulation	Selection Effect Cov (Wi, zi)	Innovation Effect $E(wi^{\Delta}zi)$
Money Market	230.00	48.61
Bond	95,275.46	285.20
Strategy	1,122,211.68	520.95
Equity	793,793.84	771.53
Index	1,421,025.35	2,062.13
Emerging Market	136,685.24	194.31
Real Estate	57,532.85	-119.41
Alternatives	90,873.35	273.24
Standardized		
Money Market	0.00	0.01
Bond	0.03	0.07
Strategy	0.30	0.13
Equity	0.21	0.19
Index	0.38	0.51
Emerging Market	0.04	0.48
Real Estate	0.02	-0.03
Alternatives	0.02	0.68

Table 18a and Table 18b: Absolute and standardized overview of partitioned change Selection and innovation effects for issuer and investment strategy

Intrapopulation Analysis for Issuer

Intrapopulation	Selection Effect Cov (Wi, zi)	Innovation Effect E(wi$^{\Delta}$zi)
BSI	-5.13	31.43
Clariden	230.74	-1,159.78
CS	54.46	24.95
Gottardo	2.73	-0.90
Gutzwiller	4.59	9.72
LODH	6.11	55.59
MI	0.14	0.32
Pictet	-321.61	963.90
Raiffeisen	-5.22	40.32
Reichmuth	3.62	68.71
Swisslife	177.90	230.26
Swisscanto	-38.34	63.39
UBS	60.65	411.70
Vontobel	-14.13	62,243.29
Wegelin	2.07	497.06
XMTCH	-46.85	12.75
ZKB	71.40	16.61
Standardized (for size)		
BSI	-0.03	0.00
Clariden	1.26	-0.02
CS	0.30	0.00
Gottardo	0.01	0.00
Gutzwiller	0.03	0.00
LODH	0.03	0.00
MI	0.00	0.00
Pictet	-1.76	0.02
Raiffeisen	-0.03	0.00
Reichmuth	0.02	0.00
Swisslife	0.97	0.00
Swisscanto	-0.21	0.00
UBS	0.33	0.01
Vontobel	-0.08	0.98
Wegelin	0.01	0.01
XMTCH	-0.26	0.00
ZKB	0.39	0.00
Group Mean	0.06	0.06

Intrapopulation
Two Sample t-Test for dependent samples

Mean	0.14
Variance	0.02
Pearson Correlation	0.08
Difference of Mean	1.00
Degrees of Freedom (df)	6.00
t-Statistic	-10.28
P(T<=t) one-tailed	0.00
Critical t-value	1.94
P(T<=t) two-tailed	0.00
Critical t-Value	2.45

Strategy Dependency:
There is signifiant evidence that Selection and Innovation Effects can be linked to investment strategy

Interpopulation
Twosample t-Test for dependent samples

Mean	0.06
Variance	0.40
Pearson Correlation	-0.08
Hypothetical Difference of Means	1.00
Degrees of Freedom (df)	15.00
t-Statistic	-5.73
P(T<=t) one-tailed	0.00
Critical t-value for one-tailed test	1.75
P(T<=t) two-tailed	0.00
Critical t-Value for two-tailed test	2.13

Firm Size Dependency:
There is significant evidence that firms with more funds can be linked to Selection Effects Innovation Effects not observable on the interpopulaton level (only one firm sign.)

Table 19a and Table 19b: Two-tailed t-Test for equality of mean in change effects of both a) issuer and b) applied asset management strategies

When analyzing Tables 18a–19b, we find that alternative investments, emerging market and index funds are more sensitive to innovation, when it comes to compare their fitness, whereas bond, equity and mixed strategies are primarily size-driven. From an issuer or funds sponsor's perspective and across strategies, innovation does not appear to be such an important factor, but size and selection are. Interestingly, despite these findings the large issuers observed are not focusing on strategies that would increase their impact as innovative, size and cost, or distribution-oriented fund providers (Tables 18a/b; 19a/b).

As partitioning effects are not yet observable across processes and capabilities, questions have arisen as to where the break lines for such a partitioning might be, assuming that the current industry logic will persist. Following the observed industry dynamics basics using the Price-Fisher accounting measures, we tried to set up a simple model and corresponding hypotheses, to dig down towards the fragile interfaces in mutual funds industrial architecture under gradual innovation dynamics (and subject to the absence of major technological disruptions).

Theory and hypotheses of evolutionary dynamics: replication of resources, routines, relations

The basic foundation of evolutionary economics is well-defined. The works of WITT (1992), DOSI AND NELSON (2001) or METCALFE (1998) and the book "Evolutionary Foundations of Economics by KURT DOPFER (2005) established the cornerstones and started an ongoing debate that spread from pure economics towards application in the management literature as well and broadened the theoretical and methodological horizons. However, consistent and coherent applications of the methods must also share a common language in terms of category definition in evolutionary economic contexts. Categorization is often classified in terms of unit of variation and unit of selection, together with an account of the actual processes involved in generating variations and selecting entities according to some designated "fitness" criterion. In addition, some kind of "inheritance" function is usually required, which describes the entity accounting for retention in order to explain patterns of persistence in a changing context. Building on their earlier work, NELSON AND WINTER introduced in 1982 their pioneering analysis of evolutionary economic processes by making the argument that selective pressures operate on companies in terms of variations in their underlying capabilities and routines – and by extension, resources (NELSON AND WINTER, 1973, 1974, 1982).

Since the seminal publication of Nelson and Winters, there has been a massive increase in interest in evolutionary processes, not just in economics. Processes of variation followed by selection and retention are now recognized in a vast array of domains, from individual development to the acquisition of behavioral routines, and from the evolution of languages through the evolution of conceptual thinking to the evolution of technologies, organizations, institutions and laws (MATHEWS, 2003). This then provides the setting for discussing evolutionary processes within the mutual fund landscape. At the outset, however, we should bear in mind the differences in concepts between economic change and evolution. Changes might be entirely in terms of stimulus and response and may range from learning to simply random reactions. What distinguishes evolutionary processes from all these is their property of blind variation (i.e. variation with unforeseen consequences) followed by selection combined with retention (or inheritance) (METCALFE, 1998). By "blind" variation STAN METCALFE means a process where actors are not in a position to anticipate or predict the consequences of their actions, since these depend on the actions of so many others in the complex system. In the following, we treat blind or random processes as what they are – error terms in the model. Bearing this in mind, we are ready to start building a basic set of hypotheses that will facilitate broad distinctions for processes and routines underlying the competitive landscape in the mutual fund markets.

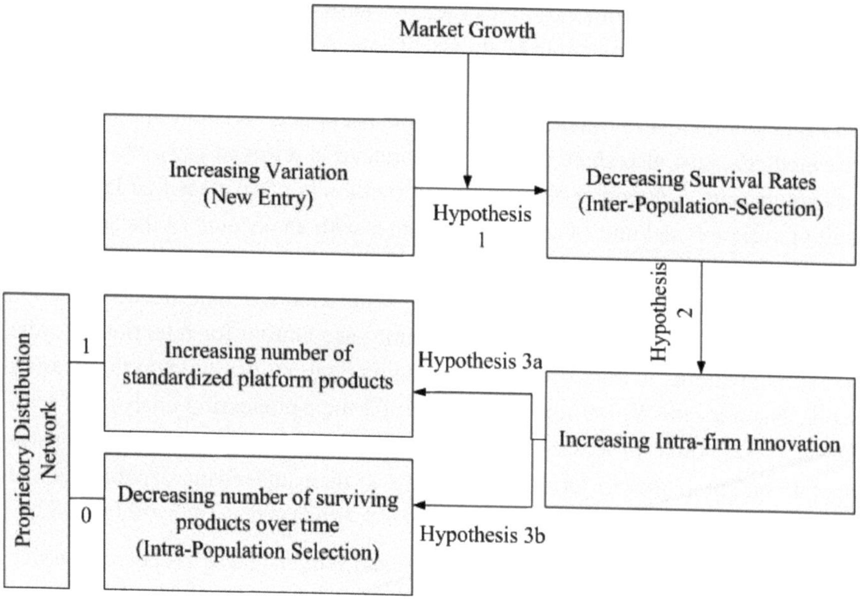

Illustration 9: Model to test for break lines in industry dynamics

Our objective is to illustrate the industry dynamics subject to the assumption of a constant stream of gradual small innovations. We argue that organizational and strategic choices reflecting this innovative environment lead at the intra-company level to process and capability adjustments and at the inter-company level to shifting competitive boundaries over time. We test whether the assumptions concerning the multi-level mutual fund market hold, given the threat of exogenous gradual innovation to incumbents, by forming the following hypotheses.

The model follows the basic concepts that underline the interplay of processes and routines as introduced in the theory of the dynamic industry literature in chapter 2. With the particular background of the mutual fund industry, it can be argued that the entry of new (innovative, i.e. high capability, low capacity) companies corresponds to an increase in variation or inter-population innovation. This increase should c. p. decrease survival rates of incumbents, as inter-population selections becomes more immanent. This relationship may be mediated by the overall market growth in the observed time span. In other words, when market growth is high, even the entry of many new and capable companies will not have as strong a selecting effect on the existing population as would be the case under constant market growth conditions and few entries. A biological reference would be that in environments with low constraints such as food shortage, variation can increase without creating additional selection pressure on the existing population. We can therefore state:

Hypothesis 1:
New entry or more generally inter-population innovation effect is significantly correlated with the increase in incumbent's inter-population selection in the following year.

The inter-population statistics and the corresponding effects follow from the methodology section and result in Table 20. Theoretical models (BUEHLER AND SCHMUTZLER, 2008) assume that incumbents react to the threat of gradual innovative entry by expanding their product base, given sufficiently high capacity and relatively low variable cost of launching a new product. This notion is supported by the observation that new products in the fund space attract new money for a fund sponsoring company (however, it could also be the case that demand for certain solutions pushes the launching of a new product (BERK AND GREEN, 2004). However, we assume that this would be the case for the new entrants, rather than for the incumbents!). We therefore state our second hypothesis: increasing inter-population selection (rivalry or competition for the capacity space occupied) leads to an increase in product variation within incumbent companies.

Table 20: Correlation effects on the inter-population level (see p. 144–145)

			Selection (Inter-Firm) t0	Selection (Inter-Firm) t1	Selection (Inter-Firm) t2	Selection (Inter-Firm) t3	Selection (Inter-Firm) t4	Selection (Inter-Firm) Mediated t0
Control (Volume)	Selection (Inter-Firm) t0	Correlation	1.000	0.161**	.112	.076	.076	1***
		Significance (2-tailed)	.	.039	.153	.333	.332	.000
	Selection (Inter-Firm) t1	Correlation	0.161**	1.000	0.603***	0.190**	0.191**	.161
		Significance (2-tailed)	.039	.	.000	.014	.014	.039
	Selection (Inter-Firm) t2	Correlation	.112	0.602***	1.000	0.287***	0.291***	.112
		Significance (2-tailed)	.153	.000	.	.000	.000	.153
	Selection (Inter-Firm) t3	Correlation	.076	0.190**	0.287***	1.000	0.997***	.076
		Significance (2-tailed)	.333	.014	.000	.	.000	.333
	Selection (Inter-Firm) t4	Correlation	.076	0.191**	0.291***	0.997***	1.000	.076
		Significance (2-tailed)	.332	.014	.000	.000	.	.332
	Selection (Inter-Firm) Mediated t0	Correlation	1.000	0.161**	.112	.076	.076	1.000
		Significance (2-tailed)	.000	.039	.153	.333	.332	.
	Selection (Inter-Firm) Mediated t1	Correlation	.161	1***	0.603***	0.190**	.191	.161
		Significance (2-tailed)	.039	.000	.000	.014	.014	.039
	Selection (Inter-Firm) Mediated t2	Correlation	.112	0.603***	0.997***	0.287***	0.290***	.112
		Significance (2-tailed)	.153	.000	.000	.000	.000	.153
	Selection (Inter-Firm) Mediated t3	Correlation	.076	0.190**	0.287***	0.999***	0.997***	.076
		Significance (2-tailed)	.333	.014	.000	.000	.000	.333
	Selection (Inter-Firm) Mediated t4	Correlation	.076	0.191**	0.291***	0.997***	1***	.076
		Significance (2-tailed)	.332	.014	.000	.000	.000	.332
	Innovation (Inter-Firm) t0	Correlation	-.169	-0.731***	-0.545***	-0.222***	-.223	-.169
		Significance (2-tailed)	.030	.000	.000	.004	.004	.030
	Innovation (Inter-Firm) t1	Correlation	-.097	-0.885***	-0.467***	-.168	-.168	-.097
		Significance (2-tailed)	.213	.000	.000	.031	.031	.213
	Innovation (Inter-Firm) t2	Correlation	-.041	-.100	-0.717***	-.110	-.114	-.041
		Significance (2-tailed)	.600	.203	.000	.159	.145	.600
	Innovation (Inter-Firm) t3	Correlation	-.046	-.053	-.055	-0.824***	-0.827***	-.046
		Significance (2-tailed)	.554	.503	.482	.000	.000	.554
	Innovation (Inter-Firm) t4	Correlation	-0.350***	-.142	-.188	-0.756***	-0.760***	-0.350***
		Significance (2-tailed)	.000	.069	.016	.000	.000	.000

Table 20: Correlation effects on the inter-population level

Selection nter-Firm) lediated t1	Selection (Inter-Firm) Mediated t2	Selection (Inter-Firm) Mediated t3	Selection (Inter-Firm) Mediated t4	Innovation (Inter-Firm) t0	Innovation (Inter-Firm) t1	Innovation (Inter-Firm) t2	Innovation (Inter-Firm) t3	Innovation (Inter-Firm) t4
0.161**	.112	.076	.076	-0.169**	-.097	-.041	-.046	-0.349***
.039	.153	.333	.332	.030	.213	.600	.554	.000
1***	0.603***	0.190**	0.191**	-0.731***	-0.885***	-.100	-.053	-.142
.000	.000	.014	.014	.000	.000	.203	.503	.069
0.602***	0.997***	0.287***	0.291***	-0.545***	-0.467***	-0.712***	-.055	-0.188**
.000	.000	.000	.000	.000	.000	.000	.482	.016
0.190**	0.287***	0.999***	0.997***	-0.222***	-0.168**	-.110	-0.824***	-0.756***
.014	.000	.000	.000	.004	.031	.159	.000	.000
0.191**	0.291***	0.997***	1***	-0.223***	-0.168**	-.114	-0.828***	-0.760***
.014	.000	.000	.000	.004	.031	.145	.000	.000
0.161**	.112	.076	.076	-0.169**	-.097	-.041	-.046	-0.350***
.039	.153	.333	.332	.030	.213	.600	.554	.000
1.000	0.603***	0.190**	0.191**	-0.731***	-0.885***	-.100	-.053	-.142
.	.000	.014	.014	.000	.000	.203	.503	.069
0.603***	1.000	0.287***	0.290***	-0.545***	-0.467***	-0.712***	-.055	-0.188**
.000	.	.000	.000	.000	.000	.000	.482	.016
0.190**	0.287***	1.000	0.997***	-0.222***	-0.168**	-.110	-0.824***	-0.756***
.014	.000	.	.000	.004	.031	.159	.000	.000
.191	0.291***	0.997***	1.000	-0.223**	-0.168**	-.114	-0.828***	-0.760***
.014	.000	.000	.	.004	.031	.145	.000	.000
-0.731***	-0.545***	-0.22***	-0.223***	1.000	0.857***	.049	.040	.100
.000	.000	.004	.004	.	.000	.531	.608	.202
-0.885***	-0.467***	-0.168**	-0.168**	0.857***	1.000	.007	.029	.066
.000	.000	.031	.031	.000	.	.933	.710	.397
-.100	-0.717***	-.110	-.114	.049	.007	1.000	-.043	.029
.203	.000	.159	.145	.531	.933	.	.586	.716
-.053	-.055	-0.824***	-0.828***	.040	.029	-.043	1.000	0.870***
.503	.482	.000	.000	.608	.710	.586	.	.000
-.142	-.188	-0.756***	-0.760***	.100	.066	.029	0.869***	1.000
.069	.016	.000	.000	.202	.397	.716	.000	.

Hypothesis 2:
Inter-population selection in time period $t_{(0)}$ is not significantly different from intra-company variation in time period $t_{(1)}$.

This can be illustrated by an economic example in which selection pressure becomes an issue (e.g. when available funds get scarce) on an inter-population level: room for experiments, e.g. the R & D budget will most probably be equally restricted. Formally, we follow this relationship by comparing the difference of means of the inter-population variables against their counterparts in the four subsequent years of our sample.

	t-value	df	p-value (2-tailed)	Mean Difference
Interpopulation				
Selection Period(0)	-7.81	170.00	0.00	-1,601.95
Selection Period(1)	-8.48	165.00	0.00	-1,246.00
Selection Period(2)	-8.11	169.00	0.00	-3,984.13
Selection Period(3)	-8.69	169.00	0.00	-3,012.50
Selection Period(4)	-8.83	170.00	0.00	-2,649.81

Table 21: One-tailed t-test on difference from mean:

Result: The mean between the two time spans is highly significantly different. Therefore hypothesis 2 stating no significant relation can be rejected. The pattern is stable over time.

One can assume that the increasing number of low degree product variation supports not only heterogeneity, but also enlarges the scope of certain transaction processes whereon the product heterogeneity is produced as minimum cost per new launch. This is because the average volume of each mutual fund must decrease (reducing scales at the direct product level) whenever new funds are launched to counter the threat of innovative entry. This clearly shows the roots of a cost-focused specialization in a core-competence concept. However, before any disintermediation process can start on this basis, the joint synergy platform of the equally jointly used processes has to be expanded. In other words, the more products an incumbent launches, the stronger its focus on platform building at fund family level (e.g. Japanese Equity Funds) must become if it wants to survive over time and take advantage of the opportunities of scale generated. This simply means that those economies of scales that are given up on the singular product level (where volume per entity decreases) must be regained through standardization and platform formation on an intermediate fund family level.

In short, if despite a shortage in funds, innovation activity persists on an intra-company population level, the necessary funds must be generated through cost savings. Cost savings can be facilitated either by reducing transaction costs or increasing the utilization rate of technology investments (i.e. on a company level – in this case by opening up the distribution platforms), or by a "variabilization" or synergy generation on a product level. We can thus postulate that either standardization is sought on a product family level or the number of products out must decrease again. Therefore, we formulate hypotheses 3a and b:

Hypothesis 3a:
The mean intra-company innovation does not correlate with the group of maximal number of standardized platform products

The number of (potential) platforms can be approximated by the number of same-fund-strategy products per issuer. When we combine the potential platforms (building on data from Table 22 and 23) and the intra-company innovation statistics, we obtain results as shown in Table 23. We calculated the model in two versions, one without an intermediating variable and one using network proxies as an intermediating variable.

Issuer	Network Index	Platform Potential	t(0)	t(1)	t(2)	t(3)	t(4)
BSI	2.43	20%	32.10	35.16	32.42	32.17	32.94
Clariden	4.78	80%	37.38	46.68	45.45	47.63	48.85
CS	4.36	1%	40.63	40.37	38.97	40.61	41.68
Gottardo	0.52	2%	22.62	23.02	24.15	25.87	35.11
Gutzwiller	0.44	100%	9.15	8.10	14.45	14.54	14.91
LODH	0.87	12%	27.62	30.27	31.91	31.69	32.46
MI	1.42	1%	10.05	10.15	10.70	10.25	10.45
Pictet	4.02	19%	102.20	110.07	116.48	124.13	127.33
Raiffeisen	1.14	40%	14.16	15.38	14.61	8.78	9.89
Reichmuth	0.81	100%	10.30	16.13	28.37	28.08	28.92
Swisslife	0.66	75%	33.61	33.66	3.66	40.50	41.64
Swisscanto	2.67	1%	31.52	29.72	29.85	40.30	40.36
UBS	13.01	2%	77.00	81.04	79.08	99.88	130.28
Vontobel	0.18	100%	152.81	16.14	224.50	226.90	318.74
Wegelin	0.05	60%	98.03	97.60	8.16	109.38	112.31
XMTCH	1.14	100%	3.55	7.40	10.95	11.25	11.57
ZKB	0.29	22%	73.76	78.15	90.33	80.07	82.15
Mean Innovation induced Change			50.30	52.73	53.91	61.70	72.17

Table 22 and 23: Calculated variables and correlation statistics for hypothesis 3a

		NW	Innovation t(0)	Innovation t(1)	Innovation t(2)	Innovation t(3)
Network	Correlation	1.00	0.22	0.33	(0.47)	0.32
	Significance	.	0.34	0.20	0.56	(0.32)
Innovation t(0)	Correlation	0.22	1.00	0.91	(0.55)	0.21
	Significance	0.34	.	0.00	0.02	(0.32)
Innovation t(1)	Correlation	0.33	0.907***	1.00	(0.44)	0.21
	Significance	0.20	0.00	.	0.08	0.30
Innovation t(2)	Correlation	(0.47)	(0.55)	(0.44)	1.00	0.25
	Significance	0.06	0.23	0.08	.	
Innovation t(3)	Correlation	0.32	(0.32)	(0.32)	0.30	1.00
	Significance	0.21	0.21	0.21	0.25	.
Innovation t(4)	Correlation	0.07	-0.72***	-0.76***	0.498**	0.624**
	Significance	0.79	0.00	0.00	0.04	0.01
Innovation Med. t0)	Correlation	0.97	0.29	0.39	(472.00)	0.37
	Significance	0.00	0.25	0.13	0.56	0.15
Innovation Med. t(1)	Correlation	0.97	0.29	0.40	(0.47)	0.36
	Significance	0.00	2.26	0.12	0.60	0.15
Innovation Med. t(2)	Correlation	0.96	0.29	0.40	(0.46)	0.33
	Significance	0.00	0.27	0.11	0.67	0.14
Innovation Med. t(3)	Correlation	0.96	0.27	0.37	(0.47)	0.39
	Significance	0.00	0.29	0.15	0.59	0.12
Innovation Med. t(4)	Correlation	0.96	0.25	0.33	(0.47)	0.40
	Significance	0.00	0.34	0.20	0.59	0.11

Table 22 and 23: Calculated variables and correlation statistics for hypothesis 3a

Innovation t(4)	NW Innovation t(0)	NW Innovation t(1)	NW Innovation t(2)	NW Innovation t(3)	NW Innovation t(4)
0.07	0.97	0.97	0.96	0.96	0.96
0.79	0.00	0.00	0.00	0.00	0.00
(0.72)	0.97	0.29	0.29	0.27	0.25
0.00	0.00	0.26	0.27	0.29	0.34
(0.76)	0.29	0.40	0.40	0.37	0.33
0.00	0.25	0.12	0.11	0.15	0.20
0.50	0.39	(0.47)	(0.46)	(0.47)	(0.47)
0.42	0.13	0.06	0.07	0.06	0.06
0.62	(0.47)	0.36	0.37	0.39	0.40
0.01	0.06	0.15	0.14	0.12	0.11
1.00	0.37	0.33	0.03	0.06	0.11
.	0.15	0.90	0.92	0.81	0.67
0.40	1.00	0.99	0.99	0.99	0.99
0.88	.	9.00	0.00	0.00	0.00
0.33	0.99***	1.00	0.99	0.98	0.99
0.90	0.00	.	0.00	0.00	0.00
0.03	0.99	0.99***	1.00	0.97	0.98
0.92	0.00	0.00	.	0.00	0.00
0.06	0.99***	0.99***	0.97***	1.00	0.96
0.81	0.00	0.00	0.00	.	0.00
0.11	.99***	0.99***	0.98***	1.00	1.00
0.67	0.00	0.00	0.00	0.00	.

The descriptive platform data can also be analyzed along correlation patterns between innovation activity and network and platform availability. The results as displayed in Table 23 support the notion that in general, there is potential for innovation (under restricted environmental conditions) to be used with platform utilization – this seems especially fruitful for non-network-owning companies.)

Hypothesis 3b:
The mean change in intra-company innovation in time $t_{(0)}$ is not significantly different from the mean change in intra-population selection in time $t_{(1)}$

Intra-population innovation should reflect increased innovation efforts in surviving companies as an alternative strategy to match lost scales as argued in hypothesis 2. The mean changes are therefore for the stable population compared over four time periods, in order to differentiate for emerging heterogeneity in terms of innovation strategies (on product level, i.e. investment strategies). Table 24 shows the corresponding results.

	t-value	df	p-value (2-tailed)	Mean Difference
Intrapopulation				
Innovation Period(0)	8.03	170.00	0.00	50.30
Innovation Period(1)	8.03	170.00	0.00	52.73
Innovation Period(2)	8.58	170.00	0.00	53.91
Innovation Period(3)	7.73	170.00	0.00	61.70
Innovation Period(4)	7.24	170.00	0.00	72.17

Table 24: One-tailed t-test on the difference from the mean

Result: The mean between the two time spans is highly significantly different. The pattern is stable over time.

Both effects, however, might by distorted by access to a proprietary distribution network that allows incumbents to ignore cost disadvantages to a certain level, as they can either save the money through more efficient hierarchical distribution channel solutions and/or through increasing the cost barrier to entry for the innovative companies who have to distribute their products to some extent through their incumbent competitors' existing sales network. Due to reduced data on this, tests on the Swiss market are not (yet) possible here. Therefore the concept is simply indicated on the model. However, we will test for such distribution effects under a disruptive innovation scenario in the following chapter exclusively.

We argue that these hypotheses support the conceptualization of partitioning industry architectures along their potential break lines, as we assume that these break lines reflect the underlying micro-foundations of routines and their related processes: processes – in which selection is based on scale and capacity utilization; routines and capabilities.

Results and Discussion

Although market architecture may be a complex interacting system made of resources, processes, routines and relations, change in industry architecture – or as we use it here – industry dynamics, reacts to a clear number of triggers: technology, regulation and customer demand. Gradual innovation-induced industry dynamics is generally defined at the level of the retail customer interface, whereas regulatory or technological change is mostly seen as a disruptive innovation event (Bátiz-Lazo and Wood, 2002; Chance and Ferris, 1991; Gentzoglanis, 2007).

We group the products within the sample market according to the characteristics "company" and "strategy". Intra-population analysis thereby focuses on the interaction of different (potentially rival) fund types within one company, while inter-population analysis focuses on the competition between multiple companies with substitutive or complementary product bases. In both analytical frameworks, we assume a constant market. We do so because it will likely be argued that every imaginable asset solution can be structured in an equal property-shaped synthetic fund solution. This approach clearly builds on rational decision making and ignores marketing issues or behavioral explanations for customer diversion. Based upon an evolutionary framework, we assume that every company will gain additional market share through above-average fitness, which is the ability to generate the best cost-based performance per risk class. Based on the Andersen or Price-Fisher setting, we would expect to find only fitness as an explanatory variable. However, we assume that size also matters due to information cost advantages for the customer, whether these are due to improved market visibility or accessibility (large branch network).

In the mutual fund context, we are dealing with a multi-submarket environment in which companies draw largely on a common resource base for their products, but also partly use the joint resources along with their competitors. As a consequence, competition can gain momentum when dealing either with same-company units or with competitors for joint resources. A fitness criterion must to some extent disentangle these relationships and form an independent variable that has a direct impact on all inter and intra-company levels based on the same grounds in order to build the base for a consistent measurement framework. This is especially true when applying measurement results to strategic decisions later on.

In order to reduce complexity, we analyze the financial service submarket "asset management". Within the asset management, we deal with the fund industry as one product market. This observation base is sufficiently large and sufficiently diverse to produce consistent results for a heterogeneous set of asset management products. Asset management products are all forms of financial service solution that meet customer demands with respect to individually defined risk-return patterns. By using exclusively funds as product proxy, we can control for net risk-return characteristics, as here – in contrast to equity or structured products – we can build upon a relatively transparent cost base (measured as TER).

The methodological concepts applied vary according to the three objectives in this paper: First, the theoretical framework by Andersen is tested by building the required equations for the sub-case of the fund industry. The goodness of fit of the theory is asserted by testing the equilibrium of the resulting equations for fund strategies and for fund issuers. Given the applicability and validity of the results, we use the model to build a causal relationship, linking inter-population selection and innovation, intra-population selection and innovation as well as supporting proxy variables for the relative influence of difference in sub-market growth.

Initially, in the descriptive set we found a strong influence of the proprietary network, i.e. integrated business models, when assessing the success of mutual fund companies in general. When drilling a little bit deeper, however, one can easily re-group the involved companies along their prima-facie business models. Thus we found that companies with a large branch network (UBS; CS; Cantonal Banks and Raiffeisen) are more clearly trying to gain market share trough size and selection effects, whereas private wealth managers position themselves more as specialists who attempt to gain market share and (distribution network) market access through distinct product innovations. Accordingly, when analyzing the independence of mutual fund product selection or innovation patterns for asset management strategy similarities or for issuer relations, we find that we do indeed have some innovation with respect to "alternative investment", "emerging market" or index-oriented (non-ETF) cost-focused products that also correlate with issuer structures. However, despite this basic product trend, there is almost no evidence that issuers position themselves equally clearly towards selection or innovation. Hence, the more or less sole selection effect is the criterion of being integrated or not. Innovation is not statistically dependent on the type of fund issuer at all. All this mirrors a relatively integrated industry architecture. When asking where trends for disintegration or change-induced re-positioning might pop up in the future, we have to model the break lines more clearly. For this, we propose a model that reflects the different levels of dynamic interaction and that lives up to emerging sets of heterogeneity which have the potential for specialization in processes and capabilities in the future.

Upon initial exploration of the relationship between new entry inter-population variation and survival rates, i.e. inter-population selection, we found a direct relationship between the two of them that holds consistently for year-to-year comparison in line with theory. Apparently, new entry or, more generally, the inter-population innovation effect is significantly correlated with an increase in the incumbent's intra-population selection. When spanning the relationship to the following year for the different cases, we find that the hypothesis does not hold for the first year, but that it is stable for the time periods 01-04. When the model was expanded by using market growth as an intermediary variable, this relationship became only slightly more explicit. The period 03-04, where the total market growth was the highest, both in absolute terms (7.12%) as well as in distance to the incumbents' growth (2.87%), marked no special impact on the underlying structure. Hence, it is fair to assume that over the observed period, capacity expansion (as induced by market growth) did not have a measurable effect on the overall industry dynamics. However, when observing these over-time patterns both with and without an intermediating variable, we found that the level of significance apparently gradually increases from period to period. This increase must to some extent be attributed to technical effects, as the distance measured increases and makes the partitioning more explicit as we expand the time series. Additionally, one could argue that the implicit opening of a potential heterogeneity gap widens over time in the absence of market disintermediation. Nevertheless, it must be noted that the theoretical gap widening and the technical aspects cannot fully be separated; hence there is no final and robust judgment possible here.

Nevertheless, when following the story of this lagged effect of increasing tension in the industrial break lines further, one can directly address the second hypothesis: a decrease in survival rates as expressed by mounting inter-population selection statistics is assumed to impact the intra-company variation in the following period. The idea behind this relation is pretty straightforward: as fewer companies are able to stay in a market (due to selection effects), the total product variety in the following period must be lower, and some companies (and products) exit and other companies will reduce their product portfolio. Thus it is not surprising that the corresponding hypothesis states that the mean inter-population selection in $t_{(0)}$ is significantly different from the mean intra-company variation in $t_{(1)}$. The consequence of this effect is a close interaction of company selection and intra-company variance in the same period, and of innovation efforts in the second period. For a mutual fund company this means that once scaling pressure increases, there are few incentives to invest in new product launches, especially not from an incumbent's position. On the contrary – it is much more pressing to restructure the product portfolio or to merge certain small funds eventually in order to generate sufficient economies of scale to stay in the market. Interestingly, in the fund industry this relation seems almost exclusively to play over economies of scale and innovation. Prices are mostly constant, even during periods of high selective pressure (although this may not be true for institutional investors who can more easily re-negotiate certain terms, but do not show up in statistics). With this, the search is on for the right response to increasing selection: hypotheses 3a and 3b therefore ask whether a portfolio restructuring or a platform or economies of scale-oriented tactic might be more successful. In order to gain a credible idea of that strategy, we formed a proxy for platform (or merger potential). This proxy is simply the share of same-strategy products per company expressed as a share of the total products managed by that company. As an example, one can think of bank Zeta that operates 15 funds; 10 of these funds are Malaysian equity funds and can be run by more or less the same fund management drawing on the identical fund research base. Hence bank Zeta has much more platform potential compared to its imaginary competitor, bank Rho which manages also 15 funds, but in vastly different segments ranging from money market, commodity and alternative investment products to Chilean equity and German bonds.

As a matter of research design, we can provide only descriptive statistics for this relationship, since with 17 fund sponsors to be aggregated; there is no robust conclusion to be drawn. However, quite consistent with expectations, we found that a high platform potential correlates with the mean innovation effect. Over time, the change attributable to innovation even increases for platform oriented fund issuers. Hence we could even make the argument that successful platform integrators have an incentive to increase their product innovation in times of selective pressure (as long as the innovation is platform-bound and the marginal cost of marginal product innovation equals or exceeds the marginal cost savings achieved on increasing economies of scale). Almost more interestingly, when we introduced the characteristic of company boundaries (i.e. a proprietary network), we found high correlations between non-network ownership and platform strategies.

With respect to the second strategy, which boils down to increasing economies of scale directly (e.g. through mergers or reduced product portfolio), hypothesis 3b asks whether a difference in the mean change in intra-company innovation equals the mean change of intra-population selection in the next period. The underlying idea is that in case of company-level focus on economies of scale, the size pressure at the company level should equalize the size pressure at the product level. Here, we find that the mean intra-company innovation and the mean intra-population selection between the two time periods are significantly different. In other words, there seems to be no consistent strategy to build economies of scale at the company level.

In summary, we have a causal relationship between innovation activity in the market and volume pressure on incumbents. This is certainly in line with expectations; the only surprising factor may be that total market growth (or capacity expansion) does not have a measurable influence for the observed period of time. Once pressure on volume increases (as expressed by more selection as a percentage of total change), innovation activity of the companies that are already in the market is affected. The difference in mean of selective pressure and the mean of innovation activity, measured as the innovation-induced change in the next period is clearly different. From this difference we can split the sample towards two possible tactics companies may use to counter the selection pressure: building economies of scale at the company level and/or building modular funds with scaling opportunities at the fund family or platform level. The potential for the first of these tactics seems to be very promising, especially for companies that do not own a large distribution network. These companies may have to expand their innovation activities to build capabilities and gain access to third party sales networks via superior products; in order to do so, they must control their cost base. Companies with proprietary networks, on the other hand, may not be equally sensitive to selection pressure (as they can boost their profits by cashing in on their sales network), or they may build economies of scale at the company level. For this, however, no clear pattern is observable.

When thinking about this empirical evidence in terms of theory, we can link the observations to pressure on processes and capabilities. Selection pressure on technology and processes leads to a change in focus, whereas innovation efforts reflect capability development to some extent. The same story can be seen from a bank versus customer perspective. On the bank side, it could be argued that when a bank has a significantly broad product portfolio that is managed in a pre-adaptive manner, below-average performance of one product will be negligible for future decisions as the money will be re-allocated automatically to a better-performing in-house product. From the customer's point of view, it is mainly a question of information and search costs. Either the absolute search cost prevents him from choosing the optimal product, or the trust in the aforementioned re-allocation mechanism does give sufficient reason for bearing the burden of the marginally increased information cost when comparing competitive products. In both cases, the interaction can be modeled with externalities: first, with the relative pressure for the bank to re-allocate, measured by the density function of the market growth; second with the information cost of the customer, measured by the externalities, e.g. of a large bank's broad branch network.

Conclusion

In this chapter, we re-visited the theories of industry dynamics and pointed out the necessity of an integrative perspective on processes and capabilities across multiple levels of analysis. We supplemented this theoretical perspective that was based primarily on the works of MATTHEWS (2001, 2003, 2006/2001) and to some extent JACOBIDES (JACOBIDES, 2005, 2008a; JACOBIDES, KNUDSEN AND AUGIER, 2006; PISANIAS AND JACOBIDES, 2006) by increasing the focus inter- and intra-company-level interaction across processes and capabilities. In a second step, we discussed measurement techniques that may be suitable to deal with the theoretically elaborated concepts. In this second part, we supplemented the multi-layer dynamic theory with evolutionary economic concepts, most notably made popular by ESBEN ANDERSEN (2003, 2004a, 2004b, 2004c) and STAN METCALFE (1995, 1998, 2001). The article re-formulated these concepts slightly in order to match the theoretical problems and applied the measure to the example of the Swiss mutual fund industry. In the descriptive section we found that the measures yield stable results for the observed population, but, that there is not much of a consistent trend for evolutionary change yet to be observed in that particular market. Therefore, we set up a formal model that was designed to reveal the hidden break lines in the current industry architecture. We found some fragile lines at the intersection of processes and capabilities, where it comes to dealing with selection pressure. There seem to be two main driving forces for future industry dynamics subject to assumptions of gradual (no regulatory and no technological change) innovation: first, ownership of a sales network is still a critical element, facilitating the appropriation of value for the company that controls customer interfaces. Second, the facts that for an independent company, this customer interface can be accessed only by means of superior performance or capabilities means that those companies must increase their innovation activity. This increased innovation activity must be financed subject to the assumption of increasing selective pressure by modularization of the portfolio. Hence, there are apparently two basic strategic directions for incumbent companies: either building a broad modularized platform that draws upon superior capabilities, or focusing on process efficiency and volume combined with a proprietary sales network. However, this is a viable concept only for incumbents with an adequate number of existing points of sale.

Appendix: Note on the Price Equation and the Fisher Theorem

(The note follows the basic line of argument that is used in METCALFE (2007) and in ANDERSEN (2004). The math is slightly modified to meet the article's objectives in terms of multi-layer analysis focus).

We look using at Price‘s equation for breaking down the change in some population average into component parts. This is now a well-known result in evolutionary population analysis (FRANK, 1998; KNUDSEN, 2004; METCALFE, 2007; PRICE, 1970, 1972).

The model is based on the idea that innovations (mutations) in the traits possessed by surviving companies/units vary individually between the initial and the terminal dates that define an interval. As any analysis with surviving companies would only dilute evidence, it is necessary to focus on three processes: (i) growth (decline), (ii) entry and exit and how they modify the population structure and (iii) innovation.

To establish this view, one can consider a population over a given interval of time with the first census date, t, and the second, t+Δt. Let $X(t+\Delta t)$ and $X(t)$ be the aggregate output rates, the sum of the outputs of all the business units in the population at the start and end of the period. Over this time span, we define g as the compound total growth rate, g_c as the growth rate of surviving companies and g_e as the growth rate of the existing company's activity.

Hence, $X_c(t+\Delta t)=X_c(t)(1+g_c)$ defined the output profile of surviving companies.

Now let $Xn(t+\Delta t)$ be the increment of output contributed by those companies that enter the population during the interval Δt, and define the flow entry rate n, such that $Xn(t+\Delta t) = n^*X(t+\Delta t)$, and, with c as a fraction of output produced by all companies that were in the market over the observed time span, and let $X_e(t+\Delta t) = (1-c)X(t)(1+g)$ be the output of exiting companies. Then it follows that

$$X(t+\Delta t) = X_c(t+\Delta t)+X_e(t+\Delta t)+Xn(t+\Delta t)$$

or

$$X(t+\Delta t) = X(t)\left\{\frac{c(1+g_c)+(1-c)(1+g_e)}{1-n}\right\}$$

With some substitutions, this becomes

$$(1+g)(1-n) = c[1+g_c]+(1-c)(1+g_c) = 1+g_0 \quad (1)$$

where g_0 is the growth rate for all business units "alive" at t, regardless of whether they will survive until $(t+\Delta t)$. When now approximating first that this same survival holds undiluted over multiple business levels (i.e. no cross-subsidies for weak entities and that in the limit e = 1-c, when e is defined the limiting value of the exit rate as Δt tends to zero, one can state that for short periods of time, one can shorten the equation to

$$g = cg_c + n - e \quad (2)^1$$

The relative fitness of the group of surviving companies is measured by g_c-g, so their relative importance in the total population changes according to the relation

$$\frac{dc}{dt} = c(g_c - g) = (1-c)g - n + e \quad (3)$$

respectively notated for subpopulations

$$\frac{dc_i}{dt} = c_i(g_i - g_c) \quad (4)$$

where

---

1 For special cases of equation 2, options to vary the relations and the implications thereof, see METCALFE (2007 p. 23ff)

$$g_c = \sum_{i=1}^{n} c_i g_i, \text{ and } c_i = X_i(t)/X_c(t)$$

or equally at the total population level

$$s_i = x_i(t)/X(t)$$

If the industry is hereby treated as a population of business units and if the respective factors at work are grouped into "selection-related processes", defined in terms of differential growth of survivors and elimination of exiting companies, and "innovation-related processes", defined in terms of new entrants and the innovation-induced development of the characteristics of the surviving companies, one may derive a common feature for all surviving and exiting entities: the characteristics that are inherent to staying in the market. This characteristic is labeled "Z", and z for the average characteristic of any population.

In line with the foregoing definitions, one can now write directly the relations for "selection processes"

$$\bar{z}(t) = c\overline{z_c}(t)+(1-c)\overline{z_e}(t)$$

where

$$\bar{z}(t) = \sum_{i=1}^{n} c_i(t) z_i(t) \text{ and } \bar{z}_e(t)$$

describe the average value of z(t) for those entities that will exit over the interval Δt. The calculation is similarly for the "innovation process", that is

$$\bar{z}(t+\Delta t) = (1-n)\overline{z_c}(t+\Delta t)+n\overline{z_n}(t+\Delta t)$$

where, $\bar{z}_n$ is the average value of z $(t+\Delta t)$ for the entrants over the interval.

The change in z follows now as

$$\Delta\bar{z} = \bar{z}(t+\Delta t)-\bar{z}(t) = \Delta\bar{z}_c + n[\bar{z}_n(t+\Delta t)-\bar{z}_c(t+\Delta t)]-(1-c)[\bar{z}_e(t)-\bar{z}_c(t)] \quad (5)$$

Equation (5) is a complete evolutionary accounting of the change in average population value of any fitness criterion and builds the foundation for the explicit Price equation that simply generalizes the above relation. Thus, the general Price equation can be written as

$$\Delta \bar{z}_c = \sum_{i=1}^{n} c_i(t+\Delta t) z_i(t+\Delta t) - \sum c_i(t) z_i(t)$$

$$\Delta \bar{z}_c = \sum_{i=1}^{n} \Delta c_i z_i(t) + \sum c_i(t+\Delta t) \Delta z_i$$

$$\Delta \bar{z}_c = \frac{1}{1+g_c} \{ \sum c_i(t)(g_i - g_c) z_i(t) + \sum c_i(t)(1+g_i) \Delta z_i \}$$

or

$$(1+g_c)\frac{\Delta \bar{z}_c}{\Delta t} = C_c(g_i z_i) + E\left[(1+g_i)\frac{\Delta z_i}{\Delta t}\right] \qquad (6)$$

Using equation (1) to introduce the notion of "entry" and "exit" into the outlined growth paths, one can re-express the relation

$$(1+g_c)\frac{\Delta \bar{z}_c}{\Delta t} = \left(\frac{1-e}{1-n}\right)[C_c(g_i z_i) + E_c\left((1+g_i)\frac{\Delta z_i}{\Delta t}\right)] \qquad (7)$$

which corresponds to the general form of the Price equation. From this form, it is now possible to adjust parameterization slightly.

Suppose now that the characteristic z_i is taken to be the growth rate g_i directly. In this case one would find

$$(1+g_c)\frac{\Delta g_c}{\Delta t} = V_c(g_i) + E_c\left((1+g_i)\frac{\Delta g_i}{\Delta t}\right) \qquad (8)$$

which is a special application of relation (7) of the Price equation, which is also known as the Fisher theorem.

All other derivatives can now easily be calculated starting from that Fisher theorem, equation (8), and applied to different levels of population analysis as illustrated in the main body of this chapter.

7 Disruptive Innovation Perspective: Why Do Electronic Markets not yet Prevail?

Introduction

Particularly in the financial industry, electronic markets have become popular alternatives to traditional market forms over the last few years. So far the discussion on how electronic markets can be used either to create new markets or to strengthen existing markets has been dominated by a search for value propositions and the observation of decreasing transaction costs in a system. Essentially, electronic markets are merely an alternative exchange mode and thereby representing a transition phase of product trading towards an electronic communication network. The implementation of a fully developed electronic financial marketplace, however, would result in more efficient pricing compared to the physical environment, greater efficiencies and financial service integration, less fragmentation, greater liquidity and a broad variety of available products.

The motivation and driving factors behind this transition have gone relatively unnoticed, especially with respect to financial service firms. Despite significant drops in transaction cost, some financial markets (e.g. structured credit) have been holding on to their established exchange regime, while others (e.g. equity) are deploying new technology and reshaping industry sub-structures. So, what allows or what constrains the effective transition of certain products to be traded on electronic markets? To answer this question it is necessary to analyze both the impact of electronic market implementation on operational / distribution cost and additional product patterns to understand their effect on market structures.

Regarding the current state of online financial services, many studies have concluded that over the past years there had been a great deal of innovation in Internet-driven financial technology with banks making use of the resulting product and delivery channel options. However, none or few empirical studies have tried to track this effect. Additionally, existing studies only focus on the firm or intra-organizational level without analyzing changes on market structures at industry level. Accordingly, we focus our analysis on mutual funds that are distributed via varying exchange regimes and try to make predictions for the developments in trading other innovative asset classes such as credit, insurance and other financial product innovations. We build our arguments on a unique empirical data set of 4,757 mutual fund products with attributes in respect to cost and fee structures, product size, complexity, standardization and underlying asset management strategy.

Generally, developments towards the Digital Economy can be analyzed along four interrelated dimensions, i.e. structures, value creation processes (e.g. reverse-marketing), products (e.g. new kinds of information products based on digitalization as a source of unbundling of traditional services), and infrastructures (i.e. either a set of technological specifications, standards, protocols, and their technical implementation, or an infrastructure of market services necessary to enable electronic commerce transactions of value creation systems) from an industry and intra-organizational perspective (ZIMMERMANN, 2000). The central argument in this paper is that the transition from one exchange form to another is not driven by added value due to technological innovations (such as the Internet), but by shifts in product design at issuance. This study contributes to the field by observing the impact of information and communication technology (ICT) on value creation structures within financial service firms at industry level.

Literature Review

Following BAKOS (1997, 2001), electronic marketplaces support an integrated process of business transactions from initial contacts and negotiation to settlement with opportunities of exchange being instantaneously observable. This definition is grounded on the diminishing level of search costs incurred on electronic markets. Furthermore, electronic market places or communication networks (ECNs) establish an integrated environment that involves many providers rather than one firm.

While financial services such as online securities trading are becoming increasingly standardized, the electronic marketplace is seen as the next stage of innovation in distributing financial assets. For many sub-markets of financial products the distribution channel is in a stage of change. Certain product classes are still stuck in hierarchically organized integrated distribution channels, others have emerged as more relational governed OTC trading, whilst the most liquid assets are exchanged over formalized institutions or (as an emerging lower cost solution) electronic market places (WESTERFELD AND ZIMMERMANN, 2008). In these cases, the determinants for successful marketplaces are clear: provide liquidity, searching capabilities, transaction reporting, compliance and enforcement, network economics and connectivity (LANCASTRE AND LAGES, 2006). The form that such a successful market place may take directly depends on governing cost, firm capabilities and product characteristics (O'HARA, 2007; O'REILLY AND FINNEGAN,

2005, 2007; VARIAN, 1998). Whilst for more established asset classes inertia and path dependency are frequently quoted when attributing a certain exchange form to a product (HARVEY AND RANDLES, 2002; KEIM AND MADHAVAN, 1997), clear determinants remain to be defined particularly for new asset classes which have not been traded on conventional markets before, e.g. credit risk.

When observing structure and value creation processes from an ICT perspective, ruptures along the cost base form a central piece of argumentation. Hence, theory of Transaction Costs Economics (TCE) that originates in institutional economics (COASE, 1993; WILLIAMSON, 1975, 1985) has been very prominently discussed in the literature. With respect to financial products, already in 1994 HESS AND KEMERER looked at the impact of ICT on industry structures within the loan industry by testing the Electronic Markets hypothesis. The authors found only little evidence of the emergence of electronic markets over hierarchies despite the availability of technology and favorable characteristics of the product (HESS AND KEMERER, 1994). STEINFIELD et al. analyzed the US home mortgage industry ten years later, focusing especially on the impact of inter-organizational systems (IOS) at the industry level. They concluded that the use of industry IOS can result in greater consolidation, increased disintegration and the use of outsourcing creating opportunities for smaller and more niche-oriented players (STEINFIELD, MARKUS AND WIGAND, 2005). Research by BATIZ-LAZO et al. concludes that increased application of telecommunications in banking markets effectively modifies external and internal banking organization (BÁTIZ-LAZO AND WOOD, 2002; JACOBIDES AND WINTER, 2005) and may lead to disintermediation effects (JACOBIDES AND WINTER, 2005).

Moreover, the transaction cost theory has been extended and applied in the field of ICT to analyze the consequences of ICT usage on firms' governance structure, also for governing disintermediated product issuance and distribution. Here, the governance structure has been interpreted as a dichotomy between markets, referring to outsourcing of an activity or relying on a pool of suppliers; and hierarchies, referring to the internalization of an activity or exclusive relationships between an organization and its sole supplier for a given input. With regard to this make-or-buy decision, firms tend to select a governance structure that minimizes total costs (BENSLIMANE, PLAISENT AND BERNARD, 2005; MATTIG, 2008). This managerial choice of governance mode is reflected in capital market reaction at the outsourcing-announcement date, which supports the notion that transaction processes are valued higher when traded over (and governed by) markets, rather than managed through hierarchies (MATTIG, 2008). Hierarchies tend to have higher production costs due to specialization effects and economies of scale applying to markets. Outsourcing and relying on market structures, however, induces additional transaction costs, i.e.

search cost (time and effort to identify contract partners and overcome information asymmetries), coordination costs (to manage the flow of goods and synchronize activities) and contractual costs (e.g. costs of negotiating, monitoring and enforcing a contract). This effect of technology on market structures was originally developed by MALONE et al. (1987) as 'Electronic Markets hypothesis'. It basically states that the use of ICT will lead to reduced transaction costs and thus to a disintermediation towards less hierarchical and more market-like governance structures.

More recently, disintermediation issues have also been addressed by the growing body of literature on industrial dynamics that emphasizes more strongly the role of societal or regulatory movements, as well as capabilities and evolutionary processes in the emergence of new industry architectures (JACOBIDES, 2005; MCGAHAN, 2004). The key element that industrial dynamic literature contributes to the discussion of the transition of exchange modes is the focus on appropriable value propositions that are generated through the transition. In other words, no actor will change the existing trading paradigm if he cannot personally benefit from the shift. This personal value gain stands in contrasts to the overall efficiency gains that might be in reach for final customers through a repositioning alternative, i.e. independently of how greatly transaction costs can be reduced in a system, the system ‚owner' will not switch unless he can personally benefit from the shift (McGahan, 2004). It appears that today the primary benefactors of ICT in mutual fund trading, however, are investors alone (FISHER AND HARINDRANATH, 2004) as there is no value of a transition captured by issuing firms.

Although the ICT discussion has already been blended successfully with financial market research, discussions have so far been dominated by a focus on the impact of ICT on transaction cost and, as an indirect effect, on financial market products. Both the question on why ICT potential is adopted (and more interestingly even, why it is not) as well as empirical studies are missing so far.

Theory

We argue that contrary to the basic assumptions of transaction cost economics and electronic market literature, it is not a mere technological innovation that spurs the diffusion of electronic markets, but rather the shift in exchange modes is due to product characteristics and market structure that allow the extraction of created value. The absence of appropriable value leads to a constraint of the electronic market hypothesis.

The underlying model reflects the notion that technological innovation, i.e. the emergence of electronic markets for financial products, reduces the cost base of a transaction. This means, the total expense ratio that can be charged for a transaction erodes as markets shift from traditional 'brokered' distribution systems towards electronic buyer-seller interaction. With respect to firms' responsiveness to this innovation two major issues stand to dispute: First, the direct transaction cost impact of distribution channels (Hypothesis 1, H1) and second, the decision to opt for a (new) form of market exchange (Hypothesis 2, H2). In other words, does technology make distribution cheaper and, if so, what drives the choice of the distribution channel besides lower distribution costs as traditional channels still exist for trading financial assets? Illustration 10 gives an overview of the model used and how the hypotheses fit into the larger framework of transaction cost economics. The model already indicates that product patterns are key to finding an answer to H2.

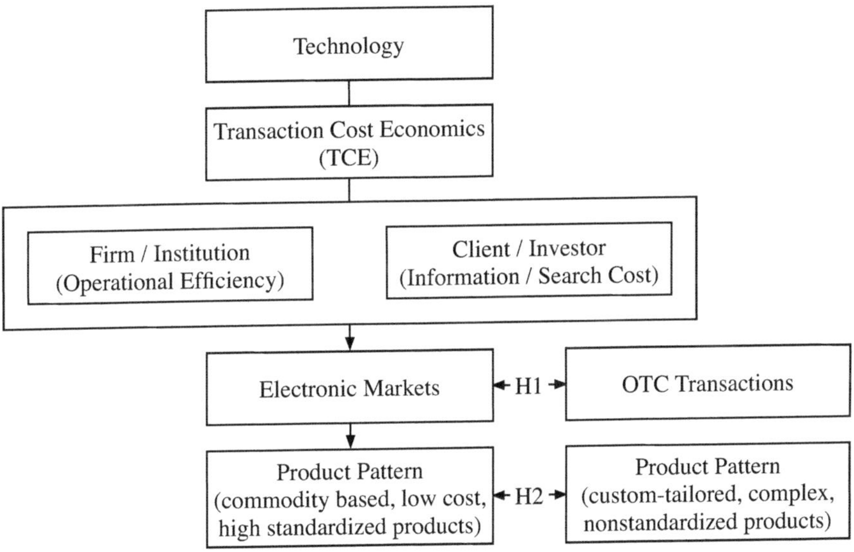

Illustration 10: Model Overview

Illustration 10 sketches the two hypotheses of this paper: Technological change affects transaction cost and thereby influences operational efficiency at the firm level and information or search cost for the potential mutual fund investor.

Consequently, we expect differences in total commission (for the investor) and spreads (for the mutual fund firm) when switching from traditional OTC trading to electronic markets. We test the first hypothesis by equalities of means. In line with the related literature, we expect that the decision to use this distribution channel is taken based on different product patterns despite cost differences in each exchange mode. We test the second hypothesis by using discriminant analyses to classify markets for corresponding patterns.

Research on market microstructure has developed theory and found empirical evidence to report the relevant attributes that reflect cost ruptures on exchange structures (O'HARA, 2007). Lower trading cost directly leads to increasing market liquidity, which again lowers average tick-size per trade and is reflected in tighter bid-ask spreads (COPELAND AND GALAI, 1983; MAYHEW, 2002). The literature lists increases in market depths (HUANG AND STOLL, 2000) and increased marginal trading or more efficient markets (DWYER, OSTERLAND, CAPELL AND REIER, 1998) as potential effects.

Secondary market trading mechanisms are generally grouped along the process of exchange and the respective technology supporting the transaction. The literature refers to three types of trading mechanisms: Over-the-counter trading (OTC), electronic communication networks and auction processes at exchanges and in specialist markets (HARVEY AND RANDLES, 2002; LEE AND CLARK, 1996). Traditional, institutionalized stock exchanges basically work along the boundaries of auction processes that are perceived as optimal for large numbers of small trade lots, whereas ECNs and OTC are the preferred choice for inter-departmental transactions or large block trades. Thus, an open market such as an ECN is widely considered to be the simplest type of a financial intermediary (STOLL, 2006) and consequently also as the most cost-efficient given the absence of prior existing surplus capacity or distinct capabilities (e.g. experienced OTC trader) that lock processes into a different exchange regime. The transfer of ownership in financial products is possible at less managerial cost (the price for transforming assets) as trade lots get larger, which leads to (managerial) price fluctuations dependent on the type of asset that is traded. The remaining administrative cost component (the mere transaction process) seems, however, not to be sensitive to product distinctiveness, but rather a function of the capacity and variable cost of the exchange system (CHORDIA, 1995). This implies that under a given exchange regime each trade (independent of product type) results in the same system cost, i.e. firm margin reflected by bid-ask-spreads. Changing from one exchange regime to another should therefore not affect product performance on top-line, but only on an after-cost yield basis. This leads to the first hypothesis that determines the cost impact of electronic markets on financial products:

Hypothesis 1:
There is no significant cost difference for buyers of funds (a) and for issuers of funds (b) between products that are traded on electronic markets versus products that are distributed over-the-counter (OTC).

Cost difference thereby can be either the total cost for a retail investor when buying a product (total commission) or the gross margin (total commission – operational cost) that the distributor levies on a product (implicit bid-ask-spread). A rejection of Hypothesis 1 would imply that cost structures are significantly different when using different exchange modes. But it would not yet explain what makes firms switch or stick to a cost-superior or cost-inferior regime. Within this closer context of the managerial decision for a transition from an OTC market towards an electronic exchange, market micro structure theory (HORTACSU AND SYVERSON, 2004) leads to three potential explanations for the product-distinct trajectories of change in distribution modes: market liquidity, product standardization / transparency and information cost.

Reduced transaction cost on electronic markets would allow more frequent trading. The literature (CHERKES, SAGI AND STANTON, 2008; DWYER et al., 1998) shows that such increased liquidity, or reduced cost per trade is mainly used by well informed, professional traders who trade at margin and ultimately enhance market efficiency. Furthermore, electronic markets go hand in hand with closed, relationship-based club trading, prominently illustrated by stock market seats on major institutionalized, traditional exchange boards. Eliminating this form of industry regulation and restriction removes the traditional barriers to entry; allowing new competitors to enter the market, add liquidity and heat up competition, primarily challenging the previously capacity-rich incumbents. Prices may thus even dip below the marginal limit under the prior institutionalized settings for electronic exchanges. This drop in margin ultimately pushes down the price per transaction at wholesale and retail level, and becomes observable in decreasing total expense ratios (CHALMERS, EDELEN AND KADLEC, 2002; HORTACSU AND SYVERSON, 2004). Therefore, Hypothesis 2 tests whether the size of a product or its different trading patterns is a potential determinant for the move towards electronic markets in financial product distribution or not.

Hypothesis 2:
The market exchange form and its corresponding cost measures are not determined by product characteristics, i.e. the complexity of a product, the degree of standardization, the size and liquidity of the products and whether the financial instrument is issued and distributed by an integrated bank or by a specialized fund firm.

Evidence from research in equity and debt markets points out an additional explanation: In the absence of someone within an existing market regime to appropriate the value created by ICT on the inter-organizational level, there needs to be an external source that presses the trading parties towards a new transaction mode. Changing regulatory requirements are the most frequently cited examples of such outside pressure (Coates and Hubbard, 2006; Khorana, Servaes and Tufano, 2005; Williams, 2000). Up to now, there are no regulatory policies in place that would force trading of mutual funds to switch to electronic markets, thus current exchange modes remain locked-in.

Methodology

Data and empirical approach

Our methodological approach focuses on mutual funds as being a financial product that is fairly comparable in terms of reporting and asset strategy patterns. A mutual fund can roughly be described as a company that invests in a diversified portfolio of securities, hence it aggregates risk-performance expectations of its customers and channels the resulting investment strategies to leverage on scale and technology. Thus, the advantages of mutual funds include not only professional management, but also diversification, variety, liquidity, affordability, convenience and ease of recordkeeping – as well as strict government regulation and full disclosure. Mutual fund trading is executed along identical rules of transaction, no matter if OTC or (electronic) exchanges are used to distribute products (Dimson and Mussavian, 1998; Khorana et al., 2005). Therefore, process arguments are not additionally checked.

To our best knowledge, this industry is currently the only financial market type that embodies traded regimes along open (electronic) market approaches as well as traditional OTC exchange.

We allocated products to the category 'electronically traded' when they were marketed in the prospectus as for sale in fund supermarkets or on electronic exchanges such as the AMEX. This is to say, we used a broad definition of electronic markets, including all kinds of electronic communication networks that reflected non-OTC exchange. We did not include the literally 'exchange traded' funds or ETFs as they represent a different category of financial products. As the mutual fund population consists of a wide set of vehicles, targeted at both retail and institutional clients, we focus on funds rated by Morningstar in order to get a relatively homogenous sample of this diverse group. Morningstar is one of the best-known agencies providing standardized fund information across national legislations. Fund attributes such as distribution channel, vehicle size (net asset value of all assets per entity, labelled NAV) and most importantly the trading cost components are obtained from the selected fund's prospectus. Accordingly, we analysed each individual fund prospectus to create a substantial and unique data set of 4,757 mutual funds. The mutual funds represent the Morningstar rated products that are allowed for trading in the largest mutual fund markets, the U.S., Luxembourg, Ireland and Switzerland.

Based on the information obtained from each fund's prospectus we calculated additional variables. For the total cost we assumed a standardized retail trade with an investor buying the minimum lot size and holding it for one year. This assumption guarantees the inclusion of all cost components and corrects for negotiation or market power arguments that might become an issue where large institutional clients are involved. Such standardization is required as the form of sales charges strongly depends on the exchange mode used to trade or distribute the funds or even the mutual fund class, i.e. funds are sometimes sold in two or more classes, with some of them being cheaper upfront but containing extra sales charges (so called load fees[2]) or extra redemption fees (CHANCE AND FERRIS, 1987, 1991). We also acknowledged the possibility of differences in a mutual fund's own trading cost. Both BAKOS (1997) and KEIM AND MADHAVAN (1997) provide detailed execution cost insights for mutual funds with respect to fund-trading activity that were applied. Also, we calculated the margin that makes the profit of a distributor or the distributing business unit in an integrated bank, i.e. the implicit bid-ask spread.

---

2 "Load fees have traditionally been viewed as a means of compensating brokers for selling mutual fund shares. [...] Funds often waive load fees on long-term investments such as retirement and pension funds." (CHORDIA, 1995, p. 15–16)

A bid-ask spread is the difference between seller and buyer price for a transaction and can be used as a proxy for the brokers margin at the same time (COPELAND AND GALAI, 1983). This margin directly depends on transaction costs, since – as shown above – when trading cost decreases, trading at margin becomes more frequent and traders become more informed, ultimately melting down the bid-ask-spread (HUANG AND STOLL, 2000). An implicit bid-ask spread represents its synthetic counterpart and is defined by ROLL (1984) under any transaction mode as the difference between the actual exchange cost and the corresponding efficient market solution. In accordance with the corresponding financial market theory (CHOU AND CHUNG, 2004) we calculated this spread as the difference between actual cost and the products' efficient fixed cost benchmark. The applied benchmark is a fixed component for administrative cost of USD 1.2 mio per fund and a variable component of 0.18 per cent on management fund size as introduced as industry average in (WERMERS, 2000) on page 1683 or in (ZERA AND MADURA, 2001) on page 245. We calculated assuming a one year, minimum lot size transaction, i.e. buying and selling at onset, respectively the end of a year in order to include all potential cost elements, such as issuance and redemption fees.

Spread and Commission Calculation	
Operational Cost Benchmark	USD 1.2 m + 0.18% NAV* = Total Operational Cost/NAV
Total Commission	Administration Fee + Issuance Fee + Redemption Fee + 12b Fee** for a trade at minimum lot size and holding period 1 year
Implicit Bid-Ask Spread	Total Commission - Operational Cost Benchmark

* NAV (Net Asset Value) indicates the size of a mutual fund, measured by the volume of assets under management
** 12b Fees are special compensations for fund distributors/brokers, named for a respective U.S. legislation

The product properties of mutual funds have been identified by HORTACSU AND SYVERSON (2004) as complexity (number of classes per fund family), liquidity in a product and degree of product standardization. The standardization degree is set by the degrees of freedom that the fund's manager has when investing in stocks or bonds. We grouped according to standardization degrees along (i) lowest degree of freedom when replicating an index, (ii) relatively high standardization where the investment strategy is defined by both the instrument's variance (e.g. pure equity or pure bond portfolio) and a regional or industry constraint, (iii) lower standardization with only instrument group (shares or bonds) or general strategy given and a class of (iv) alternative strategies that summarize all mixed and derivative strategies. A proxy for liquidity was defined as the average turnover for the last 5 years measured by net new money in-/ outflows (KARCESKI, LIVINGSTON AND O'NEAL, 2004, p. 8).

All necessary data for this calculation can be obtained from the Morningstar performance reports. As an additional control variable, we included the business model of the parenting fund firm, with a dummy variable for integrated bank-fund firms that own and manage a proprietary (traditional) distribution network and maintain relationship-based client interaction, and those that focus on fund business only without maintaining a retail network.

Validity and robustness checks

We do not introduce new measurement constructs and we control for validity of our data by comparing it to information reported by alternative mutual fund studies. Here, implied bid-ask spreads have been identified as 0.35 bps up to 0.88 bps in CHALMERS et al. (2002). Our data ranges slightly wider from 0.18 to 1.08 bps, with the mean lying at 0.8 bps. However, even though our sample contains a broader set of strategies, still some 80 per cent of our total population lie within the boundaries discussed in the literature. The remaining dispersion may be due either to different asset management strategies or due to different buying and selling assumptions (e.g. more than a one year, minimum size trade) that affect total cost measures. Additionally, we controlled for robustness by excluding sequential sub-groups for both size effects and asset management strategy.

Results and Discussion

Table 25 presents the descriptive statistics for our Morningstar sample. We include 248 issuers who market 4,757 products. Of these products, however, only 173 funds are distributed through electronic channels, whereas the majority are sold over-the-counter. Commissions amounted to 4 per cent on average with a peak at 12.9 per cent. The corresponding bid-ask margins are at 0.8 basis points on average and hence in the range of other financial product studies. From a descriptive point of view the most interesting observations are thus the combination of relatively high cost with low proportions of electronic market diffusion. As stated in the basic hypotheses, such a structure calls for an answer to whether electronic trading in the context would effectively be available at lower cost.

Descriptive Statistics

	N	Minimum	Maximum	Mean
Issuer #	4,757	1	248	
Standardization Categories	4,757	1	4	
NAV 2007	4,757	0	5,893	2,599
Min. Trade Lot	4,757	1	75,000	27,257
Commission (annual)	4,757	0.0%	4.0%	1.4%
Issuance Fee	4,757	0.0%	14.4%	3.7%
Redemption Fee	4,756	0.0%	6.0%	0.6%
12b/Distribution Fee	4,757	0.0%	2.6%	6.9%
Total Commission	4,757	3.0%	12.9%	8.0%
Spread	4,756	0.18 bp.	1.08 bp	0.8 bp

Table 25: Descriptive Statistics

For this, we run a t-test for equality of means in independent samples. Results are reported in Table 26. In line with expectations from electronic market research, the technology adapting distribution channels proved to be significantly cheaper from a retail customer's point of view (total commission) as well as more cost cautious from the distributors' margin point of view (spread). The results are stable irrespectively of whether equality of variance is assumed or not.

We control for factors mediating total commission and spread by forming control groups based on the asset management strategy employed. Different asset management strategies and their differences in trading and effective management cost are seen as the main factor to drive overall commission level (GERANIO AND ZANOTTI, 2005). Money market funds generally require low active management and are not particularly return focused but represent a more temporary form of investment. Consequently, the fees that can be generated are far lower than for other strategies, but the spread is also lower than the average of the total fund population. Quite the opposite is true for alternative investments that are based on a more long-term and return-focused notion. These funds require active management and are particularly expensive. The peak commissions are incurred here – mainly due to the fact that the asset strategy penalizes investors through prohibitively high redemption fees after one year (that decreases, though, if funds are hold for longer time frames).

Group Statistics	Market	N	Mean	Std. Deviation
Spread	Exchange	173.00	0.00	0.00
	OTC	4,583.00	0.03	0.10
Commission	Exchange	173.00	2.58	1.10
	OTC	4,584.00	5.75	1.57

t-Test	Sig.	t-value	df	Sig. (2-tailed)	Mean Differenc	Assumption
Spread	0.01	-2.09	4,754.00	0.04**	0.00	Equal Variance
		-7.45	611.04	0.00***	0.00	No Equal Variance
Commission	0	-26.31	4,755.00	0.00***	-3.17	Equal Variance
		-36.40	199.21	0.00***	-3.17	No Equal Variance

Table 26: Results of Hypothesis 1

Product Type/ Asset Management Strategy: Money Market

	Market	N	Mean	Std. Deviation
Margin/ Spread	Exchange	6	1.07bp	0.00
	OTC	122	5.99bp	0.00
Commission	Exchange	6	1.99%	0.49
	OTC	122	4.48%	2.08

Table 27a

Product Type/ Asset Management Strategy: Alternatives

	Market	N	Mean	Std. Deviation
Margin/ Spread	Exchange	49	4.38bp	0.00
	OTC	931	6.86bp	0.00
Commission	Exchange	49	2.64%	1.31
	OTC	931	5.73%	1.49

Table 28a

Product Type/ Asset Management Strategy: Equity and Bond

	Market	N	Mean	Std. Deviation
Margin/ Spread	Exchange	167.00	3.50bp	0.00
	OTC	4,461.00	9.02bp	0.00
Commission	Exchange	167.00	2.56%	1.12
	OTC	4,461.00	5.78%	1.54

Table 29a

Table 27b

t-Test	Sig.	t-value	df	Sig. (2-tailed)	Mean Difference	Assumption
Margin/Spread	1.36	0.25	0.59	126.00	0.56	Equal Variance
			0.48	5.31	0.65	No Equal Variance
Commission	7.80	0.01	(2.91)	126.00	0.00	Equal Variance
			(9.02)	17.11	0.00	No Equal Variance

Table 28b

t-Test	Sig.	t-value	df	Sig. (2-tailed)	Mean Difference	Assumption
Margin/Spread	0.13	(1.09)	978.00	0.28	0.00	Equal Variance
		(2.42)	86.90	0.02**	0.00	No Equal Variance
Commission	1.10	(14.30)	978.00	0.00***	(3.10)	Equal Variance
		(16.00)	54.69	0.00***	(3.10)	No Equal Variance

Table 29b

t-Test	Sig.	t-value	df	Sig. (2-tailed)	Mean Difference	Assumption
Margin/Spread	0.01	2.17	4,626.00	0.03**	0.00	Equal Variance
		8.74	984.71	0.00***	0.00	No Equal Variance
Commission	0.00	26.47	4,627.00	0.00***	3.19	Equal Variance
		35.65	190.49	0.00***	3.19	No Equal Variance

Tables 27, 28, 29:
Results of Hypothesis 1 for Different Asset Management Strategies

We find that even though means are different for electronically traded products compared to OTC, these differences from asset management strategies do not disturb the overall observation. Evidently, the strategy does not yield sufficient value for investors to allow for more than a minimal fee independently of the distribution fee. However, for all other strategies that engage in slightly or strongly active management the picture looks different. Alternative investment funds can command significantly lower premiums for electronically traded products on a cost (commission) base but interestingly not so on a spread base for the issuing institutions. Only in the case of non-equal variance, a 95% confidence in different spreads could be found, whereas results for commissions are significant on a 99% interval irrespective of the variance distribution assumptions. The results are similar for more mainstream products. Again, the highest significance is reported on a commission basis, where the total fees differ from 5.78% in traditional markets to 2.56% in electronic environments. As the difference is not displayed at the market-front (commission), but only internally (spread) there is room for some arguments with respect to the management cost of maintaining one or the other strategy: for instance, trading cost could be higher with increasing sophistication of the managed assets, eating into the margins of the issuer. However, with the exception of the low-cost environment in money market funds, the first hypothesis – stating no difference in cost between exchange forms – can be dismissed. This supports the well-established theory with respect to the 'electronic market hypothesis' (MALONE et al., 1987) and the expectation for a disintermediation process on the industry level. However, the result is in clear contrast to the observed market reality, i.e. the tremendous over-representation of OTC traded products. What are the implications of these patterns with respect to the electronic market discussion? Based on the second hypothesis we analyze, therefore, whether it could be one of the attributes of mutual funds (beside the form of trading) to favour OTC so clearly and at a measurable cost disadvantage. The correlation analysis (Table 30) shows the corresponding patterns. We grouped not only the direct patterns of the mutual funds but also the various cost components to check for linkages.

We found first of all that size is rather irrelevant with respect to the cost base, contrasting general assumptions with respect to economies of scale. However, size correlates positively with the degree of complexity (i.e. the number of classes) and the degree of standardization in a fund, implying that these two patterns in combination with large funds allow appropriating an above average part of the value created by any investment strategy. Furthermore, OTC traded funds are significantly larger in terms of net asset value than electronic market traded products. In contrast, higher fund complexity also mirrors keener custom tailoring of products. Thus, increasing complexity correlates positively with new money inflows into a product, independently of the fund's past performance. High new money inflows, however, also increase product liquidity. We can thus argue that the driver behind total commission is the effect of liquidity on issuance and redemption fees. Where these fees are held relatively low, in- and outflows are consequently more frequent than in fee structures that are more restrictive. Another pattern can be seen around the business model discussion. Integrated banks seem to prefer offering products with greater complexity and higher turnover in managed accounts. This can be seen as either a discretionary management decision to expand income in other business units (e.g. trading) in a less transparent setting, or as a greater tendency to tailor classes to suit the needs of particular clients, which ultimately expands the number of share classes per fund.

After analyzing correlation patterns among the market characteristics, we test for the grouping power of these patterns for either electronic trading or OTC. We do so by means of discriminant analysis on the basis of a step-wise grouping process. However, prior to the discriminant analysis we perform univariate tests of the grouping variables (Table 31) and then span the scope of our analysis factor-wise towards a multivariate setting that reflects our second hypothesis and the main mutual fund characteristics as defined in SYVERSON AND HORTACSU (2004).

Our analysis points out that the strongest impact on the choice of the distribution model is the liquidity of the products, followed by spread, past performance, standardization and issuer (see Table 33). Using these patterns, it is possible to group 96.3% of the total sample correctly for trading form. These results confirm significant levels obtained in the course of the canonical functions. When assessing which factors increase the probability for a mutual fund to be traded electronically, we find similar evidence as discussed in the correlation analysis. Liquidity spread size and past performance are already significant when looking for patterns that allow us to classify for electronic market versus OTC traded products. As seen in the correlation analysis, spread size and past performance thereby do not have additional explanatory power, as the first may be a functionality of distribution choice and the latter a driver for liquidity, which in itself is already an important factor. Beside product patterns, the role of the issuer is noteworthy here. It seems that the probability of being traded electronically alters – independently of product features, when the funds are set up by certain issuers. This may reflect pricing and distribution strategies of these issuers. It appears that there is no competitive or electronic market hypothesis driven choice to use the cheaper distribution channel, but rather the choice is made first at the discretion of the issuer and second, based on product characteristics. There is no evidence for electronic markets fostering higher transparency and price competition in the observed market.

Correlation Matrix		NAV 2007	Fund Complex	Standardization Dummy	In-/Outflow after Performance	Turnover of existing fund shares/
Size (NAV 2007)	**Correlation**	**1.00**	**0.00**	**0.02**	**-0.02**	**-0.01**
	Significance (2-tailed)	.	0.90	0.18	0.13	0.36
Stucture (Fund Complex)	**Correlation**	**0.00**	**1.00**	**0.08**	**0.01**	**0.05**
	Significance (2-tailed)	0.90	.	0.00***	0.32	0.00***
Standardization Dummy	**Correlation**	**0.02**	**0.08**	**1.00**	**0.00**	**-0.06**
	Significance (2-tailed)	0.18	0.00***	.	0.88	0.00***
In/Outflow after Performance	**Correlation**	**-0.02**	**0.01**	**0.00**	**1.00**	**0.02**
	Significance (2-tailed)	0.13	0.32	0.88	.	0.14
Turnover of existing fund shares/	**Correlation**	**-0.01**	**0.05**	**-0.06**	**0.02**	**1.00**
	Significance (2-tailed)	0.36	0.00***	0.00***	0.14	.
Liquidity	**Correlation**	**0.00**	**-0.07**	**-0.02**	**0.01**	**0.67**
	Significance (2-tailed)	0.94	0.00***	0.11	0.44	0.00***
Commission (annual)	**Correlation**	**0.00**	**-0.01**	**-0.02**	**0.00**	**0.03**
	Significance (2-tailed)	0.86	0.43	0.18	0.83	0.02**
Min. Trade Lot	**Correlation**	**0.00**	**-0.01**	**-0.02**	**0.00**	**-0.02**
	Significance (2-tailed)	1.00	0.47	0.09*	0.98	0.16
Issuance Fee	**Correlation**	**0.00**	**-0.01**	**0.02**	**0.01**	**0.10**
	Significance (2-tailed)	0.84***	0.46	0.30	0.62	0.00***
Redemption Fee	**Correlation**	**-0.01**	**0.10**	**-0.01**	**0.01**	**-0.03**
	Significance (2-tailed)	0.44	0.00***	0.52	0.60	0.05**
12b/Distribution Fee	**Correlation**	**0.00**	**0.02**	**0.03**	**0.01**	**-0.06**
	Significance (2-tailed)	0.73	0.14	0.07*	0.68	0.00***
Cost fo a Transaction	**Correlation**	**-0.02**	**0.07**	**0.02**	**0.00**	**0.16**
	Significance (2-tailed)	0.18	0.00***	0.12	0.93	0.00***
BusinessModel (BM)	**Correlation**	**0.00**	**-0.02**	**-0.07**	**0.01**	**0.01**
	Significance (2-tailed)	0.94	0.15	0.00***	0.47	0.68
Spread	**Correlation**	**-0.01**	**0.07**	**-0.01**	**0.00**	**0.09**
	Significance (2-tailed)	0.60	0.00***	0.57	0.73	0.00***

Control for:	Issuer #	Sign. Level	90% indicated by * 95% indicated by ** 99% indicated by ***
Observation (n) / df:	4734		

Table 30: Correlation Analysis of Product Patterns

Liquidity	Commission (annual)	Min. Trade Lot	Issuance Fee	Redemption Fee	12b/Distribution Fee	Per New Transaction	BM	Spread
0.00	**0.00**	**0.00**	**0.00**	**-0.01**	**0.00**	**-0.02**	**0.00**	**-0.01**
0.94	0.86	1.00	0.84	0.44	0.73	0.18	0.94	0.60
-0.07	**-0.01**	**-0.01**	**-0.01**	**0.10**	**0.02**	**0.07**	**-0.02**	**0.07**
0.00***	0.43	0.47	0.46	0.00***	0.14	0.00***	0.15	0.00***
-0.02	**-0.02**	**-0.02**	**0.02**	**-0.01**	**0.03**	**0.02**	**-0.07**	**-0.01**
0.11	0.18	0.09*	0.30	0.52	0.07*	0.12	0.00***	0.57
0.01	**0.00**	**0.00**	**0.01**	**0.01**	**0.01**	**0.00**	**0.01**	**0.00**
0.44	0.83	0.98	0.62	0.60	0.68	0.93	0.47	0.73
0.67	**0.03**	**-0.02**	**0.10**	**-0.03**	**-0.06**	**0.16**	**0.01**	**0.09**
0.00***	0.02**	0.16	0.00***	0.05**	0.00***	0.00***	0.68	0.00***
1.00	**0.00**	**-0.02**	**0.09**	**-0.14**	**0.00**	**0.03**	**0.11**	**-0.06**
.	0.92	0.17	0.00***	0.00***	0.89	0.03**	0.00***	0.00***
0.00	**1.00**	**0.00**	**-0.03**	**-0.01**	**0.02**	**0.02**	**0.03**	**0.00**
0.92	.	0.80	0.04**	0.59	0.15	0.12	0.08*	0.79
-0.02	**0.00**	**1.00**	**0.01**	**0.03**	**0.02**	**0.02**	**0.02**	**0.00**
0.17	0.80	.	0.67	0.08*	0.09*	0.21	0.09*	0.77
0.09	**-0.03**	**0.01**	**1.00**	**-0.49**	**-0.11**	**0.68**	**0.04**	**0.00**
0.00***	0.04**	0.67	.	0.00***	0.00***	0.00***	0.00***	0.88
-0.14	**-0.01**	**0.03**	**-0.49**	**1.00**	**-0.06**	**0.20**	**0.01**	**0.00**
0.00***	0.59	0.08*	0.00***	.	0.00***	0.00***	0.59	0.82
0.00	**0.02**	**0.02**	**-0.11**	**-0.06**	**1.00**	**-0.08**	**-0.01**	**-0.03**
0.89	0.15	0.09*	0.00***	0.00***	.	0.00***	0.59	0.02**
0.03	**0.02**	**0.02**	**0.68**	**0.20**	**-0.08**	**1.00**	**0.05**	**0.01**
0.03**	0.12	0.21	0.00***	0.00***	0.00***	.	0.00***	0.63
0.11	**0.03**	**0.02**	**0.04**	**0.01**	**-0.01**	**0.05**	**1.00**	**-0.06**
0.00***	0.08*	0.09*	0.00***	0.59	0.59	0.00***	.	0.00***
-0.06	**0.00**	**0.00**	**0.00**	**0.00**	**-0.03**	**0.01**	**-0.06**	**1.00**
0.00***	0.79	0.77	0.88	0.82	0.02**	0.63	0.00***	.

Univariate Discriminant Tests

Analysis Case Processing Summary

Unweighted Cases	N
Valid	4,736.00
Missing or out-of-range group codes	0.00
At least one missing discriminating variable	21.00
Both missing or out-of-range group codes	0.00
Total	4,757.00

Tests of Equality of Group Means

	Wilks' Lambda	F	df1	df2
Issuer #	1.00	13.12	1.00	4,734.00
Fund Complex	1.00	0.32	1.00	4,734.00
Standardization Dummy	0.99	29.07	1.00	4,734.00
NAV 2007	1.00	0.65	1.00	4,734.00
Past Performance	1.00	0.99	1.00	4,734.00
Total Commission	1.00	3.78	1.00	4,734.00
Spread	1.00	3.54	1.00	4,734.00
Liquidity	1.00	9.42	1.00	4,734.00
Strategy	1.00	0.64	1.00	4,734.00
Business Model	1.00	0.01	1.00	4,734.00

Table 31: Univariate Discriminant Tests

Canonical Analysis

Function	Eigenvalue	% of Variance	Cumulative %	Canonical Correlation
1	0.02	100.00	100.00	0.12

a. First 1 canonical discriminant functions were used in the analysis.

Wilks' Lambda	Wilks' Lambda	Chi-square	df	Sig.
1	0.98	74.22	5.00	0.00

Standardized Canonical Discriminant Function Coefficients

Issuer #	-0.39	***
Standardization Dummy	-0.61	***
Perfomance t-3	0.68	***
Spread	0.32	***
Liquidity	0.88	***

Table 32: Univariate Test and Canonical Discriminant Analysis

Analyzing the results, especially the outcome of the first hypothesis test may be explained by inertia. Even though the cost advantage of electronic markets is measurable, traditional markets prevail, which might indicate that it takes more time for market structures to adjust, as competition is probably not sufficiently intense yet. However, not only the observed market's feature as one of the most dynamic financial markets (KHORANA et al., 2005) sheds doubt on this explanation but even more so the results from observing the various product patterns and their interaction with the trading form. Additionally, similar arguments could be found when reading about the situation prior to electronic markets; so, already in the 1960's, excessive mutual fund fees and the absence of price competition allegedly persisted because: (1) investment advisors did not compete for contracts to manage mutual funds; (2) advisors controlled the boards of directors of mutual funds, protecting advisors against dismissal and giving boards very little independent power to contest the fees charged to shareholders; and (3) advisors denied investors' transparency on the fees they were paying (COATES AND HUBBARD, 2006).

Stepwise Discriminant Analysis

Step	Entered	Wilks' Lambda	df1	df2	df3	Exact F-Statistic	df1	df2
1	Standardization Dummy	0.99	1.00	1.00	4,734	29.07	1.00	4,734
2	Issuer #	0.99	2.00	1.00	4,734	19.67	2.00	4,733
3	Liquidity	0.99	3.00	1.00	4,734	17.33	3.00	4,732
4	Past Performance	0.99	4.00	1.00	4,734	16.89	4.00	4,731
5	Spread	0.98	5.00	1.00	4,734	14.96	5.00	4,730

At each step, the variable that minimizes the overall Wilks' Lambda is entered.
a. Maximum number of steps is 20.
b. Minimum partial F to enter is 3.84.
c. Maximum partial F to remove is 2.71.
d. F level, tolerance, or VIN insufficient for further computation.

Step	Number of Variables	Wilks' Lambda	df1	df2	df3	Exact F-Statistic	df1	df2
1	1.00	0.99	1.00	1.00	4,734	29.07	1.00	4,734
2	2.00	0.99	2.00	1.00	4,734	19.67	2.00	4,733
3	3.00	0.99	3.00	1.00	4,734	17.33	3.00	4,732
4	4.00	0.99	4.00	1.00	4,734	16.89	4.00	4,731
5	5.00	0.98	5.00	1.00	4,734	14.96	5.00	4,730

Table 33: Stepwise Discriminant Analysis

Classification Results

Classification Processing Summary

Processed		4757
Excluded	Out-of Range	0
	Missing	1
Used in Output		4756

Prior Probabilities for Groups

Market Dummy	Prior Unweighed	Cases Used in Analysis
0	0.96	4563.00
1	0.04	173.00
Total	1.00	4736.00

Classification Function Coefficients

Market Dummy	0	1
Issuer #	0.02	0.02
Standardization Dummy	6.17	5.59
Past Performance	-0.09	-0.05
Spread	66.40	132.64
Liquidity	-0.03	0.09
(Constant)	-11.06	-12.31

Predicted Group Membership

		0	1
Count	0	4581.00	2.00
	1	173.00	0.00
%	0	99.96	0.04
	1	100.00	0.00

a. 96.3% of original grouped cases correctly classified.

Table 34: Classification Results

These arguments clearly point towards the idea of integrated banks that systematically leverage upon their relational ties in the mutual fund market, their existing (large) retail customer base and their other business units, such as securities trading, whilst upholding non-transparent product markets (low standardization and high complexity) and (CHORDIA, 1995) fee structures. Supply and demand of customized relational classes seem to go beyond the cost aspects of the sole transaction process. This marks an apparent difference between products traded OTC compared to products traded on electronic exchanges. As we showed, both the variance of the product patterns and the respective influence of variables on spread levels are significantly different for the two exchange forms. Clearly, theory tells us that electronic markets are more transparent (BAKOS, 1991, 1997; GROVERI AND TENG, 2001) than opaque OTC trading. This should apply equally for commission and spread awareness. For instance, COPELAND AND GALAI (1983) point out that increased information and transparency directly reduce bid-ask spreads in financial markets. Although marketing or relational and performance expectation factors might have an influence on lowering such effects (WALDFOGEL AND CHEN, 2007), reported differences are systematic and significant. Furthermore, results from earlier studies (HORTACSU AND SYVERSON, 2004) indicate that even under homogenous performance expectations (in his case for S&P-500 index funds) fees paid by investors vary strongly. There is clear evidence that large players earn rents from non-transparency in pricing structures when distributing OTC instead of using electronic markets. Given the results, two potential arguments can be thought of, namely product patterns or industry structures.

The first explanation for this puzzle is grounded on product pattern observation and states that OTC trading does not primarily reflect higher cost of distribution but is much more a customized way of product issuance. In this line of argumentation, mutual funds would not be treated as secondary financial markets, but each buyer of a fund would constitute a primary emission of a new tranche. That is especially relevant where larger buyers dominate markets and where complex fund classes are effectively produced for customized trading (e.g. with respect to taxation issues), hence demand-driven and not necessarily (commission) cost-sensitive (LESSEIG, LONG AND SMYTHE, 2002). The remaining, less customized, plain-vanilla tranches of a tailor-made issuance might then be sold through the same OTC channel to retail clients, irrespective of price considerations. This is due to the fact that marginal fund charges for an additional plain-vanilla class of a tailor-made complex class are close to zero (COATES AND HUBBARD, 2006; KARCESKI et al., 2004).

The second explanation is based on electronic market characterization. In line with (PHILIPP O'REILLY AND FINNEGAN, 2005), it might be sensible to rethink the construct of an electronic market for mutual funds. Whilst BAKOS (1997) emphasizes the function of markets to aggregate, to match suppliers and customers, to provide trust and interorganizational market information, current electronic market places may not yet live up to these demands. In most electronic supermarkets or exchanges, a function to aggregate buyers and amalgamate their large and heterogeneous demands into negotiation power is not yet given (WILLIAMS, 2000). Even more so, if we adapt the concepts used by DAI AND KAUFFMANN (2002), or more explicitly by SOH AND MARKUS (2002): Value proposition, product-market focus, value activities, ownership and market structure. It appears that existing electronic marketplaces are not yet able to create value, and hence offer a value proposition, in the mutual fund market. Accordingly, OTC-tailoring dominates the market despite a cost disadvantage. This may only change if products traded OTC and via electronic markets become more comparable in terms of either their properties or their fees structures. Also, electronic trading platforms need to add clear value propositions, for instance by aggregating (retail) customers' demand more efficiently than the relationship-based process in OTC trading. For the time being, search costs remain too high for retail investors compared to the direct access afforded to large investors to traditional distribution networks. Similar results can be taken from evidence in mutual fund marketing in Scandinavia (KNUUTILA, PUTTONEN AND SMYTHE, 2006).

Conclusion

In this chapter we discussed the idea that the use of ICT lowers transaction cost in a system and we applied these assumptions to the mutual fund market as an exemplary case for trading financial products on electronic markets. In a second step, we did not expand the discussion towards market disintegration as in previous studies, but rather attempted to answer the question why disintermediation and electronic trading might not (yet) dominate the industry space despite its clear cost advantages. We found clear differences in product patterns between products that are traded on traditional channels and those solely traded electronically. The choice for or against a distribution system is heavily influenced by the issuer of a product and directly links to an issuer's distinct pricing and distribution policies. Alternative dominant patterns are liquidity, standardization and the strategies applied. Looking more closely at the interrelation of these product patterns, especially at the 'complexity of a fund structure', the number of different fund classes is significant, which means that products traded OTC and products traded on electronic channels are effectively different. We expanded this observation towards a discussion of whether electronic marketplaces might currently lack a clear value proposition compared to traditional exchange forms.

With respect to financial products, our results not only give insights into the structure of the mutual fund industry but might also be interesting for understanding structures on other secondary markets such as credit derivatives and structured credit. Traditional markets did not exist for these products, with electronic trading being the prevailing market form. However, even in these new markets, hybrid structures have been emerging lately that indicate a tendency to trade complex structures off the electronic platforms in alternative, relationship-intense trading forms. Given the results from the empirical analysis discussed here, it would seems important that electronic platforms are able to add value and find substantial value propositions to prevent complex trading from moving into club-markets. This is especially important as complex product patterns lead to less cost transparency and trigger inefficient markets, which is a regressive step in market development.

With respect to electronic markets, we conclude, following the central argument in this paper, that the transition from one exchange form to another is not driven by added value due to technological innovations (such as the Internet), but by shifts in product patterns and value propositions within these product offerings. The key value proposition of mutual funds to most investors seems not to be just a risk-return relationship but a customized way to meet diversification, management and cash flow structure goals (e.g. with respect to taxation), which is achieved by customized class formation. A firm issuing mutual funds can capture this customization value more effectively by engaging in hierarchical structuring and trading of the products. Thus, even if transaction cost may be reduced, mere cost considerations are not strong enough to shift competitive boundaries, because the issuer captures the boundaries' value in the customization process and has no competitive pressure to reduce or change its transaction cost base. For electronic markets the observation also implies that it is not primarily the standardization of products that fosters electronic markets but transactional value that stipulates standardized products. This leaves room for predictions for trading other innovative asset classes such as credit, insurance and other financial product innovations. Also here, the products' value propositions lie primarily in offering distinct cash flow structures. As long as market participants have no incentive to cut execution cost in structuring deals, transactional elements such as electronic trading places will be of minor importance for the overall volume traded.

8 Operational Risk Perspective: Governance Across the Widening Disintermediation Gap

In the previous chapters, we discussed the dynamics of the mutual fund markets and elaborated on potential break lines in the industrial architecture. In this context industrial dynamics have a two-fold implication: First, they pinpoint the fundamental building blocks and emphasize dependencies of processes from capabilities in times of change, which can define the boundaries of a firm under changing environments. Second, by the very action of redefining these firm boundaries, dynamics at industry level starts to re-balance established value distributions and aligned organizational set ups. This leads sometimes to value migration across the value chain, but almost in every case to new intermediary markets that emerge at the former process interfaces. Such new markets urge for a change in the process-flow: Whilst previously the processes were monitored by hierarchies and shaped by transaction cost perspective, markets force entities to move towards the use of price as the main factor, not only for allocation, but also for governance. As control shifts, the nature and perception of operational risk changes along. By moving towards markets, firms forego some of their ability to get actively involved in the traded services. Cost and time of intervention increases as information is not following the intra-firm interfaces anymore, but is spreading beyond efficient hierarchical structures towards inter-firm markets. This generally leads to the notion (and perception) of intermediary markets such as processes outsourcing, as being more risky. Explicitly, the shift in management approach increases operational risk and the move to markets adds – to some extent – market risk as a new issue to be managed. On the other hand, however, increasing depths of markets over time are one factor that can clearly reduce operational risk per firm, as the real-options to change (not only when prices are too high, but also where quality does not live up to expectations) are becoming more valuable to the firm's risk management.

In the mutual fund industry, disintermediation has not yet really seen what people expected only a few years ago in terms of disintermediation. Despite an increasing awareness for some elements of decoupling, e.g. with respect to white-labeling processes in mutual fund set up, and the fact that a number of larger banks have (partially) opened their platform, the complex and large operational block that links product origination and distribution remains so far monolithic. Certainly, there is the offer of most of the larger firms to insource part of these services, furthermore, there exist a number of large international players in the field, e.g. StateStreet, but most small and mid-sized market participants continue to rely on inhouse solutions for virtually everything. Nevertheless, as in times of crisis demand side pressure tends to invert established value chains at a higher pace, this situation could face change soon enough.

Now, assuming that the process of disintermediation got started, what is the relevant decision base for these firms? Should they simply team up with the large international players or should they look for a more custom-tailored solution? There are two main elements in drafting an answer on this: Scale and risk. Whilst size in operations certainly is a key factor that allows technology investments, standards and efficient handling, risk is a more subtle concept. In disintermediation most firms often quote first the risk of becoming dependent of a (larger) partner who basically is competing on the product side, whilst he is offering services to third parties on the operational level. Second, more directly, there is operational risk involved. As soon as processes have to be opened, they change from in-house processes towards inter-firm interfaces. A side effect of this is higher information requirements, clearer rules and a non-fully controllable handling as soon as the activity arrives in one's partners' facilities. To some extent the risk can be managed by drafting clear and transparent agreements (SLAs), nevertheless, literature generally agrees that operational risk increases along distintermediation of industries in general (ZAIRI, 1997).

There is up to today no measurable evidence for the mutual fund industry. Low-profile cooperation in white-labeling or in limited opening of distribution platforms in large international firms could hence only be tracked with case study designs and not yet measured in a more systematic approach. In order to complement our earlier works with evidence for guiding strategies and concepts to handle arising challenges, we rely on a related industry. We observe a set of reactions and the management of these processes based on small entities' decisions in Swiss retail banking. Swiss retail banking is still in an early stage of disintermediation and finds itself confronted with comparable problems in defining cooperation: Large dominant players that are competing vis-à-vis smaller entities in an industry that is clearly sensitive to economies of scale. We therefore assume that the lessons to be learnt are comparable, mainly due to the similarity in trends and legal requirements, just as well as in shifts in market structure (large incumbents who dominate the market and offer selected sourcing opportunities). One field where lessons can be learned is outsourcing governance. The impact can be illustrated by a short quote: „Outsourcing success – it's all in Governance" reported LAUREN BIELSKI in the ABA Banking Journal (2006) and indeed the examination of outsourcing has been a domain of IS research, as well as of strategy research for several years now. Thereby it focused on the following three fields: Why should a company outsource?, What should it outsource? And how should it outsource? (GELLINGS, 2007). Our research aims at contributing to the third question as to the issue of how to outsource, which is closely related to governance of outsourcing. The article is strongly linked to the 40-Hawaii Conference Proceeding on Outsourcing Relationships. Whilst the focus there was on the 'how to do' of outsourcing, such as the structuring of the relationship and subsequently the management of arrangements (Gellings, 2007), we shall focus on a specific form of outsourcing (business process outsourcing), and group the management of observed business outsourcing initiatives along four modes of governance. The focus will thereby not be on operational issues such as the right contract clauses, but rather on the appropriate ownership and governance structure in a BPO (business process outsourcing) agreement. We measure the expected rigor of this governance mode by market reaction on the announcement, and contrast the findings to executive's observed practice. Backed by expert interviews, we discuss the question as to whether and why difference in governance mode is perceived differently by the market, and how this might link into the future practice of outsourcing in business process management. The main argument is that the nearer outsourcing services are to the market, the lower the cost from a governance point of view. Pushing this idea to the limit leads to the notion of traded services as an emerging trend.

The key contribution of this chapter is to present a governance mode framework that allows discussing recent outsourcing agreements in the Swiss retail banking industry, respectively the lack thereof, when compared to expert-predictions, and to link the findings to implications for business process outsourcing in practice.The remainder of the paper is organized as follows: Section two will sketch the conceptual scope and present the key definitions before introducing the existing theoretical background. In section three and four, we present the base cases and the method applied, whilst section five discusses the results and conclusion.

Background

The chapter bases its argument on previous findings on outsourcing and governance, and places them into the context of business process management (BPM-)practice. Speaking with Zairi (1997), BPM is concerned with all aspects of business operations where there is high leverage and potential for added value. Processes therefore have to be modeled and managed, whilst performance has to be measured. Following an outsourcing decision, these processes have to be newly defined and proper performance metrics must be installed. This is to ensure an undisrupted workflow and a stable operational risk environment. This role is attributed to the BPO-governance. The general importance of governance structure within any outsourcing relationship has already been emphasized by various researchers (CLARK, ZMUD AND MCCRAY, 1995; DAVIS, 1997; DIBBERN, GOLES, HIRSCHHEIM AND JAYATILAKA, 2004). These researchers identify agency problems as underlying cause for potential disruptions and stress that an efficient relationship management with a well-organized governance structure is an important success factor to attain expected benefits. For example, CLARK, ZMUD AND MCGRAY (1995) explicitly state that the "truly critical success factors associated with successful outsourcing are those associated with (vendor) governance". GELLINGS (2007) consequently showed that the important tool therefore is to be seen in contracts as management tools meant to align interests and minimizing agency costs; thus forming the primary vehicle through which IS outsourcing relationships is governed in BP practice. However, existing literature on outsourcing relationship remains largely focused on this operational or contractual level of performance and risk control. It describes, analyzes and evaluates contractual clauses to monitor performance through e.g. Balanced Scorecards or specifically defined Key Performance Indicators (KPI's), and sets rules for an undisrupted workflow through clauses such as Service Level Agreements (SLAs), penalty reward systems, pricing, benchmarking, audits and more. LACITY AND HIRSCHHEIM (1993) or KERN AND WILLCOCKS (2000) provide a good and broad overview. Thus, BP-governance traditionally combines operational performance measurement and quality monitoring as a means to reduce contract-induced risks (REBERNIK AND BRADAC, 2006). Especially in the context of the banking industry, (operational) risk governance is a key driver, as it affects direct regulatory capital. This is either positive as risk is mitigated, or negative as an increased equity layer is required (AUBERT, PATRY AND RIVARD, 1998, 2001). Thus, successful outsourcing governance has the potential to influence not only operational performance, but also to leverage on the equity value. Several empirical studies have been conducted that illustrate this direct risk-performance relationship: HUNTON et al. (2000) analyzed a sample of 77 information systems IS outsourcing announcements (non-bank) between 1990 and 1997. They found evidence that capital markets react positively on the announcements, and abnormal returns were greater for smaller firms than for larger firms (defined by the market value). GLASSMAN (2000) examined 27 companies which undertook large information technology outsourcing initiatives between 1993 and 1999. He found an average gain in shareholder value of 5.7% over the general market trend, two months prior, to two months after the announcements. Based on the study by GLASSMAN (2000), ALBRIGHT (2003) extended the timeframe to cover a data set of 45 deals from 1993 until 2002. The effects were proven similarly positive. Another event study by FARAG, KRISHNAN (2003) examined purely information technology outsourcing deal announcements between January 1994 and August 2001. They concluded that capital markets react positively to IT outsourcings announcements of IT industry firms and service industry firms. They found positive market reactions to strategic sourcing projects, but not for cost-cutting projects. Similarly, Wonseok and GALLIVAN (2004) analyzed a sample of 97 information technology outsourcing deal announcements between 1998 and 2001. In contrast to prior research, they found only weak evidence with respect to investors' positive reaction to IT outsourcing announcements, but more specifically, they detected that abnormal returns are negatively associated with asset specifics, and with contract size. Whilst these results speak quite strongly in favour of outsourcing, a study by GILLEY AND RASHEED (2000) that focused on the effect of outsourcing of peripheral and near-core tasks on a firm's financial and non-financial performance displayed a different truth: They found no significant direct effect of outsourcing, but conclude that outsourcing interaction with corporate strategy suggests a positive performance. In this strategic sense, outsourcing agreements are meant as an instrument to coordinate less specific tasks for a firm's success with less capital and control costs, whilst at the same time ensuring undisrupted workflow with reduced transaction costs. The optimal degree of outsourcing governance is thus to be seen as an equilibrium between cost of capital intense equity stakes in the outsourcing agent, and efficiency oriented saving potential (LAUPER, 2005; MCIVOR, 2005). Direct transaction costs are also relevant with respect to the direct transaction process (LEE AND DALE, 1998).

To conclude these findings, it seems clear that there must be something in outsourcing that drives performance; if not outsourcing itself than some variable related to it. When focusing now on the specific case of retail banks, these results do have another implication: Apparently strategic relevance or specifics of assets and transaction size are important factors shaping future performance after striking outsourcing deals. Bearing in mind that outsourcing naturally inherits a great deal of risk, the capital markets are assumed to pay special attention to a combination of these issues. This led us to the focus of this research project: Do executives anticipate risks in the outsourcing deal (at least in line with other market participants)? Do those risks outweight the potential chances (e.g. higher earning potentials) arising from outsourcing initiatives? And are these judgments reflected by market prices and do they deviate?

We focused our discussion on the financial services industry, whereby we have taken a spechial look at banking and providers of services for banks. The industry seems especially valuable to the endeavour as there is a common assumption within the banking industry that the sector is at the eve of a substantial disintegration process of its value chain. Similar processes could earlier on be identified in the textile or in the automotive industry (BACHMANN AND LANCE, 2006).

Theory

As indicated in the background literature, outsourcing problems are understood mostly through transaction cost theory (McIvor, 2005), the resource-based view (Penrose, 1995) or agency theory (Jensen and Meckling, 1976). Whilst most previous set ups focused on one of the approaches, empirical evidence suggests that a combination of the factors might be of the highest explanation power (Gilley and Rasheed, 2000; Lee and Dale, 1998). In order to take into account these theories in practice, governance is in the BPM-context often discussed by applying a five axe concept proposed by the IT Governance Institute (ITGI) originally (Weil and Ross, 2005): This framework discusses governance along the dimensions of strategic alignment and value management (resource based view), performance and risk measurement (agency theory) and resource management (transaction cost theory). Given this framework, optimal governance should be expected to balance these five axes soundly. Accordingly, BPM practice focuses on structuring, managing and measuring outsourcing partnerships along these axes on the managerial level. Given equal strategic importance, executives would be expected to form governance decisions based on the parameters of transaction cost and risk. Risk thereby is controlled by the definition of scalable, standardized SLAs as indicated in Illustration 11. The number of partners involved in an outsourcing scheme is thus not relevant from a risk governing point of view; transaction costs are reduced, however at the expense of increased coordination cost which is in line with BPM practice. Holding equity ownership in the outsourcing partner should however not affect risk variables, but rather the transaction cost side. Ownership thus should be disentangled from governance.

When holding strategic relevance and SLA agreements on the operational level constant, a risk-control function such as ownership and the scope of the sourcing network can be described along the dimensions driving the implied costs: Transaction and information costs, dependent on the scales in a BPO agreement, or the number of participating firms, as well as coordination costs or more specifically overinvestment thereof. We sketch the first dimension along Joint-Venture structures (dyadic) to network structures, whilst the second dimension is modeled by equity ownership versus market coordination of the contractual agreements. The theoretical core of this paper's argument rests on agency theory assumption, which is asymmetric information in the ex-ante and ex-post stage of an outsourcing agreement. This theoretical framework has managed to shape the discussion on many problems having a cooperative structure (Eisenhardt, 1989, p. 57) successfully in the past. Particularly when discussing a field amidst risk and organization, such as outsourcing structures where the rich array of applications of the theory, allow drawing on as many facets of the corresponding literature. All decision patterns generally suffer from the classical three aspects: Moral hazard, Adverse Selection and Imperfect commitment as the client is faced with the problem to choose an agent (outsourcer), motivate and coordinate its decisions and behaviours with those of its own organization. Explicitly moral hazard is faced (EISENHARDT, 1989; JENSEN AND MECKLING, 1976). Adverse Selection occurs where principals cannot observe ex-ante the characteristics of its agents. It might therefore happen that outsourcing offers extremely competitive terms that lure a principle into a long term relationship despite the fact that the agent cannot sustain the promised services after a couple of years. Having out sourced in such a relationship could turn out for the principle to be costly. Operational risk of disruption in processes and transaction capabilities cease to run and eventually even put him out of the market. As governance methods such as ITIL or COBIT only manage in a BP-practice sense the ex nunc or ex post relationships, executive decisions are faced beyond managerial governance methods and at a higher degree of uncertainty. In this environment, risks are greater the more specific the outsourced service is. Having said that we acknowledge that the competitive environment in the business process outsourcing industry, as well as the ability to re-build out contracted services are two key intermediating factors for outsourcing relationships.

In this context, agency theory is of practical relevance in this decision-state in two ways: First, business process outsourcing (BPO) providers are positioning themselves in the market in a way to consciously signal certain governance features to potential customers. Secondly, especially banks, willing to outsource certain services employ agency theoretical considerations to choose the right partner. Therefore, executive's BPO decisions gain a meta-level dimension beyond operational SLA structuring. On this meta-level available information and expected cost factors are seen as the main decision factors and form the modes of governance framework. Viewing cooperation as information sharing implies the possibility of both the moral hazard and adverse selection. Cooperation needs to overcome asymmetric private information and to a requisite minimum of shared, common, public information (REBERNIK AND BRADAC, 2006). By choosing the combination of equity ownership to the number of outsourcing partners, they move within modes of governance. Interestingly, these two layers ex-ante and ex-post, respectively their attributes show interestingly entangled features. As a result of the analysis of the underlying cases, we found a strong correlation between equity-ownership and individual SLAs (where the two owners are the only participants in the agreement) and more standardized (multi-partner targeted) market solutions. In this paper we restrict focus on the meta-layer of governance, which is described by the ownership and membership structure rather than by SLA design (although correlations are evident). The market for outsourced contracting in the Swiss banking industry (as any market) can be described along the dimensions "dyadic" or "network based" and the traded services along the distinctions "near commodity" or "specific". In practice we observe the following: Banks out source specific services to partially equity controlled BPO's and near-commodity to more network or market based independent BPO's. In this framework, BPO initiatives display or change operational risk features of the underlying processes ex-ante in the form of management decisions, respectively market announcements. As risk is relevant for banks both as a means for uninterrupted service (GEWALD AND FRANKE, 2007) production as well as a major cost factor under the prejudices of general capital requirements, it is of high relevance both for executives as well as for the market to signal those risks ex-ante in a transparent way. Thus, outsourcing announcements help evaluating asymmetries in risk features more rigorously. Furthermore, operational risks can be lowered the more standardized the bank services are, and the easier the bank can switch suppliers, in case of service disruption. This allows the bank to mitigate partially the risk to the BPO service provider. In the context of outsourcing and asymmetric information, we assume that operational risk should be lower were banks source out on a standard way to BPO's that are replaceable – thus not equity controlled and within a market of alternatives and strong corporate governance schemes. We thus assume that an announcement for outsourcing has a stronger impact where the ex-ante expectation of good governance is high and where BPO provider offer services "at market" (with transparent pricing and standardized products). This is because a track record in a competitive environment signals good governance more credibly than a less transparent joint venture. One has to bear in mind that players in the financial service industry tend to be more risk averse than in other industries, be it through culture or through respective regulations. The thereby raised coordination and control costs, contrast with uncertainty in potential future gains from sourcing or from forming sourcing networks. In this environment, stringent corporate governance measurements can eventually stimulate the formation of new sourcing linkages as transparent, but where trust is enhanced and coordination costs are reduced. Thus risk adjustment of expected savings is an inherent part of the decision function for entering into BPO initiatives. If factors such as anticipated risk, contract size and other variables are to affect performance, one should assume that the respective data is also ex-ante considered by the responsible executives when forming an BPO initiative, as well as by markets, when evaluating the announced initiatives and adjusting stock prices accordingly to the (new) inherent firm value perception. Beside, risk features and asymmetric information strategy literature teaches us that only non-core processes have been sourced out. We take this to be true for this model as well (PHUSAVAT, CHAISAKUL AND TAKALA, 2005). We thus assume the decision function for entering into BPO initiatives to be defined by cost-benefits only at the highest level of aggregation. On a second layer, cost is to be seen as a variable, dependent of standardization of the process and monitoring, the inherent additional operational risk and the availability of efficient evaluators just as well as alternatives to switch to, in case of business disruption. This perspective reflects also the findings outlined in chapter 7. Furthermore, this decision is only true under the conditionality of non-uniqueness of the involved resources for the firm. One therefore can conclude that two dimensions are of interest for the evaluation of governance modes: Being "at market" with standardized and exchangeable products, or being part of a less transparent "club", most extremely a joint venture style outsourcer. Sources of operational costs associated with membership in certain modes of governance are frequently summarized under the term coordination cost, whilst sunk costs for the uprising or repositioning as such is ignored for the economic decision process (KUADA, 2002). We show that this optimization process results in stable governance schemes that contribute to the operational performance of the networks and thus may serve as a valuable instrument for risk management in sourcing decisions. Especially the scope of a sourcing partner broadens standardized procedures and corporate "network" governance mechanisms (KRAUT, STEINFIELD, CHAN, BUTLER AND HOAG, 1999), seem to be crucial to success. We therefore treat network scope versus dyadic interaction as the second dimension in the mode of governance scheme.

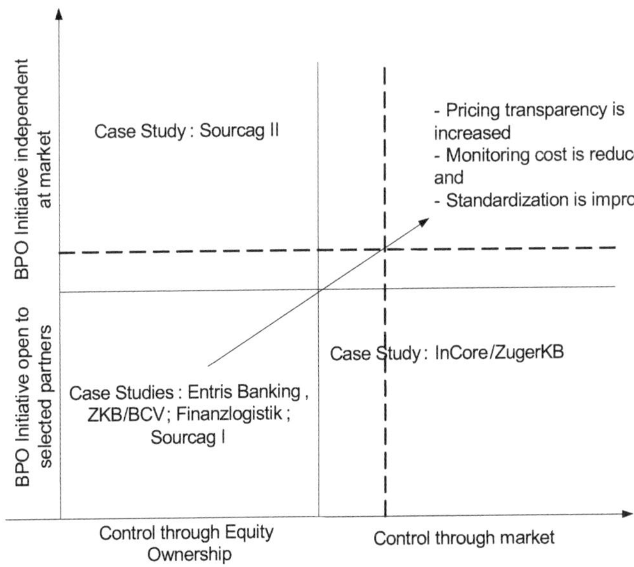

Illustration 11: Modes of governance for BPO Meta structures

When turning towards the more "hands-on" view of outsourcing processes one sees that BPO initiatives are set up on a meta structure – meaning an ownership and control layer rather than on the project management and operational control layer that is managed by the choice of optimal contract decisions and surveillance – normally designed as contractual agreements. This separation is not necessarily true for banks or other large out-contractors. In cases of large contract volumes or perceived barriers such as operational risk, one often observes that the subunits that were entrusted with the business process before the sourcing decision are, at least for some time, employed by the BPO provider to ensure smooth and undisrupted operations during the transition phase. Along the transfer of their employees and their processes, especially banks have been observed to take equity stakes in the provider firms (as it happened in most of the herein observed cases) in order to close asymmetric information induced gaps, and ensure that their risk management standards are met, as well as the service firms strategic objectives which later on can be altered along the banks positioning, thereby enhancing real options available. Such behaviour leads to either dyadic (one-to-one relationships) or network relationships. A mixed form is seen in constellations that are featured by a broad network, coordinated by an integrator company virtually offering turnkey business process outsourcing solutions to a wide set of customers. These three forms obviously can be characterized by different risk-return and different cost-return patterns. The potential gain from outsourcing is higher the more scale-sensitive parts of a value chain are sourced towards a reliable partner at low coordination and ongoing transaction costs, which is capable of extracting a maximum of value from the insourced processes. This again strengthens our concept of the governance mode dimensions "network or market" and "dyadic", but adds to others, namely whether to hold equity stakes or not after a completed BPO initiative.

To sum up, the theory is generally well developed when it comes to comparing governance modes shifts with respect to distinctiveness or specifics of a sourced resource, based on standards of strategy research (LACITY AND HIRSCHHEIM, 1993; PHUSAVAT et al., 2005; QUELIN AND DUHAMEL, 2003) on the ex-ante meta layer as well as through operational governance methods (PHUSAVAT et al., 2005; REBERNIK AND BRADAC, 2006). However, in the observed industry, business process sourcing announcements refer to identical and not strategic labelled services. On the other side, cost and risk factors are the decisive variables. Especially in areas with low added value per single transaction and high cost per transaction, the implied control costs are critical. Outsourcing here is walking on a thin line as the internal cost of coordination and control for an agreement soon might outweigh beneficial effects from scales and standardization. Thus, the nearer a BPO initiative is to market the lower the marginal internal cost for control and the higher the standardization is, which corresponds to lower weighted operational cost. The same is true for network relationships, which is why we identify the intersection "network at market" as the preferred mode of governance on the Meta frame for BPO initiatives.

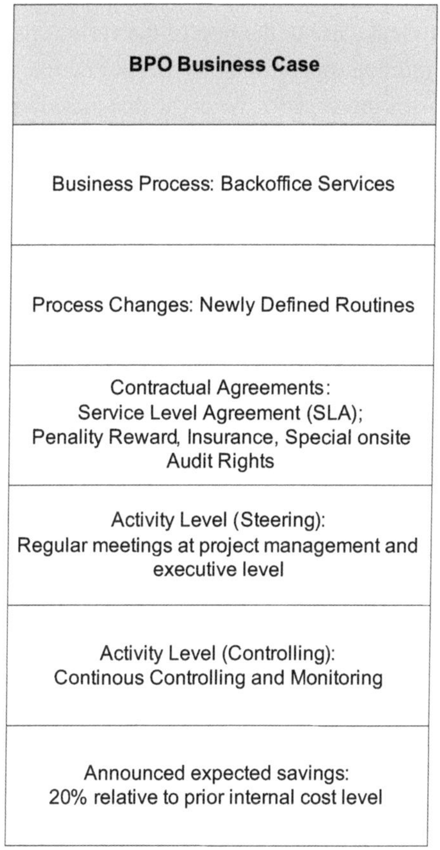

Illustration 12: Aligning interests based on contractual agreements: A uniform framework as applied identically in all observed BPO cases

These risks and their costs of monitoring are the critical factors allowing for business process outsourcing in banks. Once an optimal mode of governance is identified on the meta level (i.e. in the absence of unique resources, a market-based outsourcing relationship), one should expect it also to become the preferred choice when looking for a specific governance solution, independent whether it is assessed from a management or from a market' perspective.

Consequently, joint value creation is optimized wherever the underlying governance mode aligns best interest of all parties to generate maximum scale on a common platform, to make use to the best of the various partners different specializations and to minimize (operational) risk that emerge in any disintermediated production processes more easily. We argue that these conditions are met best in market oriented and network-based governance modes. Under these configurations, the group of partners is sufficiently large to build upon the benefits of size, the dependency is minimal and the task of coordinating the processes is allocated to the price function, reducing transaction cost to a minimum. Relationships that follow this setting should be judged superior to simple dyadic relationships and also superior to (costly) equity based means of control.

Research Method

This section explains our research approach that was based on expert interviews with CEO's and responsible project managers for BPO's in the Swiss retail banking industry and market data from the Swiss Stock exchange (SWX). We structured the analyzed cases along four modes of governance, previously identified through market observation and evaluated by expert interviews. We selected those cases based on the analysis of BPO announcing press releases for retail banks quoted at the Swiss stock exchange. We than selected the herein used sample of comparable BPO initiatives in terms of same sourced processes. We back tested those findings by questioning the experts at the initial phase of the interviews. Based on the broad literature available, we saw a positive relationship between outsourcing and performance as given at the onset. As we had a sample of cases that shared the basic characteristics in governance at the contractual level, and at the announced expected savings from the BPO initiative, we implicitly controlled for the relevant factors. We however did not control the size of the transaction, although WONSEOK AND GALLIVAN found evidence for this to be relevant (WONSEOK AND GALLVIAN, 2004). The reason for not controlling for transaction size was that in the given sample, the companies sourcing in the dyadic modes had always comparable size (in terms of assets, transaction volume and profit margin at time of the initiative's start). The only deviations from this homogeneity were seen in the cases "InCore" and "Sourcag II". Both represent unique positions in the governance mode scheme and are not directly compared to each other. It is to mention here that according to the interviews the homogeneity in expected savings stems exactly from the fact that the partners in transaction combined comparable volumes each time they announced a BPO initiative.

Having set up this framework as initiated in the theory part, we now start to test the market performance as a re-test to find positive outsourcing-announcement effects. Given such effects, we take it that the market has adopted the information and acts as a valid instrument for measuring the signalling effect of the different governance mode's perception (PHUSAVAT et al., 2005). We then move on to measure how the signalling of one or the other mode of governance to be applied did affect the respective stock's above-market performance. We measure above market performance by combining the stock-value appreciation at different points in time with a comparables benchmark. This benchmark is based on all the retail banks quoted at the Swiss stock exchange, except for the two largest UBS and Credit Suisse. These two were not included, since the Swiss retail business accounts for only a small part of the respective stock assets and valuation. Thus including them would clearly distort the results. We did not weigh the stock by their transaction volume, because the small sample of retail stock available compared to the observed cases would lead to distortions by the very effects to be measured. We knew that from every case analyzed, only one partner was quoted, and thus used this partner to indicate as a proxy sensitive to the BPO initiative's impact. Furthermore, all BPO initiatives were strategically relevant for the involved banks and gained considerable attention in the media. As the preconditions apart of governance mode were identical, our model set up suggests that out performance should be higher, the stronger the market supervision of a deal is, and the less equity ownership the out contracting partners had to commit. As we strongly based the theoretical body on agency theory, it is to bear in mind that in this context that agency theory virtually is split into two camps (JENSEN AND MECKLING, 1976) leading to differences in interpretation: On the one side BARNEY AND OUCHI (1986) argued that agency theory emphasizes how capital markets can affect the firm, whereas other authors made no reference to capital markets at all (EISENHARDT, 1989).

This paper adapted the prior view and used capital markets as an independent scale of measurement for outsourcing announcements. We tested both for "no above normal returns" of outsourcing companies compared to market, and for structural breaks in valuation before and after the deal announcement. The relationship should hold if measured for outsourcing effects as a whole and mainly also for the differences in the four modes of governance. We will test so for varying time windows:

First for the announcement date compared to one day prior (one announcement was on January 1, 2007; the respective dates for the calculation are December 29, 2006 and January 3, 2007 as these were the last and the next trading days). We re-ran the tests for the timeframe 3 days prior and after announcement, and 30 days prior and after announcement. At latest in the 3 day time frame the information should be worked in the price and over the pre and post 30 day frame, the valuation of the observed stock should display significant differences in valuation if the assumptions were to be correct.

Cases

The cases relevant for this project were the business project outsourcing initiatives of BCV (Banque Cantonale Vaudois) and ZKB (Zürcher Kantonalbank), RBA group and BEKB (Berner Kantonalbank), the two cantonal banks of Basle (Sourcag I), the extension of Sourcag I by means of acquiring additional customers at the market (Sourcag II) and the set up of InCore, a service bank established by the privately owned Maerki Baumann group with its customer Zuger Kantonalbank. The cases were largely identical by strategic objective and largely driven by scales in operations for unanimously not-strategic labelled back office functions. All cases involved the outsourcing of business services to a new provider that was, however, set up prior by the involved partners as a custom tailored, separate legal entity. The processes were not – as in non business process outsourcing usual – adopted from one of the partners, but rather redesigned from scratch. We therefore speak of business process outsourcing also in the dyadic-modes that otherwise might also be labelled joint ventures. The key difference is that the properties for BPO are met according to bmp.org definitions.

Empirical Support for the argument

Assuming that management is incentivized by capital markets, one should expect that not only reaction to outsourcing in general, but also the specific mode of governance applied, reflects in stock market reaction. We therefore observed stock market reaction at announcement date for all the different case studies. We relied upon an event study that follows tracks a singular event's announcement over a decreasing series of time windows (BENNER, 2007). Consequently we tested first, if the stock reaction at sourcing announcement positive (i.e. is there a significant outperformance of the market over a 3, 7 and 30 day event window). A positive announcement effect would be in line with the theory, however, it would not yet be an indication for governance choice, as positive effects can also relate to expectations on increased operational efficiency, i.e. cost savings. Therefore, we test in a second step whether there is any significant difference in the announcement effect of same governance groups, respectively, whether there is such a difference across modes of governance.

Due to the limited number of samples this cannot be a stable indication in itself, but may support executive interview and theoretical notions.

The empirical evidence as displayed in Table 36 and 37 confirms the basic argument. Outsourcing is seen positive in general, but the mode of outsourcing clearly displays differences. However, there is one important caveat required here: Even though the tests are stable with respect to the number of trades executed in the observed time windows, the number of "cases" per mode is too restricted to generalize the empirical findings. In this, one needs to continuously rely on theory and case study evidence.

Table 36: Announcement effects

Outperformance at Announcement

Event	Bank-Stock	Governance	Event	Mean Benchmark	Std. Deviation	z-Statistic	Critical z-Value	Decision
BCV/ZKB	BCV	Mode 1	-0.42%	0.57%	0.006	6.042	z>1.645	Reject Ho
Finanzlogistik	CA	Mode 1	0.02%	1.40%	0.008	7.133	z>1.646	Reject Ho
ENTRIS	BEKB	Mode 1	-0.49%	0.74%	0.016	3.026	z>1.647	Reject Ho
Sourcag II	KB BS	Mode 2	-0.13%	0.00%	0.005	1.945	z>1.648	Reject Ho
InCore	KB Zug	Mode 3	-0.13%	1.07%	0.008	5.501	z>1.649	Reject Ho
Sourcag I	KB BS	Mode 1	-0.22%	2.05%	0.012	7.606	z>1.650	Reject Ho

One-tailed Test; Level of Significane 5%; Number of trades: n = 15

Ho: The observed event of the sensitive bank at announcement date is not significantly different from the benchmark
Alternative Hypothesis: The stock of the sensitive bank did significantly outperform the market at announcement date
Decision rule: Reject Ho if test z > + 1.645

Outperformance over 3 days prior to 3 days post announcement

Event	Bank-Stock	Governance	Event	Mean Benchmark	Std. Deviation	z-Statistic	Critical z-Value	Decision
BCV/ZKB	BCV	Mode 1	0.30%	0.02%	0.005	-2.097	[-1.96; 1.96]	Reject Ho
Finanzlogistik	CA	Mode 1	0.15%	-0.25%	0.004	-4.303	[-1.96; 1.96]	Reject Ho
ENTRIS	BEKB	Mode 1	0.41%	-0.26%	0.004	-6.535	[-1.96; 1.96]	Reject Ho
Sourcag II	KB BS	Mode 2	0.34%	-0.21%	0.004	-4.840	[-1.96; 1.96]	Reject Ho
InCore	KB Zug	Mode 3	1.95%	-0.06%	0.006	-9.909	[-1.96; 1.96]	Reject Ho
Sourcag I	KB BS	Mode 1	1.12%	-0.78%	0.004	16.958	[-1.96; 1.96]	Reject Ho

Ho: The observed event of the sensitive bank at announcement date is not significantly different from the benchmark
Alternative Hypothesis: The stock of the sensitive bank did significantly outperform the market in time window [+/- 3]
Decision rule: Reject Ho if test $z > +1.645$

Outperformance over 30 days prior to 30 days post announcement

Event	**Bank-Stock**	**Governance**	**Event**	**Mean Benchmark**	**Std. Deviation**	**z-Statistic**	**Critical z-Value**	**Decision**
BCV/ZKB	BCV	Mode 1	0.29%	0.08%	0.005	1.546	[-1.96; 1.96]	Accept Ho
Finanzlogistik	CA	Mode 1	0.10%	-0.06%	0.004	-1.682	[-1.96; 1.96]	Accept Ho
ENTRIS	BEKB	Mode 1	0.18%	-0.06%	0.004	-2.246	[-1.96; 1.96]	Reject Ho
Sourcag II	KB BS	Mode 2	0.12%	0.15%	0.004	0.186	[-1.96; 1.96]	Accept Ho
InCore	KB Zug	Mode 3	0.21%	-0.15%	0.006	-2.163	[-1.96; 1.96]	Reject Ho
Sourcag I	KB BS	Mode 1	-0.06%	-0.33%	0.004	-2.372	[-1.96; 1.96]	Reject Ho

Two-tailed Test; Level of Significane 5%; Trades: $n = 95$

Ho: The observed event of the sensitive bank at announcement date is not significantly different from the benchmark
Alternative Hypothesis: The stock of the sensitive bank did significantly outperform the market in time window [+/- 30]
Decision rule: Reject Ho if test $z > +1.645$
Assumption: The Variance of Stock Prices are normally distributed at announcement date

Table 37: Difference in Modes of Governance

Difference in Equality of Means across Modes of Governance

Equality of Mean Mode 1 versus Mode 2	**Modal Change**	**Mean Benchmark**	**Std. Deviation**	**z-Statistic**	**Critical z-Value**	**Decision**
Scenario Announcement	0.48%	0.00%	0.006	-2.955	[-1.96; 1.96]	Reject Ho
Scenario 3 Prior/ 3 Post	0.49%	0.34%	0.005	-1.170	[-1.96; 1.96]	Accept Ho
Scenario 30 Prior/ 30 Post	0.13%	0.12%	0.005	0.002	[-1.96; 1.96]	Accept Ho

Equality of Mean Mode 1 versus Mode 3	**Modal Change**	**Mean Benchmark**	**Std. Deviation**	**z-Statistic**	**Critical z-Value**	**Decision**
Scenario Announcement	0.48%	1.07%	0.016	2.445	[-1.96; 1.96]	Reject Ho
Scenario 3 Prior/ 3 Post	0.49%	1.59%	0.004	10.639	[-1.96; 1.96]	Reject Ho
Scenario 30 Prior/ 30 Post	0.13%	0.21%	0.004	0.842	[-1.96; 1.96]	Accept Ho

Equality of Mean Mode 2 versus Mode 3	**Modal Change**	**Mean Benchmark**	**Std. Deviation**	**z-Statistic**	**Critical z-Value**	**Decision**

Scenario Announcement	-0.42%	0.57%	0.006	6.042	[-1.96; 1.96]	Reject Ho
Scenario 3 Prior/ 3 Post	0.02%	1.40%	0.008	7.133	[-1.96; 1.96]	Reject Ho
Scenario 30 Prior/ 30 Post	-0.49%	0.74%	0.016	3.026	[-1.96; 1.96]	Reject Ho

One-tailed Test; Level of Significane 5%; Trades n: 15; 36; 95

Mixed Evidence on the short term, but clearly signifiant different in means over a [+/- 30 day window]

Results and Discussion

We displayed the results by first addressing the insights from the expert interviews on the theory and the framework of governance modes, whilst than looking at the "facts" in the market through the capital market's lenses. We concluded by discussing the different views on BPO governance and the lessons for practice that could be drawn. Discussions during the executive interviews revealed that the experts generally agreed with both the idea of the split of governance into a Meta model of ownership and control layer, and an operational contractual layer as well as on the theoretical background and the structuring of the meta-governance along the four modes of governance. Interestingly enough, when speaking about positioning within these four modes of governance and future strategic initiatives for the outsourcing providers, there was some consent that the firms should and would move towards "market", although they strongly relied on their mostly dyadic outsets. This situation was explained mainly by two arguments: First, the (involved) experts brought forward the need to exert direct control in order to ensure the commitment with banking regulation and to cope with arising issues of operational risk management. Second, the executives indicated that so far, no market existed and as long as no one moved in this fourth preferred field of the governance matrix, the others would be trapped in their inferior positions.

If the first argument can be treated as somewhat contradicting to previously accepted theory and may be at least partially disguising the willingness or ability to reposition oneself, the second argument reminds of a game theoretical trap. However, if we refer to the case of InCore that has moved towards market, but failed to attract additional customers so far by this positioning we might remind ourselves of the result of Wonseok and Gallivan (2004) who stress the role of size in transactions. As in the dyadic transactions more or less equally sized partners met, InCore would most probably draw either smaller partners (in less favourable negotiation positions) or larger partners (with apparent pride on their systems) into an outsourcing agreement. Thus, in an environment (currently) shaped by strong margins, the pressure to re-position oneself with respect to business process outsourcing may not have been strong enough. However, with view to the modes of governance, one can conclude that the framework seems to hold, as well as the implied decision function for the executives. Quite in line with agency theory the story goes that risk can ex-ante be reduced best when closing the asymmetric boundaries with quasi-vertical equity control (Barney and Ouchi, 1986). However, when turning towards cost-risk relationships, realizing scales by attracting new partners, or even towards possible gains from diversification effects in the risk portfolio, the picture looks different. When asking executives on their decision prior to enter into BPO initiatives, the dominant answer is not "by means of strategic rigor", but rather by mere "cost-benefits analysis". However, if this were true, it might be hard to argue for the current market structure that can be observed in Switzerland or in other (European) countries. The dominance of strongly integrated entities is too obvious to be neglected (BACHMANN AND LANCE, 2006). When referring to strategic literature for structuring the discussion, the point was raised that outsourcing relationship and governance thereof generally focuses on core or non-core, respectively unique or commodity resources of a firm, which seems to be in clear contrast. We make the point that this contrast stems from the difference in the ability to mitigate risks through outsourcing agreements (on the equity respectively market dimension) and to minimize coordination and monitoring costs (on the dyadic, respectively network dimension). The signalling effect displayed when chosen one of the governance modes implied by these dimension has an impact on market evaluation of the goodness of the chosen strategy. We labelled capital markets the independent institution to assess the goodness of fit, of a certain form of outsourcing governance comparable to the discipline of capital market corporate governance on the intra-firm level of analysis. By applying the markets perspective, we found first of all evidence that the outsourcing announcement had a positive effect on the stock prices of the involved banks that were forecasted. This is quite in line with the previous findings in literature, as we had implicitly controlled for size and strategy (ALBRIGHT, 2003; BOUCHAIB AND RIVARD, 2003; BURRINGTON, 2007). Furthermore, we found that the positive reaction was stronger and more persistent in the cases of market solutions. When this issue was addressed in executive-level interviews, we received two alternative explanations: First of all, all officers agreed unanimously that in the current industry environment it is seen as standard procedure to take a stake in the outsourcer. The reasons executives gave This was reasoned for by indicating improved control means (only for the outsourcer taking a stake in the insourcer) and by a general thrive for independence of the involved banks in a stable and currently high-margin environment (all officers). Contrary to the first point, transactions at arms' lengths were commented on, as not stronger in terms of control rights compared to equity stakes. Furthermore, they saw the fact that banks continued to hold equity stakes in the insourcing providers as a reason for new potential customers not to join an existing partner, but rather to form a joint venture of their own. Thus, they saw besides operational risks, also future expected savings (in the form of forgone scale-effects) were at risk. In our opinion, a further argument has to be met with respect to press coverage after an outsourcing agreement. Certainly the joint venture of ZKB and BCV has found a broader audience than the Entris-deal, a matter of broadness of the involved partner's owner base. A similar argument could be true for the case of Zuger KB and InCore. However, stock market reaction at announcement date indicates that the signalling effect in fact is received by market participants, so why not by executives?

We find that executives clearly define a market – network mode of governance as the preferred position for their firm. This objective seems to be consistent with market expectation. However, managers are normally observed to move towards this position in practice. A possible reason could be seen in the fact that the move towards the market involves uncertainty that only can be overcome at high (information) cost, as long as the market does not exist. This however is contradicted by the positive market reaction to the InCore announcement. Outsourcing success does not seem to be directly linked to (contractual) ex-post governance methods. Results from both, market reaction as well as from executive objectives, hint towards a preferable position with lower cost and equal risk. In such a setting tight governance methods of hierarchical or equity-based control is reduced in favour of a more fluid surveillance scheme that is coordinated by the (near-)market. The market with such a concept also provides an additional feature of increased flexibility in terms of switching options for certain services. The lesson to be learnt for practice is therefore to build additional degrees of freedom by reducing switching costs in the market. As ex-ante uncertainty factors are equal to asymmetric information features in the agency theory, a means to reduce risks could be the broadening of public information by applying market functions as an efficient independent monitoring agency when signalled properly. Finally, market solutions foster standards that again reduce switching costs, and costs from disruption in the BP workflow. Consequently, all the interviewed companies agreed in stating that their primary objective is to move towards a market for processes. Accordingly, even Banks and BPO providers that today form dyadic joint ventures see their choices only as a first step towards such a market. We find that the capital markets to tight governance structures and equity stakes prefer this increased tradability of services. These results contradict well established concepts. Although governance probably still matters in BP outsourcing agreements, it might not necessarily be linked so firmly to success as BPM literature previously assumed. Especially the availability of public information is in this context a variable that has to be taken into account, especially as market solutions with low switching costs and high public information content appear to offset highly specific governing costs – making "tradable" processes a superior choice to bilaterally sourced processes.

9 A Conclusion from a Practitioners' Perspective

This thesis we discussed how changing market structures in the mutual fund industry can be understood, described and influenced. Firstly, we provided a short overview of the mutual fund industry, its basic structure, its value chain and its dominant processes that evolved along that value chain. Secondly, the nature and lines of argument of the industrial dynamics literature were presented. We used one of the concepts from this research tradition, the economics of entry, in order to observe how all the other aspects of the industry structure (e.g. the intra-firm level relations and the inter-firm interactions) connect and can be affected. This approach was underlined by a formal model and corresponding propositions.

To summarize, the model started with a basic and simplified cash flow function for a mutual fund provider that was placed in an environment with low barriers to entry at the product level and, a steady build-up of capacity with resulting characteristics of high sunkness that incumbent firms accumulate over time. This sunkness together with the relative cost of entry shapes the logic of the market. This market logic results in three basic roles to analyze entry and assess its marginal cost: the first role is played by incumbents with existing products, the second refers to newly launched products by incumbents and the third to the new products launched by ex-novo entrants. All these three roles obviously have to cope with different marginal cost to launch a new product. Besides, however, all products that could eventually been launched are easy to be copied and hence can largely be seen as commodities.

When an incumbent optimizes his position under these conditions, he can either do so by adjusting his product portfolio or by redefining its firms' boundaries along the vertical value chain. The vertical value chain is thereby closely interlinked with the capacity investments that have been committed to (some) of the links of the chain over time. At this point, we introduce a second aspect of asymmetry based on process-efficiency rooted in transaction economics and hierarchical control and developed routines and capabilities. We argue that management decisions can only influence the transaction cost lever (at least in the short and mid-term, which we cover with our data). Nevertheless, both these sources of differentiation are (asymmetrically) interlinked. This implies a strong integration of transaction cost and capability arguments and provides a strong theoretical argument for the corresponding organizational discussion (FELIN, ABEL 2008). Besides theoretical impact, however, it is also of practical relevance. For instance, a decision to increase the process capacity would always have a positive mediation (or feedback) effect on capability formation. This feedback effect would lead to advantages for industry players who rely on capability that finally make it easier to form proprietary capacity and guarantee a strategic advantage. Hence, we can argue that integrated incumbent have a stable advantage both in terms of process-efficiency as well as where it comes to new capability building.

When linking these two elements, we arrive at the basic model that guides this thesis. Incumbents profit (relatively) more from capacity expansion as they can appropriate value from the efficiency gains realized. With respect to capability expansion, the gains for incumbents are even higher, especially when talking about product origination capabilities. Here, increasing spillovers are combined with the relative lower cost of launching the products.

We assume therefore that incumbents might follow to basic strategies when facing the threat of (innovation based) new entry. If the likelihood of market disruption is low, a constant expansion of the product portfolio lowers also the potential entrant's cash-flow prospects and decreases the marginal cost of the tactical move by incumbents. Such gains can be realized in cases where the scope from platform effects can offset the loss from reduced economies of scope. The consequence is twofold: first of all, the minimum scales efficiency (MES) shifts steadily north and the industry structure settles at an equilibrium that would - under static assumptions - be sub-optimal in terms of economies of scale. According to this argument, the stronger the role of incumbents in the market historically has been, the lower the average scales should be today; and they are indeed, as a comparison of average funds under management between the U.S., Europe or Asia shows (Table 6, chapter 2).

Conclusion

The conclusion can be outlined by following the initial objectives of…

…one theoretical model to understand the market dynamics. Chapter 5 discusses the industrial organization and the multi-segment competition characteristics of the mutual fund industry. From a leading incumbent's organizational perspective, there is one dominant strategic response to each type of innovation. Grounded in the theoretical concepts of the seminal work of BAIN (1956), we show that different types (endogenous or exogenous) innovation erode different types of market barriers asymmetrically, and that asymmetry correlates with the fund-specific multi-market characteristics. This can be illustrated, when looking at different levels of management decisions in response to new competitors that are entering a market and that build their entry decision upon either specific

capabilities (or gradual innovation), or upon superior cost structures (capacity adjustments) in the aftermath of disruptive innovation events. In more classical terminology, management seems to link its decisions to horizontal diversification when dealing with gradual innovation and to vertical diversification when it is confronted by innovations that are more disruptive in nature. New markets and thus new business models are required to stay in the market in both cases. From a theory point of view, the key contribution is a joint model that captures both horizontal product decisions as well as vertical integration scope. Thereby, the connex of resource and process literature is stressed and used to mimic the influence on market disintermediation.

...one measurement framework for empirical work to track the dynamics. Here, we propose a measurement technique that meets the requirements of the characteristic of change assumed in our theoretical model. We build a measure based on evolutionary accounting for gradual or incremental innovation, and a measure based on mark-up spreads for discontinuous or disruptive types of change.

In this context, we first addressed the events under gradual innovation. The thesis relied on an application of evolution metrics as proposed by ANDERSEN (2004).We perform this analysis based on a sample from the Swiss Fund industry. Results suggest significant relationships to industrial change, especially when focusing on "specialization routines" and, on a conceptual level, when looking at the dynamic properties of the market environment. Therefore, this form of "evolution metrics" allows us to discuss economic problem sets and identify first evidence of break-lines along the joint process-capability building blocks of the industry architecture.

Second, we address the cases of disruptive innovation. We discuss the reasons for stickiness in the key bottleneck of the fund industry, i.e. its distribution function in chapter 7. We track the movement from exchange modes from over-the-counter (OTC) based exchange towards electronic markets for financial products. The transition is analyzed along the shifting cost structures per trade, measured by the implicit bid-ask spread (or the mark-up charged for access to the distribution network). The results indicate that certain product patterns facilitate, allow or constrain the effective transition towards electronic markets and products that remain in the OTC trading scheme, whereby the results also emphasized the role of network control for value appropriation. The key contribution was in the further developing of measurement approaches and in the empirical identification of building blocks or modules which form breaking lines for disintermediation and the evolution of new markets. The importance of network control that was put forward in the distribution network discussion is the focus of chapter 8.

Referring to developments in retail bank operations, we look at the challenge of bridging widening gaps in operational risk as disintermediation moves forward, and we evaluate different modes of governance to do so. The thesis concludes with a summary and an integrated framework to discuss the arising options from a management's perspective.

...*one application framework* for strategic discussions, we engage in a more practice oriented way of looking at the results.

A practice-oriented perspective

A practice-oriented perspective on mutual fund firm strategies, industry structure and accounts of competition unveils a number of problems that are observable in ongoing intra-firm rivalry and decreasing margins, despite (or better because) of a high growth rate of the overall industry (and low barriers to entry for standard products and easily copied investment strategies). Consistent with corporate strategy, the immediate consequence is that mutual funds lose ground in comparison to alternative (collective) investment schemes or even direct investments. This problem is accentuated as exchange fees for all investors are decreasing (driven by both stock market competition and the emergence of discount brokers), and hence, per unit cost of asset management and risk sharing (diversification) are gradually eroded. This reduction in trading and in the risk sharing cost lowers the incentive for potential customers to pay for management fees under collective investment schemes. In particular for standardized products that trade sufficiently liquidly and for which information flows are diffused efficiently. Skilled managers move towards the more risky and less liquid spaces. The result is that new forms of collective investments gain in prominence; the first type of emerging investment schemes are those that are designed for a more standardized asset management strategy and focus on executing simple (e.g. index-based-) strategies at the lowest cost. These products are often exchange traded (so called ETFs or exchange traded funds). The second answer to the challenge of the decreasing trading cost is to move into more sophisticated product categories. A typical phenotype that stands for this reaction are hedge-funds, which allow more discretionary trading in less liquid market environments, but allow for the involved management to justify the corresponding premium. In this environment, classical mutual funds seem to be confronted with a typical "stuck-in-the-middle" problem (MUELLER-STEWENS AND LECHNER, 2003).

Mutual fund market comparisons are often static and cannot credit this ongoing competition (COATES AND HUBBARD, 2006). But, from an industry perspective, the competitive notion is a challenge. Industry dynamics seem to push either towards low cost processing or high sophistication services. As the demand moves from balanced mutual fund products to specialist (cost or performance-based) services, so do the suppliers. An increasing number of boutiques are (re-)shaping the competitive landscape (KPMG, 2007) and offering distinct product or support services. This clearly has an impact on the incumbents' business models as well. The problem for the firms in the market is that without significant reshaping of their organization, the economic fundamentals do not seem to be as attractive as they were in the past. When summarizing the competitive dynamics even more, one can refer to a simple reconfiguration of established processes and trained routines might well jeopardize the very capabilities that formed the competitive advantages. The issue is to judge which capabilities have to be developed and retained in the first place, and where future investments should flow to in order to stay competitive as a firm. Is it an advantage to keep going with integrated solutions or should a switch towards certain steps of the value chain be considered? What are the consequences of such a separation for the different contributors throughout the mutual fund value chain? And after all – why not simply staying in the "middle" as this is a well-known ground?

In fact, there is certainly also a strong argument for staying in the "middle" as this market is not simply going to disappear or being replaced by ETFs, hedge funds or direct investments. The reason for this is simply regulations that keep traditional mutual fund strategies in the market. In legal terms, mutual funds and other forms of collective investment schemes are discussed either along a separation of customers or along a separation of product (types). These products are generally grouped in fund-families that consist of a group of products with similar asset strategies and a single fund advisor (Deutsche Bank, 2006). For the first ones, the basic difference is made between individual (retail) investors and institutional investors (Lakonishok, Shleifer, Vishny, Hart and Perry, 1992). This differentiation is important as legal provisions in most regulatory environments differentiate for so-called "qualified investors" and other investors. The qualification argument is bound to the notion of either "institutionalism", and direct or indirect supervisory through the financial authorities that are assumed to have an increased risk-taking capacity (Fischer and DenOtter, 2007). Accordingly, the products are grouped as being eligible for general or for selected investors only under collective investment regulations – or products that are not regulated, but only supervised under the corresponding legal frameworks. Investor (and investment) regulations do thus exert a strong influence on the boundaries of differentiation. This strength of the legal constraint forms the reason to also start discussions on drivers of change at both the firm and the industry level along the customer separation between qualified (institutional investors) and retail clients. The needs of the two groups can then be observed through the lenses of (increased efficiency) in the financial intermediation process, tailored to each segments' needs. The middle market here is very interesting because the bulk of the volume is managed here. However, to be successful, the industry logic has to somehow be turned towards a structure more comparable to that of the U.S. than to the European landscape. This means, firms in the middle have to turn away from building scope and platforms, and they must rely on reached sufficient economies of scales, e.g. through M&A activity. It is doubtful that this strategy will prove to be successful as long as the underlying dynamics of new entrants keeps determining the pace of competition.

From an industry practitioner's perspective, the whole idea of industry dynamics may be seen too theory driven. Nevertheless, some indication with respect to future directions in the industry development still needs to be provided, just the same as the distinction made between large integrated, large international, mid-sized and small content providers is required. The results of this thesis allow a preliminary framework to be drawn to discuss direction of change and potential impacts. However, it cannot provide the "one and only" solution, because firms are heterogeneous and, depending on their size, their financial capacities and their team's capabilities, they are bound in their decision-making. Nevertheless, we hope to provide a basic outline with this work. We graphically summarized our conclusions for this in table 13.

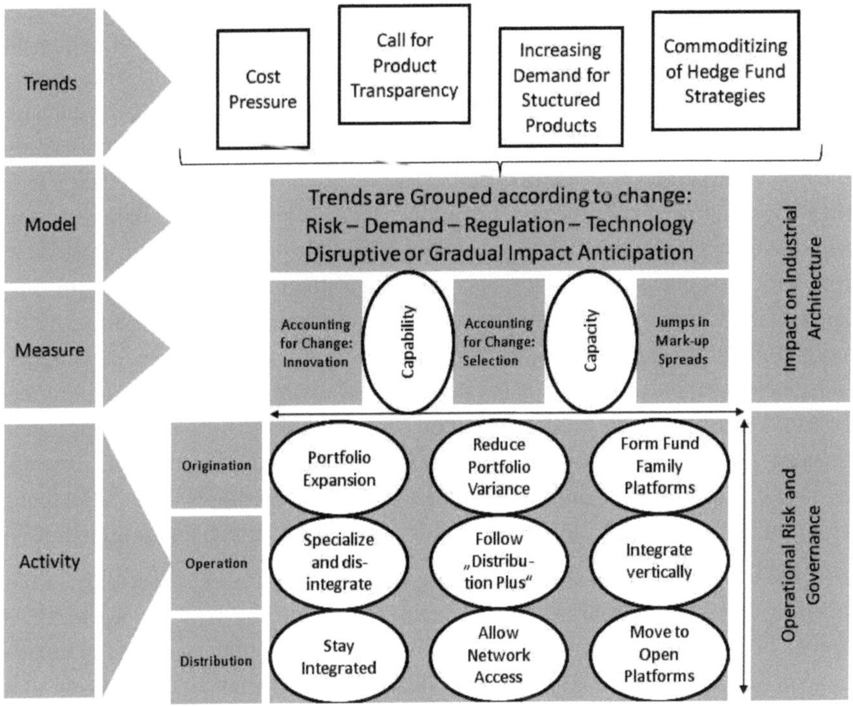

Illustration 13: An integrated Framework for Strategic Applications

As introduced, the model applied throughout the thesis and the corresponding measurement techniques developed can be used as guidelines when setting up a basic framework for decision-making in the mutual fund industry. With respect to application of the findings, there are two important contributions: first, the year-long discussion in the financial service industry can be institutionalized by expanding the horizon from a process and transaction perspective, which is in line with current discussions in the literature (JACOBIDES, 2008; NIGHTINGALE, 2008; WOLTER AND VELOSO, 2008) and second, the concepts allows a move beyond the theory into measuring some of the discussed aspects.

From a managerial perspective, the interesting point can be seen in the formation of joint building blocks that hold the strings of transaction cost oriented processes and innovative capabilities together. These building blocks can be seen in modular segments, mainly on the operational level of the value chain, and they are represented by modular fund family platforms that integrate (related) research and trading activity, but do not require proprietary support functions. Whilst this aspect corresponds largely to the very basic notion of "forming" comparative advantages by focusing on bundles of resources and capabilities, the clear emphasis on the process-capability node that basically calls for only building such advantages under the ex-ante constraint of efficiency primacy is new and will eventually also be industry specific. Nevertheless, an application of the concepts leads to some observations that are new and even puzzling. One driver for change that affects innovative capabilities on the product segment of the value chain and calls for increasing portfolio variance may at the same time urge the firms to close their distribution channels more rigorously and shield their exclusivity. The flip-side can be seen when assuming disruptive innovation, which is expected to result in more modular product design one the one end and in open platforms at the other end. The evolution of platforms is one key trend along the dynamic traits of the market. For example in fund distribution, the gradual opening up of traditional channels for instance led to a growing number of intermediaries (that fuel the platforms with new products and compensate the owner accordingly). We could think on a trend very much like this in the nexus of trading-research and origination.

In both redesigns of the architecture, the most interesting aspects lie in the "middle". For these firms, generally seen as being in the least favorable position in strategic management literature, the choice of available options is broadest. Simplified "advise" of reducing product portfolio variance, of engaging in a "product plus" focus when being confronted with gradual openings of the distribution platforms clearly lies at the heart of the idea of the emergence of industry networks. Within these network discussions, we found two elements to be most critical for success: First of all, it seems that depending on the pre-change setting (i.e. the capability and capacity endowment) of the incumbents affected, the options of change need not necessarily to point towards network concepts for all the covered parts of the value chain. Certainly, the key argument hereby will be made that disintermediation and focus along the value chain will be the first step to be taken. However, as our discussions showed this does not need to be true, as those processes that can be "cut" more easily during the disintermediation processes may often be closely interwoven with capabilities required for performing the one task in which the firms specialize. Local networks along the continuation of certain business (i.e. to some extent even duplication of processes) may in this context be a much more suitable and looked for alternative. This is even more true when looking at the second interesting implication – the widening of operational risk and the choices in governance that emerge. Along the four basic modes of governance discussed in chapter 8, it becomes clear that – despite theoretical supremacy – full network models that are traded at the market have a difficult standing in practice. One explanation for this might be found in the linkages between the different activities, another one, just in the absence of a sufficiently deep (in terms of trading one would say liquid) market for these services that would allow the switching of suppliers at low cost. For now, the role of "trust" and the importance of "similarity and adaptation" as a pre-condition for disintermediation/ network formation remain key issues according to the interviewed practitioners.

As the market dynamics gain in pace and the discussed trend towards platforms not only for distribution, but also towards asset management platforms (i.e. joint platforms or families for structured, fund, and base asset modules), the need for specialization, not only for certain modules, but even more so for distinct steps in the production field increase in importance. An initial move in this direction could be seen in the increased offerings of "white labeling" solutions by large incumbents to new entrants. In this context, one important remark may be that "execution has often been neglected in the past, or has not given the attention necessary as long as fees were high enough and structures not fully transparent". Apart of the field of operation, distribution channels will probably keep their importance. This will remain a constant fact becaue even under the assumption of technological disruption, most players seem not to have an incentive to move towards more open (e.g.) electronic platforms. The cost-benefit ratios for the small niche players are apparently insufficient, and it is no surprise that there is no incentive for the large incumbents to give up their traditional stronghold.

Summary

In summary, the key contribution of any thesis should be in line with the scientific objective that motivated the research. We expected to observe, classify and analyze the reaction patterns of mutual fund firms to different types of market innovation, and to use these findings to extend the contingency framework to design business strategies in this special field of financial services. Thus, we had three objectives: "Understanding", "Explaining" and "Influencing".

"Understanding": What is the industry structure in the mutual fund industry like? What are the drivers of competitive dynamics in the mutual fund industry? We outlined the basic logic of the industry and its structure in chapter 2. Based on the theoretical tradition of the industrial dynamics literature (chapter 4) and the industry structure, we concluded that the key driving dimensions of the financial service environment, namely demand, risk, technology and regulation, hold for mutual funds. Furthermore, we divided these effects according to their potential impact as incremental (resulting from gradual exogenous innovation) or discontinuous as (resulting from disruptive exogenous innovation).

"Explaining": How do firms react to innovation under this kind of competitive dynamics? How does this interplay affect market evolution in the mutual fund industry? Or how can industry structures (equilibria) be explained based on the presented theory? In order to meet the challenge of explaining the responsiveness of firms and the effects of change on industry architecture, we developed a basic model for the mutual fund industry in chapter 5. The key contribution of this model its ability to illustrate how process and capability functions can interact, but that this interaction is asymmetrical in nature. This effect influences the response sets depending on the type of innovation (but also depending on the resource and capability endowments prior to the innovation event). Based on this model, we explain distinct traits under the assumption of gradual or disruptive change. For a gradual innovation setting, there seem to be two main driving forces for industry dynamics. First, ownership of a sales network continues to be a critical element, facilitating the appropriation of value for the company that controls customer interfaces. Second, the fact that for independent companies, this customer interface can be accessed only by means of superior performance or capabilities, implies that these firms need to improve their innovation activity (which can be in product origination, but in fact also in operational execution). The need to finance these innovation activities can be argued to be a prime driver for a move towards low-capital intense efficiency improvements, i.e. the move towards platforms. For a disruptive setting, the key questions are for or against opening up an exclusive system. We find that this choice is strongly influenced by the characteristics of the products that are meant to be traded or distributed in the end. Beside aspects such as liquidity, standardization and basically product knowhow, the complexity (i.e. the modularity of share and share class structures are key elements. Furthermore, we could show that as a result of the economic logic in the market there are few reasons for the involved firms to respond to changing conditions by moving towards fully open solutions, simply because they cannot appropriate the additional value that might be saved through such a move.

"Influencing": What lessons can be learnt for strategy and policy formation? Both from a theoretical stance as well as for the distinct case of the mutual fund industry. With respect to "influencing", the contribution of the thesis can be found in the evaluation of modes of governance deemed suitable once intermediation processes get started. This result contributes both to theoretical discussions about optimal governance structures, as well as it hints towards difficulties in implementing such "optimal" solutions in everyday practice. Furthermore, we integrate the model and the empirical results into a joint framework. This basic framework can be used for discussion and may hopefully also influence the structuring of strategic options in mutual fund firms.

References

ABELL, P., FELIN, T., AND FOSS, N. J. (2008). Building micro-foundations for the routines, capabilities, and performance links. Managerial and Decision Economics, 29(6), 489–502.

ABERNATHY, W. J., AND CLARK, K. B. (1985). Innovation – mapping the winds of creative destruction. Research Policy, 14(1), 3–22.

ABERNATHY, W. J., AND UTTERBACK, J. M. (1988). Patterns of Industrial Innovation. In M. L. Tushman and W. I. Moore (Eds.), Readings in the Management of Innovation (pp. 25–36). New York: Harper Business.

ABIRU, M., NAHATA, B., RAYCHAUDHURI, S., AND WATERSON, M. (1998). Equilibrium structures in vertical oligopoly. Journal of Economic Behavior and Organization, 37(4), 463–480.

ADMATI, A. R., AND PFLEIDERER, P. (1990). Direct and indirect sale of information. Econometrica, 58(4), 901–928.

AGARWAL, R., AUDRETSCH, D., AND SARKAR, M. (2008). The process of creative construction: Knowledge Spillovers, Enterpreneurship and Economic growth. Paper presented at the 25th Celebration Conference 2008.

AGHION, P., AND HOWITT, P. (1992). A model of growth through creative destruction. Econometrica, 60(2), 323–351.

AGHION, P., AND HOWITT, P. (1998). Endogenous Growth Theory. Cambridge, MA.: MIT Press.

ALBRIGHT, C. (2003). Outsourcing for Outsized Gains. Marakon Associates.

ALLEN, F., AND SANTOMERO, A. M. (1998). The theory of financial intermediation. Journal of Banking and Finance, 21, 1461–1485.

AMIT, R., AND SCHOEMAKER, P. (1993). Strategic assets and organizational rent. Strategic Management Journal, 14, 33–46.

ANDERSEN, E. S. (1991). Schumpeter's Vienna and the Schools of Thought. Aalborg University.

ANDERSEN, E. S. (1996). Theories of Localised Resource-Based Growth and Development: From Marshall to New Evolutionary Economics. Paper presented at the Regional Development Based on Forest Resources: Theories and Practices, Joensuu.

ANDERSEN, E. S. (2003). A note on Price's equation for evolutionary economics: Deviation, interpretations, and simple applications.

ANDERSEN, E. S. (2004). Evolutionary econometrics: From Joseph Schumpeter's failed econometrics to George Price's general evometrics and beyond. Paper presented at the Economic Transformation of Europe (ETE).

ANDERSEN, E. S. (2004a). Evolutionary Econometrics: From Joseph Schumpeter's Failed Econometrics to George Price's General Evometrics and Beyond. DRUID.

ANDERSEN, E. S. (2004b). Evolutionary econometrics: From Joseph Schumpeter's failed econometrics to George Price's general evometrics and beyond. Paper presented at the Economic Transformation of Europe (ETE).

ANDERSEN, E. S. (2004c). Population Thinking and Evolutionary Economics Analysis: Exploring Marshall's Fable of Trees.

ANDERSEN, E. S. (2006). Appraising Schumpeter's "Essence" after 100 Years: From Walrasian Economics to Evolutionary Economics.

ANDERSON, S. P., AND ENGERS, M. (2005). Participation Games: Market Entry, Coordination and the Beatiful Blonde. CEPR Industrial Organization Paper, DP5241.

ARIEW, A., AND LEWONTIN, R. C. (2004). The Confusions of Fitness. British Journal of Philosophy, 55, 347–363.

ARNOLD, S. J. (1983). Morphology, Performance and Fitness. Journal of Theoretical Biology, 23(2), 347–361.

ATTESLANDER, P. (2000). Methoden der empirischen Sozialforschung (7th ed.). Berlin [a.o.]: deGruyter.

AUBERT, B., PATRY, M., AND RIVARD, S. (1998). Assessing the Risk of IT Outsourcing. Proceedings of the 31 Hawaii International Conference on System Sciences.

AUBERT, B., PATRY, M., AND RIVARD, S. (2001). Managing IT Outsourcing Risk: Lessons Learned. Cahier du CReSI, 01(11), 10–21.

BACHMANN, R., AND LANCE, C. (2006). Vertrauen in Macht in zwischenbetrieblichen Kooperationen. In J. Sydow (Ed.), Management von Netzwerkorganisationen: Gabler.

BAIN, J. S. (1956). Barriers to new competition, their character and consequences in manufacturing industries. Cambridge, MA.: Harvard University Press.

BAKOS, Y. (1991). A Strategic Analysis of Electronic Marketplaces. MIS Quarterly, 15(3), 295–310.

BAKOS, Y. (1997). Reducing Buyer Search Costs: Implications for Electronic Marketplaces. Management Science, 43(12), 1676–1692.

BAKOS, Y. (2001). The emerging landscape for retail e-commerce. The Journal of Economic Perspectives, 15(1), 69–80.

BALDWIN, C. Y. (2008). Where do Transactions Come From? Modularity, Transactions, and the Boundaries of Firms. Industrial and Corporate Change, 17(1), 155–195.

BALDWIN, J. R., AND GORECKI, P. K. (1989). Measuring the Dynamics of Market Structure: Concentration and Mobility Statistics for the Canadian Manufacturing Sector. Annales d'Economie et de Statistique, 15/16, 315–332.

BARNEY, J. B. (1986). Types of Competition and the Theory of Strategy: Toward an Integrative Framework. Academy of Management Review, 1(4), 791–800.

BARNEY, J. B. (1989). Asset stocks and sustained competitive advantage – a comment. Management Science, 35(12), 1511–1530.

BARNEY, J. B. (1991). Firm resources and sustained competitive advantage. Journal of Management, 17, 99–120.

BARNEY, J. B. (1991). Strategic factor markets: Expectations, luck and business strategy. Management Science, 32, 1231–1241.

BARNEY, J. B. (1991a). Firm resources and sustained competitive advantage. Journal of Management, 17, 99–120.

BARNEY, J. B. (1991b). Strategic factor markets: Expectations, luck and business strategy. Management Science, 32, 1231–1241.

BARNEY, J. B., AND OUCHI, W. G. (1986). Organizational Economics. San Francisco: Jossey-Bass.

BATIZ-LAZO, B. (2007). Competitive effects of IT Innovation on Bank Strategy: 1985–1995. RePEc Archive.

BÁTIZ-LAZO, B., AND WOOD, D. (2002). An Historical Appraisal of Information Technology in Commercial Banking. Electronic Markets, 12(3), 192–205.

BAUM, J. A. C. (1996). Organizational ecology In S. R. Clegg, C. Hardy and W. R. Nord (Eds.), Handbook of organizational studies (pp. 77–114). Thousand Oaks, CA.: Sage.

BAUMOL, W. J., PANZAR, J. C., AND WILLING, R. D. (1982). Contestable Markets: An Uprising in the Theory of Industry Structure. American Economic Review, 72(1), 1–15.

BAUMOL, W. J., PANZAR, J. C., AND WILLING, R. D. (1982). Contestable Markets: An Uprising in the Theory of Industry Structure. American Economic Review, 72(1), 1–15.

BENNER, M. J. (2007). Financial market reactions following technological discontinuities: a non-event study in two industries. Industrial and Corporate Change, 17(1), 109–154.

BENSLIMANE, Y., PLAISENT, M., AND BERNARD, P. (2005). Investigating Search Costs and Coordination Costs in Electronic Markets: A Transaction Costs Economics Perspective. Electronic Markets, 15(3), 21–224.

BERGER, A. N., DEMSETZ, R. S., AND STRAHAN, P. (1999). The consolidation of the financial service industry: Causes, consequences, and implications for the future. Journal of Banking and Finance, 23, 135–194.

BERGSTRESSER, D., CHALMERS, J. M., AND TUFANO, P. (2004). Assessing the costs and benefits of brokers in the mutual fund industy. Havard Business School and University of Oregon.

BERK, J., AND GREEN, R. C. (2004). Mutual Fund Flows and Performance in Rational Markets. Journal of Political Economy, 112(6), 1269–1295.

BERNET, B. (2003). Institutionelle Grundlagen der Finanzintermediation. München: Oldenbourg.

BERNET, B. (2006). Marktevolution und Marktarchitektur im Firmenkreditgeschäft. BIT, 1, 23–32.

BESANKO, D., DRANOVE, D., SHANLEY, M., AND SCHAEFER, S. (2003). Economics of Strategy. New Jersey: Wiley.

BIELSKI, L. (2006). Outsourcing – its all in Governance. ABA Banking Journal, 3, 12–21.

BINDEMANN, K. (1999). Vertical integration and incentives to innovate. International Journal of Industrial Organization, 21, 457–488.

BONACCORSI, A., AND GIURI, P. (2001). The long-term evolution of vertically-related industries. International Journal of Industrial Organization, 19, 1053–1083.

BOOT, A. W. A., AND SCHMEITS, A. (2005). The competitive challenge in banking. Amsterdam Center for Law and Economics.

BORENSTEIN, S. (1989). Hubs and High Fares: Dominance and Market Power in the U.S. Airline Industry RAND Journal of Economics, 20, 344–365.

BORENSTEIN, S. (1992). The evolution of airline competition. The Journal of Economic Perspectives, 6, 45–74.

BOTHER, M. S. (2003). Competition and social influence: The diffusion of the sixth generation processor in the computer industry. American Journal of Sociology, 108, 1175–1210.

BOUCHAIB, B., AND RIVARD, S. (2003). The information technology outsourcing risk: a transaction cost and agency theory-based perspective on Decision Sciences and Management Information Systems. Journal of Information Technology, 18(3), 211–221.

BRANDON, R. N. (1990). Adaptation and Environment. Princeton: Harvard University Press.

BRESSER, R. K., ESCHEN, E., AND MILLONING, K. (2001). Internet-Banking verdirbt Filialbanken das Geschäft. Harvard Business Manager.

BUEHLER, S., AND SCHMUTZLER, A. (2005). Asymmetric Vertical Integration. Advances in Theoretical Economics, 5(1).

BUEHLER, S., AND SCHMUTZLER, A. (2008). Intimidating competitors – Endogenous vertical integration and downstream investmient in successive oliopoly. International Journal of Industrial Organization, 26(247–265).

BURRINGTON, P. R. H. (2007). Commercial implications of operational risk for service-based contracts. BT Technology, 18(3), 58–67.

BURT, R. S. (1992). Structural holes: The structure of competition. Cambridge, M.A.: Harvard University Press.

CACCIATORI, E., AND JACOBIDES, M. G. (2005). The Dynamic Limits of Spezialization: Vertical Integration Reconsidered. Organizational Science, 26(12), 1851–1883.

CARHART, M. M. (1997). On Persistence in Mutual Fund Markets. Journal of Finance, 52(1), 57–82.

CARROLL, G. R. (1985). Concentration and Specialization: Dynamis of niche width in populations of organizations. American Journal of Sociology, 90(6), 1262–1283.

CARROLL, G. R., AND HANNAN, M. T. (2000). The demography of corporations and industries. Princeton, NJ.: Princeton University Press.

CARROLL, G. R., AND SWAMINATHAN, A. (2000). Why the microbrewery movement? Organizational dynamics of resource partitioning in the American brewing industry after Prohibition. American Journal of Sociology, 106, 715–762.

CARROLL, G. R., BIGELOW, M., SEIDEL, D., AND TSA, L. (1996). The fate of De Novo and De Alio producers in the American automobile industry. Strategic Management Journal, 17, 117–138.

CARROLL, G. R., DOBREV, S., AND SWAMINATHAN, A. (2002). Organizational Processes of resource partitioning. Research in Organizational Behaviour, 24(1), 1–40.

CETORELLI, N., AND GAMBERA, M. (2001). Banking Market Structure, Financial Dependence and Growth: International Evidence from Industry Data. Journal of Finance, 56(2), 617–648.

CHALMERS, J. M., EDELEN, R. M., AND KADLEC, G. B. (2002). On the Perils of Financial Intermediaries Setting Security Prices: The Mutual Fund Wild Card Option. The Journal of Finance, 56(6), 2209–2236.

CHANCE, D. M., AND FERRIS, S., P. (1991). Mutual fund distribution fees: An empirical analysis of the impact of deregulation. Journal of Financial Services Research, 5(1), 25–42.

CHEN, I. (2005). Vertical Disintegration. Journal of Economics and Management Strategy, 1, 209–233.

CHEN, Y. (2001). On vertical mergers and their competitive effects. RAND Journal of Economics, 32, 667–685.

CHERKES, M., SAGI, J., AND STANTON, R. (2008). A Liquidity-Based Theory of Closed-End Funds. Review of Financial Studies.

CHIPTY, T. (2001). Vertical Integration, market foreclosure, and consumer welfare in the cable television industry. American Economic Review, 91, 428–453.

CHORDIA, T. (1996). The structure of mutual fund charges. Journal of Financial Economics, 41, 3–39.

CHOU, R. K., AND CHUNG, H. (2004). Decimalization, Trading Cost, and Information Transmission between ETFs and Index Funds.

CHRISTENSEN, C. M. (1997). The Innovator's Dilemma: When New Technologies Cause Great Firms to Fall. Boston, MA.: Harvard Business School Press.

CHRISTENSEN, C. M., JOHNSON, M. W., AND RIGBY, D. K. (2002). Foundation for Growth: How to Identify and Build Disruptive New Businesses. MIT Sloan Management Review, 43(3).

CHRISTENSEN, C. M., VERLINDEN, M., AND WESTERMAN, G. (2002). Disruption, Disintegration, and the Dissipation of Differentiability. Industrial and Corporate Change, 11(5), 955–993.

CLAESSEN, S., AND LAEVEN, L. (2004). Waht drives banking competition? Some international evidence. Journal of Money, Credit and Banking, 36(3), 563–583.

CLARK, T. D., ZMUD, R. W., AND MCCRAY, G. E. (1995). The outsourcing of Information Services: Transforming the Nature of business in the Information Industry. Journal of Information Technology, 10, 221–237.

COASE, R. (1993). The Nature of the Firm. Oxford: Oxford University Press.

COASE, R. H. (1937). The nature of the firm. Economica, 4, 386–405.

COATES, J. C., AND HUBBARD, G. R. (2006). Competition and Shareholder Fees in the Mutual Fund Industry: AEI American Enterprise Institute o. Document Number)

COATES, J. C., AND HUBBARD, G. R. (2006). Competition and Shareholder Fees in the Mutual Fund Industry: Evidence and Implications for Policy. American Enterprise Institute for Public Policy Research.

CONSOLI, D. (2005). Changing boundaries and structure of a technological system: Lessons from UK Retail Banking.

COPELAND, T. E., AND GALAI, D. (1983). Information Effects on the Bid-Ask Spread. The Journal of Finance, 38, 1457–1469.

CYERT, R. M., AND MARCH, J. G. (1992). A Behavioral Theory of the Firm (Second ed.). Cheltenham: Wiley-Blackwell.

D'AVENI, R. (1999). Strategic supremacy through disruption and dominance. Sloan Management Review, 40(3), 127–135.

DAI, Q., AND KAUFFMANN, R. J. (2002). Business Models for Internet-Based B2B Electronic Markets. International Journal of Electronic Commerce, 6(4), 13–30.

DAVIS, K. J. (1997). IT Outsourcing Relationships: An Exploratory Study.

DELL'ARICCIA, G., IGAN, D., AND LAEVEN, L. (2008). Credit Booms and Lending Standards. IMF Working Paper in Draft Form.

DENOTTER, M. (2007). Fondsgeschäft und KAG. Swiss Fund Association (SFA).

DEUTSCHE BANK. (2006). EU Asset Management. Frankfurt: DB Research o. Document Number)

DEUTSCHE BANK. (2007). Industrialization of financial services. Frankfurt o. Document Number)

DIAMOND, A. M. (2007). Searching for Schumpeter in Amazon. Paper presented at the 34th Annual Meeting of the History of Economics Society.

DIBBERN, J., GOLES, T., HIRSCHHEIM, R., AND JAYATILAKA, B. (2004). Information Systems Outsourcing: A Survey and Analysis of Literature. The Data Base for Advances in Information Systems, 35(4), 60–102.

DIEKMANN, A. (1995). Empirische Sozialforschung. Reinbeck: rowohlts enzykopädie.

DIERICKX, I., AND COOL, K. (1989). Asset Stock Accumulation and Sustainability of Competitive Advantage. Management Science, 35(12), 1504–1513.

DIMSON, E., AND MUSSAVIAN, M. (1998). A Brief History of Markets and Efficiency. European Financial Management.

DIXIT, A. (1980). The role of investment in entry deterrence. Economic Journal, 90(1), 95–106.

DOPFER, K. (2005). The Evolutionary Foundations of Econmics. Cambridge: University Press.

DOSI, G. (1988). The nature of the innovation process. In G. Dosi, J. Freeman, R. R. Nelson, G. Silverberg and L. Soete (Eds.), Technical Change and Economic Theory. Brighton: Wheatsheaf.

DOSI, G., MALERBA, F., AND ORESNIGO, L. (1994). Evolutionary regimes and industrial dynamics. In L. Magnussen (Ed.), Evolutionary and Neo-Schumpeterian approaches to Economics. Boston: Kluwer Academics.

DOSI, G., NELSON, R. R., AND WINTER, S. (2001). Introduction: the nature and dynamics of organizational capabilities. In G. Dosi, R. R. Nelson and S. Winter (Eds.), Nature and Dynamics or Organizational Capabilities (pp. 1–21). New York: Oxford University Press.

DREZE, J. H., AND SHESHINSKI, E. (1984). On industry equilibrium under uncertainty. Journal of Economic Theory, 33(1), 88–97.

DUCA, J. V. (2001). The Rise of Stock Mutual Funds. Southwest Economy/ Federal Reserve Bank of Dallas, 2(1), 4–9.

DUFFY, J., AND HOPKINS, E. (2004). Learning, Information and Sorting in Market Entry Games: Theory and Evidence. Games and Economic Behaviour, 51(1), 31–62.

DWYER, P., OSTERLAND, A., CAPELL, K., AND REIER, S. (1998). The 21s century stock market. Business Week, August 10, 66–72.

DYER, J. H., AND SINGH, H. (1998). The relational view: Cooperative Strategy and sources of interorganizational competitive advantage. Academy of Management 23(4), 660–679.

EISENHARDT, K. M. (1989). Agency Theory: An Assessment and Review. Academy of Management Review, 14(1), 57–74.

EISENHARDT, K. M., AND MARTIN, J. A. (2000). Dynamic capabilities: what are they? Strategic Management Journal, 21, 1105–1122.

FARAG, N. I., AND KRISHNAN, M. S. (2003). The Market Value of IT Outsourcing Investment announcements: An Event-Study Analysis. AMCIS Proceedings 206.

FELIN, T., AND HESTERLEY, W. S. (2007). The Knowledge-based View, Nested Heterogeneity, and New Value Creation: Philosophical Considerations on the Locus of Knowledge. Academy of Management Review, 32(1), 195–218.

FERRIS, S., P., AND CHANCE, D. M. (1987). The Effect of 12b-1 Plans on Mutual Fund Expense Ratios: A Note. The Journal of Finance, 42(4), 1077–1082.

FISCHER, G., AND DENOTTER, M. (2007). KAG Atlas. Zurich: Niocolussi.

FISHER, J., AND HARINDRANATH, G. (2004). Regulation as a barrier to electronic commerce in Europe: the case of the European fund management industry. European Journal of Information Systems, 13, 260–272.

FISHER, R. A. (1958). The Genetical Theory of Natural Selection. New York: Dover Books on Biological Science.

FISHER, R. A. (1999). The genetical theory of natural selection: A complete Variorum Edition. Oxford: University Press.

FLIGSTEIN, N. (2001). The Architecture of Markets: An Economic Sociology of the Twenty-First Century. Princeton: University Press.

FORSGREN, M., HAGG, L., HAKANSSON, H., JOHANSON, J., AND MATTSON, L. G. (1995). Firms in Networks: A New Perspective on Competitive Power. Oxford: University Press.

FRANK, S. A. (1998). Foundations of Social Evolution. New Jersey: Princeton University Press.

FREIXAS, X., AND ROCHET, J.-C. (1997). Microeconomics of Banking. Cambridge, MA.: MIT Press.

FUDENBERG, D., AND TIROLE, J. (1984). The fat-cat effect. American Economic Review, 74, 361–366.

GAVETTI, G. (2005). Cognition and hierarchy; Rethinking the microfoundations of capabilties' development. Organizational Science, 16(6), 399–617.

GAVETTI, G., AND LEVINTHAL, D. (2004). The Strategy Field from the Perspective of Management Science: Divergent Strands and Possible Integration. Management Science, 50(10), 1309–1318.

GELLINGS, C. (2007). Outsourcing Relationships: The contract as IT Governance Tool. Proceedings of the 40th Hawaii International Conference on System Sciences.

GENTZOGLANIS, A. (2007). Technological and Regulatory Changes in the Financial Industry in the MENA Region: Competitiveness and Growth. Université du Québec à Montréal.

GERANIO, M., AND ZANOTTI, G. (2005). Can mutual funds characteristics explain fees? Journal of Multinational Financial Management, 15, 354–376.

GEROSKI, P. (1991). Market Dynamics and Entry. Oxford: Basil Blackwell.

GEROSKI, P., AND MASSON, R. (1987). Dynamic market models in industrial organization. International Journal of Industrial Organization, 5, 1–14.

GEWALD, H., AND FRANKE, J. (2007). The risk of business process outsourcing: a two-fold assessment in the German banking industry. International Journal of Electronic Finance, 1(4), 420–441.

GHOSHAL, S., AND MORAN, P. (1996). Bad for practice: A crititique of the transaction cost theory. Academy of Management Review, 21(1), 13–47.

GILLEY, M. K., AND RASHEED, A. (2000). MAking More by Doing Less: An Analysis of Outsourcing and its Effects on Firm Performance. Journal of Management, 26(4), 763–790.

GLASSMANN, D. (2000). IT Outsourcing and Shareholder Value. Stern Steward.

GLAUS, A. (1997). Anlagefonds – Typen, Funktionen und nationale Märkte. University of St. Gallen (HSG), St. Gallen.

GOEKE, C., AND GERSCH, M. (2007). Wertschöpfungstiefe und innovative Geschäftsmodelle am Beispiel des Bankensektors. Berlin: VDM Verlag.

GOETZMANN, N. W., AND MASSA, M. (2002). Index fund Innovations and stock market growth. Journal of Business, 3, 64–75.

GOODNIGHT, C., SCHWARTZ, J. M., AND STEVEN, L. (1992). Contextual Analysis of Models of Group Selection, Soft Selection, Hard Selection and evolution. The American Naturalist, 140(5), 743–761.

GRINBLATT, M., AND TITMAN, S. (1992). The Persistence in Mutual Fund Performance. Journal of Finance, 47(5), 1977–1984.

GROVERI, V., AND TENG, J. T. (2001). E-Commerce and the information market. Communications of the ACM, 44(4), 79–86.

GUPTA, A., KNOTT, A. M., AND HOOPES, D. G. (2005). Design of routines for replication. Paper presented at the SMS Meeting.

HAEMMERLI, H. (2003). Transformation und Herausforderungen der Fondsbranche. Private, 3, 36–37.

HAKANSSON, H., AND SNEHOTA, I. (1989). No business is an island: the network concept of business strategy. Scandinavian Journal of Management, 5(3), 187–200.

HAMILTON, W. D. (1964). The genetical evolution of social behavior. Journal of Theoretical Biology, 7, 1–16.

HAMMOND, P. J. (2007). Schumpeterian Innovation in Modellling Decisions, Games and Economic Behavior. Stanford University.

HANNAN, M. T., AND FREEMAN, J. (1989). Organizational ecology. Cambridge, M. A.: Harvard University Press.

HARVEY, M., AND RANDLES, S. (2002). Markets, the organization of exchanges and instituted economic process – an analytical perspective. ESCR Center for Innovation and Competition, University of Manchester.

HEISLER, L., AND DAMUTH, J. (1987). A method for analyzing selection in hierarchically structured populations. The American Naturalist, 130(4), 582–602.

HELFAT, C. E., FINKELSTEIN, S., MITCHELL, W., PETERAF, M. A., SINGH, H., TEECE, D. J., et al. (2007). Dynamic Capabilities: Understanding Strategic Change in Organizations. Boston, MA.: Blackwell.

HENDERSON, R. M., AND MITCHELL, W. (1997). The interactions of organizational and competitive influences on strategy and performance. Strategic Management Journal, 18, 5–14.

HESS, C. M., AND KEMERER, C. F. (1994). Computerized Loan Origination Systems: An Industry Case Study of the Electronic Market Hypothesis. MIS Quarterly, 251–265.

HILL, C. W. J. (1997). Establishing a standard: Competitive strategy and technological standards in winner-take-all industries. Academy of Management Executive, 11(2), 7–25.

HOFFMANN, M., AND MATTIG, A. (2009). From Organizational Economics towards Organizational Capabilities – An integrative Perspective. University of St. Gallen.

HORTACSU, A., AND SYVERSON, C. (2004). Product Differentiation, Search Costs, and competition in the mutual fund industry: A Case Study of SANDP 500 Index Funds. The Quarterly Journal of Economics(May), 403–456.

HOSKISSON, R. E., HITT, M. A., WAN, W. P., AND YIU, D. (1999). Swings of a pendulum: THeory and research in strategic management. Journal of Management, 25, 417–456.

HUANG, R., D., AND STOLL, H. R. (2000). Tick Size, Bid-Ask Spreads and Market Structure. Paper presented at the PACAP/FMA Conference.

HUNTON, J., RECK, J., AND HAYES, D. (2000). The Market's Reaction to Information Systems Outsourcing Announcements. Journal of Information Systems 14, 2, 109–125.

ICI. (1996). Mutual Fund Statistics for the Bank Distribution Channel. Washington: Investment Company Instituteo. Document Number)

ICI. (2007). Mutual Fund Statistics for the Bank Distribution Channel. Washington: Investment Company Instituteo. Document Number)

ICI. (2008). A Review of Trends and Activity in the Investment Company Industry: ICI Organization.

INGRAM, P., ROBINSON, J., AND BUSCH, M. L. (2005). The intergovernmental network of world trade: IGO connectedness, governance, and embeddedness. American Journal of Sociology, 111, 824–858.

IVKOVICH, Z. (2001). Is blood thinker than water? Spillovers in mutual fund families. Yale School of Management.

JACOBIDES, M. G. (2005). Industry change through vertical disintegration: How and why markets emerged in mortgage banking. Academy of Management Journal, 48(3), 465–498.

JACOBIDES, M. G. (2008). How capability differences, transaction cost and learning curves interact to shape vertical scope. Organizational Science, 19(2), 306–326.

JACOBIDES, M. G. (2008a). How capability differences, transaction cost and learning curves interact to shape vertical scope. Organizational Science, 19(2), 306–326.

JACOBIDES, M. G. (2008b). Playing football in a soccer field: Value chain structure, institutional modularity and success in foreign expansion. Managerial and Decision Economics, 29(2–3), 2257–2276.

JACOBIDES, M. G., AND BILLINGER, S. (2006). Designing the Boundaries of the Firm: From "Make, Buy, or Ally" to Dynamic Benefits of Vertical Architecture. Organizational Science, 17(2), 249–261.

JACOBIDES, M. G., AND WINTER, S. (2005). The co-evolution of capabilities and transaction costs: explaining the institutional structure of production. Strategic Management Journal, 26(5), 395–413.

JACOBIDES, M. G., KNUDSEN, T., AND AUGIER, M. (2006). Benefiting from innovation: Value creation, value appropriation and the role of industry architectures. Research Policy, 35, 1200–1221.

JACOBIDES, M. G., WINTER, S., AND KASSBERGER, S. M. (2006). A Marshallian Model of Efficiency Profits. London Business School and the Wharton School.

JANSEN, J. (2003). Coexistence of strategic vertical separation and integration. International Journal of Industrial Organization, 21, 699–716.

JARILLO, C. J. (1988). On Strategic Networks. Strategic Management Journal, 9(1), 31–41.

JENSEN, M. C., AND MECKLING, H. (1976). Theory of the Firm: Managerial Behaviour, Agency Costs and Ownership Structure. Journal of Financial Economics, 3, 305–360.

JOHANSON, J., AND MATTSON, L. G. (1994). The markets-as-network tradition in Sweden. In G. Laurent, G. L. Lilien and B. Pras (Eds.), Research traditions. Boston, M.A.: Kluwer Academic.

JOHNSON, D. R., AND HOOPES, D. G. (2003). Managerial cognition, sunk costs, and the evolution of industry structures. Strategic Management Journal, 24(10), 1057–1068.

JORDAN, J. S., AND RADNER, R. (1982). Rational expectations in microeconomic models: An overview. Journal of Economic Theory, 26(2), 201–223.

KAMIEN, M., AND SCHWARZ, N. (1982). Market Structure and Innovation. Cambridge: University Press.

KAPLAN, S., AND HENDERSON, R. M. (2005). Inertia and Incentives: Bridging Organizational Economics and Organizational Theory. Organizational Science, 16, 509–521.

KARCESKI, J., LIVINGSTON, M., AND O'NEAL, E. S. (2004). Mutual Fund Brokerage Commissions.

KARIM, S., AND MITCHELL, W. (2000). Path-dependent and path-breaking change: Reconfiguring business resources following acquisitions in the U.S. medical sector, 1978–1995. Strategic Management Journal, 21(10–11), 1061–1081.

KAY, J. (1993). Foundations of Corporate Success. Oxford: Oxford University Press.

KEIM, D. B., AND MADHAVAN, A. (1997). Transactions Costs and Investment Style: An Inter-Exchange Analysis of Institutional Equity Trades. Journal of Financial Economics, 46(3), 265–292.

KEMPF, A., AND RUENZI, S. (2004). Tournaments in Mutual Fund Families. Center for Financial Research (CFR).

KERN, T., AND WILLCOCKS, L. (2000). Contracts, Control and Presentation in IT Outsourcing: Research in Thirteen UK Organizations. Journal of Global Information Management, 2, 37–58.

KESSIDES, I. (1986). Advertising, sunk costs and barriers to entry. Review of Econmics and Statistics, 12, 1043–1074.

KETCHEN, D. J., SNOW, C. C., AND HOOVER, V. L. (2004). Research on Competitive Dynamics: Recent Accomplishements and Future Challenges. Journal of Management, 30(6), 779–804.

KHORANA, A., AND SERVAES, H. (1999). The determinants of mutual fund starts. Review of Financial Studies, 12, 1034–1074.

KHORANA, A., AND SERVAES, H. (2000). What drives market share in the mutual fund industry. SSRN.

KHORANA, A., SERVAES, H., AND TUFANO, P. (2005). Explaining the Size of the Mutual Fund Industry around the World. Journal of Financial Economics, 78, 145–185.

KING, A., AND TUCCI, C. L. (2002). Incumbent Entry into New Market Niches: The Role of Experience adn Managerial Choice in the creation of dynamic capabilities. Management Science, 48(2), 171–186.

KIRZNER, I. M. (1985). Enterpreneurial Discovery and the Competitive Market Process: An Austrian Approach. Journal of Economic Literature, 35(1), 60–85.

KLEPPER, S. (1996). Entry, Exit, Growth, and Innovation over the Product Life Cycle. American Economic Review, 86(3), 562–583.

KLEPPER, S. (2002). Firm survival and the evolution of oligopoly. RAND Journal of Economics, 33(1), 37–61.

KLEPPER, S., AND THOMPSON, P. (2005). Submarkets and the Evolution of Market Structure. Florida International University.

KNUDSEN, T. (2004). General selection theory and economic evolution: The Price equation and the genotype/phenotype distinction. Journal of Economic Methodology, 11, 14–173.

KNUUTILA, M., PUTTONEN, V., AND SMYTHE, T. (2006). The effect of distribution channels on mutual fund flows. Journal of Financial Service Marketing, 12(1), 88–96.

KOGUT, B., AND ZANDER, U. (1992). Knowledge of the firm, combinative capabilities, and the replication of technology. Organizational Science, 3, 383–397.

KOPPENHAVER, G. (1999). Circle unbroken: bank-affiliated money market funds. Paper presented at the Bank Structure and Competition, Chicago.

KORPELA, M., AND PUTTONEN, V. (2006). Mutual fund expenses: Evidence on the effect of distribution channels. Journal of Financial Service Marketing, 11(1), 17–29.

KPMG. (2007). The State of the Investment Management and Fund Industry (Europe) o. Document Number)

KPMG. (2007a). The State of the Investment Management and Fund Industry (Europe) o. Document Number)

KPMG. (2007b). The State of the Investment Management and Fund Industry (U.S.) o. Document Number)

KRAUT, R., STEINFIELD, C., CHAN, A., BUTLER, B., AND HOAG, A. (1999). Coordination and Virtualization: THe Role of Electronic Networks and Personal Relationships. Organizational Science, 10(6), 722–740.

KREPS, D., AND SCHEINKMAN, J. (1983). Quantity Precommitment and Bertrand Competition yield Cournot Outcomes. Bell Journal of Economics, 14, 326–337.

KUADA, J. (2002). Outsourcing and Offshoring: Some Theoretical Perspectives. Aalborg University.

LACITY, M. C., AND HIRSCHHEIM, R. (1993). The Information Systems Outsourcing Bandwagon. Sloan Management Review, Fall, 73–86.

LAKONISHOK, J., SHLEIFER, A., VISHNY, R. W., HART, O., AND PERRY, G. L. (1992). The Structure and Performance of the Money Management Industry. Brookings Papers on Economic Activity. Microeconomics, 1992, 229–391.

LANCASTRE, A., AND LAGES, L. F. (2006). The relationship between buyer and a B2B e-marketplace: Cooperation determinants in an electronic market context. Industrial Marketing Management, 35(1), 774–789.

LANGLOIS, R. N., AND ROBERTSON, R. N. (1995). Innovation, Networks and Vertical Integration. Research Policy, 24(4), 543–562.

LAUPER, U. (2005). Wertorientierte Netzwerksteuerung, neue Werttreiber für Unternehmen in Wertschöpfungsnetzen. Bern: Haupt.

LEE, H. G., AND CLARK, T. H. (1996). Impacts of Electronic Marketplace on transaction Cost and Market Structure. International Journal of Electronic Commerce, 1(1), 127–149.

LEE, R. G., AND DALE, B. G. (1998). Business process management: a review and evaluation. Business Process Management Journal, 4(3), 214–225.

LESSEIG, V. P., LONG, M., D., AND SMYTHE, T. I. (2002). Gains to Mutual Fund Sponsors offering multiple share class funds. The Journal of Financial Research, 25(1), 81–98.

LEVINTHAL, D. (2006). The Neo-Schumpeterian theory of the firm and the strategy field. Industrial and Corporate Change, 15(2), 391–394.

LEVINTHAL, D., AND MYATT, J. (1994). Co-Evolution of Capabilties and Industry: The Evolution of Mutual Fund Processing. Strategic Management Journal, 15(Special Issue: Competitive Organizational Behaviour), 45–62.

LEWONTIN, R. C. (1974). The Genetic Base of Evolutionary Change. New York: Columbia Press.

LIPPMAN, S. A., MCCARDLE, K. F., AND RUMELT, R. P. (1991). Precis of Heterogeneity under Competition. Economic Inquir, 29, 774–782.

LUKACH, R., PLASMANS, J., AND KORT, P. (2005). Innovation, strategies in a comopetitive dynamic setting. Center for Economic Studies.

MAKADOK, R., AND BARNEY, J. B. (2001). Strategic Factor Market Intelligence: An application of Information Economics to Strategy Formulation and Competitor Intelligence. Management Science, 47(12), 1621–1638.

MALONE, T. W., YATES, J., AND BENJAMIN, R. I. (1987). Electronic Markets and Hierarchies. Communications of the ACM, 30(6), 484–467.

MASSA, M. (2003). Mutual fund competition and stock market liquidity. London Stock Exchange.

MATHEWS, J. A. (2001). Competitive Interfirm Dynamics within an Industrial Market System. Industry and Innovation, 8(1), 79–107.

MATHEWS, J. A. (2003). Competitive dynamics and economic learning: an extended resource-based view. Industrial and Corporate Change, 12(1), 115–145.

MATHEWS, J. A. (2006/2001). Resources, Routines, and interfirm Relations: Enterpreneurial and Evolutionary Dynamics within an Industrial Market System. Paper presented at the Danish Research Unit on Industrial Dynamics (DRUID) Conference.

MATTHEWS, K., AND THOMPSON, J. (2005). The Economics of Banking. Chichester: John Wiley and Sons.

MATTIG, A. (2008). Modes of Governance in Business Process Outsourcing: Executive versus Market's Perspective. Paper presented at the Proceedings of the 41th Annual Hawaii International Conference on System Sciences.

MATTIG, A., AND WUEST, P. (2008). Architektur und Evolution von Finanzdienstleistungsmärkten am Beispiel des Schweizerischen Anlagefondsmarktes. University of St. Gallen.

MAYHEW, S. (2002). Competition, Market Structure, and Bid-Ask Spreads in Stock Option Markets. The Journal of Finance, 57(2), 931–958.

MCGAHAN, A. (2004). How Industries Change. Harvard Business Review(October), 1–9.

MCIVOR, R. (2005). The influence of transaction cost economics and the resource based view on the outsourcing process. Paper presented at the 16th Annual Conference of POMS.

MEHRA, A. (1996). Resource and Market Based Determinants of Performance in the U.S. Banking Industry. Strategic Management Journal, 17, 307–322.

MESA MANAGEMENT. (2008). Active vs. Passive Mutual Fund Strategies: A Fee Comparison. Retrieved July 20, from http://www.mesamgmt.com/images/cost_table.gif

METCALFE, S. (1995). The Desing of Order: Notes on Evolutionary Principles and teh Dynamics of Innovation. Revue Economique, 46, 327–346.

METCALFE, S. (1998). Evolutionary Economics and Creative Destruction. London: Routledge.

METCALFE, S. (2001). Evolutionary approaches to population thinking and the problem of growth and development. In K. Doepfer (Ed.), The Evolutionary Foundations of Economics. St. Gallen.

METCALFE, S. (2006). Enterpreneurship: An evolutionary approach. In M. Casson, B. Yeung and N. Wadeson (Eds.), Oxford Handbook on Enterpreneurship. Oxford: University Press.

METCALFE, S. (2007). Accountig for Economic Evolution: Fitness and the Population Method. CRIC.

MUELLER-STEWENS, G., AND LECHNER, C. (2003). Strategisches Management: Wie strategische Initativen zum Wandel führen. Stuttgart: Schaefer-Poeschel.

NELSON, R. R., AND WINTER, S. G. (1973). Toward an evolutionary view of economic capabilities. American Economic Review, 63, 440–449.

NELSON, R. R., AND WINTER, S. G. (1974). Neoclassical vs evolutionary theories of economic growth. Critique and prospectus. Economic Journal, 84, 886–905.

NELSON, R. R., AND WINTER, S. G. (1982). An Evolutionary Theory of Economic Change. Cambridge, MA.: Harvard Univesity Press UP.

NIGHTINGALE, P. (2008). Meta-paradigm change and the theory of the firm. Industrial and Corporate Change, 17(3), 533–583.

O'HARA, M. (2007). Optimal Microstructures. European Financial Management, 13(5), 825–832.

O'REILLY, P., AND FINNEGAN, P. (2005). Performance in Electronic Marketplaces: Theory in Practice. Electronic Markets, 15(1), 23–37.

O'REILLY, P., AND FINNEGAN, P. (2007). Electronic Marketplaces as market system Intermediaries: An exploratory study and characteristics framework. Paper presented at the 15th European Conference on Information Systems.

OTTEN, R., AND BAMS, D. (2002). European Mutual Fund Performance. European Financial Management, 8(1), 75–101.

OXERA. (2006). Current Trends in Asset Management. European Union.

PANZAR, J. C., AND WILLIG, R. D. (1977). Economies of Scale in Multi-Output Production. The Quarterly Journal of Economics, 91(3), 481–493.

PENROSE, E. (1995). The Theory of the Growth of the Firm. New York: Wiley.

PETAJISTO, A. (2003). The Decentralization of Information Processing in the Presence of Interactions. Review of Economic Studies, 70, 667–695.

PHUSAVAT, K., CHAISAKUL, S., AND TAKALA, J. (2005). Management Outsourcing Activities: Roles of Performance Measurement. Paper presented at the ICPR Conference.

PISANIAS, N., AND JACOBIDES, M. G. (2006). Unfulfilled Promises: Why Information Technology Failed to Transform the Re-insurance Sector. Leverhulme and London Business School.

PODOLNY, J. M., STUART, T. E., AND HANNAN, M. T. (1996). Networks, knowledge, and niches: Competition in the worldwide semiconductor industry, 1984–1991. American Journal of Sociology, 102, 659–689.

POWELL, W. W. (1990). Neither Market Nor Hierarchy: Network Forms of Organization. Research in Organizational Behaviour, 12, 295–336.

PRAEST, M. (1999). Evolutionary Patterns of Technological Competence Accumulation: A Measurement Proposition. Paper presented at the European Meeting on Applied Evolutionary Economics.

PRICE, G. R. (1970). Selection and Covariance. Nature, 227(520–521).

PRICE, G. R. (1972). Fisher's Fundamental theorem made clear. Annals of Human Genetics, 36, 129–140.

PRICE, G. R. (1995). The nature of selection. Journal of Theoretical Biology, 175, 389–396.

QUÉLIN, B., AND DUHAMEL, F. (2003). Bringing together Strategic Outsourcing and Corporate Strategy: Outsourcing Motives and Risks. European Management Journal, 21(5), 647–661.

QUÉLIN, B., V., AND CLAUDE-GAUDILLAT, V. (2005). Innovation, New Market and Governance Choices of Entry: The Internet Brokerage Market Case. Paper presented at the Conférence Internationale de Management Stratégique.

RADNER, R. (1991). Dynamic games in organizational theory. Journal of Economic Behavior and Organization, 16, 289–304.

RADNER, R. (2006). Neo-Schumpeterian and other theories of the firm: a comment and personal retrospective. Industrial and Corporate Change, 15(2), 373–380.

RAFF, D. (2001). Competition, Innovation, and Strategy in the Financial Services Industry. Wharton.

RAMOS, S. B. (2007). The Size and Structure of teh World Mutual Fund Industry. European Financial Management, 0(0), 1–34.

RAMOS, S. B. (2009). The Size and Structure of the World Mutual Fund Industry. European Financial Management, 15(1), 145–180.

REBERNIK, M., AND BRADAC, B. (2006). Cooperation and opportunistic behavior in transormational outsourcing. Kybernetes, 35(7/8), 1005–1013.

RILEY, J. (1990). International Government Finance and the Amsterdam Capital Market 1740–1815. Cambridge: University Press.

ROBERTSON, A., AND HILL, W. G. (1966). The effect of linkages on limits to artifical selection. Genetical Research, 8(3), 269–294.

ROLL, R. (1984). A Simple Implicit Measure of the Effective Bid-Ask Spread in an Efficient Market. The Journal of Finance, 39(4), 1127–1139.

ROSENBLOM, R. S., AND CHRISTENSEN, C. M. (1994). Technological Discontinuities, Organizational Capabilities, and Strategic Commitments. Industrial and Corporate Change, 3(3), 655–685.

ROUWENHORST, G. K. (2004). The Origins of Mutual Funds. Yale School of Management.

RUMELT, R. P. (Ed.). (1984). Towards a Strategic Theory of the Firm (Reprinted in Foss, Nicoloj J., Resources Firms and Strategies: A Reader in the Resource-Based Perspective. Oxford University Press, 131–145 ed.). Englewood Cliffs, N.J.: Prentice-Hall.

RUMELT, R. P., SCHENDEL, D., AND TEECE, D. J. (1991). Strategic Management and Economics. Strategic Management Journal, 12(2), 5–29.

RUSSEL, R. (2007). An Introduction to Mutual Funds Worldwide. New York: Wiley

SALINGER, M. A. (1988). Vertical mergers and market foreclosure. Quarterly Journal of Economics, 103, 345–356.

SANCHEZ, R. (1996). Strategic Product Creation: Managing new interactions of technology, markets and organizations. European Management Journal, 14(2), 121–138.

SANTOS, F. M., AND EISENHARDT, K. M. (2005). Organizational Boundaries and Theories of Organization. Organizational Science, 16(5), 491–508.

SAVIOTTI, P. P. (1998). On the dynamics of appropriability, of tacit and of codified knowledge. Research Policy, 26(7–8), 843–856.

SAVIOTTI, P. P. (2001). Variety, Growth and Demand. Journal of Evolutionary Economics, 13, 119–142.

SAVIOTTI, P. P. (2006). A theoretical approach to the construction of technology output Research Policy, 13(3), 141–151.

SCHERER, F. M. (1980). Industrial market structure and economic performance. Chicago, IL.: Rand-McNally.

SEC. (2008). An Introduction to Mutual Funds. Retrieved June 15, 2008, from http://www.sec.gov/investor/pubs/inwsfmf.htm

SENGUPTA, J. (2007). Dynamics of Entry and Market Evolution. Santa Barbara: Palgrave macmillan.

SHY, O., AND STENBACKA, R. (2003). Market structure and diversification of mutual funds. Journal of Financial Markets, 6, 607–624.

SIGGELKOW, N. (2003). Evolution toward Fit. Administrative Science Quarterly, 47, 125–159.

SLADE, M. (1998). Beer and the tie: dd divestiture of brewer-owned public houses lead to higher beer prices? Economic Journal, 108, 565–602.

SOH, C., AND MARKUS, L. M. (2002). Business-To-Business Electronic Marketplaces: A Strategic Archetypes Approach. Proceedings of the Twenty-Third Conference on Information Systems, Barcelona.

STEINFIELD, C., MARKUS, M. L., AND WIGAND, R. (2005). Exploring Interorganizational Systems at the Industry Level of Analysis: Evidence from the US Home Mortgage Industry. Journal of Information Technology, 20(4), 224–233.

STIGLER, J. (1951). Market Exchange or Vertical Integration: An Empirical Analysis. Review of Econmics and Statistics, 67(2), 327–331.

STOLL, H. R. (2006). Electronic Trading in Stock Markets.

SUTTON, J. (1998). Technology and Market Structure. Cambridge, MA.: MIT Press.

SUZUMURA, K. (1995). Entry and cost reduction: Comment. Japan and the World Economy, 7(4), 411–418.

TEECE, D. J., PISANO, G., AND SHUEN, A. (1997). Dynamic capabilities and Strategic Management. Strategic Management Journal, 18(7), 509–533.

TIROLE, J. (1988). The Theory of Industrial Organization. Cambridge, MA.: MIT Press.

VANWEGBERG, M. (1992). Capacity as a Commitment Insturment in multi-segment market competition. In A. VanWitteloostuijn (Ed.), Market Evolution – Competition and Cooperation. Limburg: Kluwer.

VANWITTELOOSTUIJN, A. (1995). Market Evolution – Competition and Co-operation. Limburg: Kluwer.

VARIAN, H. R. (1998). Effect of the Internet on Financial Markets.

VIVES, X. (2001). Competition in the Changing World of Banking. Oxford Review of Economic Policy, 17(4), 535–547.

WALDFOGEL, J., AND CHEN, L. (2007). Does Information undermine brand? Information intermediary and preference for branded web retailers. Journal of Industrial Economics, 54(4), 425–449.

WALTER, I. (1998). The Global Asset Management Industry: Competitive Structure, Conduct and Performance. Leonard N. Stern School of Business, Department of Economics.

WALTER, I. (1999). The Global Asset Management Industry: Competitive Structure, Conduct and Performance. Financial Markets, Institutions and Instruments, 8(1), 1–78.

WALTER, I. (1999a). The Asset Management Industry in Europe: Competitive Structure and Performance under EMU. Paper presented at the Conference on the Future of Asset Management.

WALTER, I. (1999b). The Global Asset Management Industry: Competitive Structure, Conduct and Performance. Financial Markets, Institutions and Instruments, 8(1), 1–78.

WALTER, I., AND SISLI, E. (2006). The Asset Management Industry in Asia: Dynamics of Growth, Structure, and Performance. Leonard N. Stern School of Business, Department of Economics.

WALTER, I., AND SISLI, E. (2007). The Asset Management Industry in Asia: Dynamics of Growth, Structure, and Performance. Financial Markets, Institutions and Instruments, 16(1), 1–77.

WEIL, P., AND ROSS, J. (2005). How top performers manage IT decision rights for superior results. Boston, M.A.: Harvard Business School Press.

WERMERS, R. (2000). Mutual Fund Performance: An Empirical Decomposition into Stock-Picking Talent, Style, Transaction Costs, and Expenses. The Journal of Finance, 40(4), 1655–1695.

WERNERFELDT, B. (1984). A resource-based view of the Firm. Strategic Management Journal, 5(2), 171–180.

WESTERFELD, S., and ZIMMERMANN, H.-D. (2008). E-Business Tools for active Credit Risk Management – A Market Analysis. Paper presented at the Proceedings of the 41th Annual Hawaii International Conference on System Sciences.

WILLIAMS, D. J. H. (2000). E-Commerce and Mutual Fund Supermarkets. Dublino. Document Number)

WILLIAMSON, O. E. (1975). Markets and Hierarchies. New York: The Free Press.

WILLIAMSON, O. E. (1985). The Economic Institutions of Capitalism: Firms, Markets, Relative Contracting. New York: The Free Press.

WILLIAMSON, O. E. (1991). Strategizinig, economizing, and economic organization Strategic Management Journal, 12(8), 75–94.

WILLIAMSON, O. E. (1999). Strategy research: Governance and competence perspectives. Strategic Management Journal, 20(12), 1087–1108.

WINCHESTER, S. (2005). A Crack in the Edge of the World: America and the Great California Earthquake of 1906. San Francisco: Harper Collins.

WITT, U. (1992). Evolutionary Concepts in Economics. Eastern Economic Journal, 18(4), 405–419.

WOLTER, C., AND VELOSO, F. M. (2008). The Effects of Innovation on Vertical Structure: Perspectives on Transactions Costs and Competences. Academy of Management Review, 33(3), 586–605.

WONSEOK, O., AND GALLVIAN, M. J. (2004). An empirical assessment of transaction risks of IT outsourcing arrangements: An event study. Proceedings of the 37th Hawaii International Conference on System Sciences.

YUE QINGYUAN, L., AND INGRAM, P. (2008). Structure, Affect and Identity Bases of Organizational Competition and Cooperation. The Academy of Management Annals, 2(1), 275–303.

ZAIRI, M. (1997). Business process management: a boundaryless approach to modern competitiveness. Business Process Management Journal, 3(1), 64–80.

ZERA, S., P., AND MADURA, J. (2001). The empirical relationship between mutual fund size and operational efficiency. Applied Financial Economics, 11, 243–251.

ZHAO, X. (2001). Entry Decision by Mutual Fund Families.

ZIMMERMANN, H.-D. (2000). Understanding the Digital Economy: Challenges for new Business Models. Paper presented at the Proceedings of the 2000 Americas Conference on Information Systems (AMCIS).